TRAVELS WITH A TYPEWRITER

MICHAEL FRAYN

Travels with a Typewriter

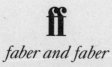

faber and faber

First published in 2009
by Faber and Faber Limited
Bloomsbury House, 74–77 Great Russell Street,
London WC1B 3DA

Typeset by Faber and Faber
Printed in England by Mackays of Chatham, Chatham, Kent

A CIP record for this book
is available from the British Library

ISBN 978–0–571–24089–0

2 4 6 8 10 9 7 5 3 1

Contents

Introduction

The first article I ever wrote, so far as I can recall – the first *anything* – was a school essay on 'The House I Should Like to Live in When I Am Grown Up'. I can't now remember anything about the essay itself, but it certainly had one sign of originality – the drawing I did to go with it, which showed not the iconic dolls' house that children usually draw, but a boldly Art Deco structure (this was somewhere around the end of the 1930s) with flat roof, white stucco walls, and long horizontal windows that curved around the corners. I must have been six or seven years old, so I had presumably written things before, but this one has stuck in my mind because of my father's comment when he read it: 'Perhaps you ought to be a journalist.'

I don't suppose this was very seriously intended. My father was not much given to parental encouragement in the modern manner. Certainly not of my various literary activities, and by the time I was old enough for the question of my future career to have any practical significance he thought I ought to follow in his footsteps and become a salesman. Nearly thirty years went by before he showed any further signs of enthusiasm for my work. But the damage had been done, because from then on a journalist is what I wanted to be.

I also wanted to be a writer, of course, but this seemed too far-fetched an ambition to announce to the world – and too nebulous a one to express, even to myself, since I had no idea what it was I wanted to write. I wrote my first plays a year or two later, to provide my home-made puppets with material, but I don't think it occurred to me that there might one day be a living in it. I started (though I never finished) a novel – about children sailing dinghies in the Lake District, even though I had never seen a dinghy, or for that matter the Lake District, outside the works of Arthur Ransome – and later filled various exercise books with poetry, even though I had never come across the concept of metre; but I can't recall ever seeing a career structure in novels or poetry. I had brief passing infatuations in my early teens with other possible futures, as an industrial chemist or commercial photographer, both a great deal more fanciful, given my general lack of practical ability, than any possible literary ambitions. But it was to the idea of being a journalist that I always returned.

I'm not quite sure what I expected the work to be like. I was brought up reading the old *News Chronicle*, a decent Liberal paper that died of either decency or Liberalism or both shortly after I got into the profession. Their star reporter was James Cameron. I wish I could say that I remember his pieces, but I don't – only my first sight of the man himself. I was an undergraduate by this time, and doing a vacation job interpreting for a delegation of Soviet students. One of the items in their programme was a visit to the *Chronicle* offices in Bouverie

Street, where we stood in a kind of visitors' gallery, gazing through a soundproof window into the newsroom. And suddenly my Russian customers were forgotten, because there, unbelievably, he was, as slim and darkly handsome as a film star, in immaculate white shirt, narrow Donegal tweed trousers, and suede shoes, hands impatiently on hips, pacing up and down the newsroom like a caged tiger, visibly the star of some great inaudible drama of newspaper life.

Did I see myself as treading in Cameron's tense footsteps when I left university the following year and got a six-month try-out in the reporters' room of the *Manchester Guardian*? My own first footsteps there were very different – they were waterlogged. I started on twelve guineas a week (this was 1957), and couldn't afford a second pair of shoes, so the holes I had accumulated during my three years on a student grant remained unrepaired, and for six months I squelched around in two permanent shoefuls of Manchester's famous rain. When at last I got a rise, then certainly I made sure the new shoes were suede, and I eventually got the white shirt and the Donegal tweed trousers to go with them. They never quite fitted in with *Guardian* style, though, and they earned the particular scorn of Mac, the tough-talking, soft-hearted night news editor, who threatened to send me to cover a big warehouse fire, as soon as one could be found, where trousers, shirt, and shoes alike would be ruined by clouds of burning ash and rivers of molten molasses.

The dark tigerishness I never managed to emulate. Just as well, perhaps; we were not darkly tigerish in the reporters' room. Our style was suggested by the furnishings – two telephones for the entire room, kept shut away in soundproof cabins, and ancient typewriters balanced on even more ancient desks that were sloped for writing by hand, so that the typewriters vibrated their way down them as you worked, and fell painfully into your lap. Our speciality was 'colour reporting', and it was our well-crafted essays, we liked to feel, that gave the paper its distinctive character and tone.

What constituted 'colour' I have never stopped to ask myself until I wrote that last paragraph. It seemed self-evident at the time. It was the idiosyncratic, the odd, the whimsical, particularly anything connected with the folk traditions of the industrial north-west. The annual processions through the city known as Whit Walks, for instance; last surviving clogmakers and railway knockers-up; anything to do with cowheel and black pudding; though we also raised quizzical eyebrows at the amusing intrusions of modern life into this dour world – saunas, science, strip clubs. Our star reporter was Norman Shrapnel, who looked like a retired Indian Army officer, and who was so famously shy that he contrived to get all his stories without speaking to anyone; he was said to have locked himself in a lavatory once to avoid a press officer who was too pressing in his eagerness to help.

Every now and then Harry Whewell, the day news editor, would emerge from his office and survey us, the corner of his mouth twitching wryly at the thought of some extraordinary unconsidered aspect of the world that had just come to mind. 'Michael, you're not doing anything, I can see. Have you ever thought what they do with cows' stomachs in other parts of the country? If they don't eat tripe, do they just throw them away? Are we wasting millions of pounds year? Have a word with one or two slaughterhouses and see if there's anything in it.'

At the head of our copy, when we were working within the Manchester city limits, we wrote 'BOOR', which the typesetters expanded to 'By Our Own Reporter'. Everywhere else we were 'FOSC' – 'From Our Special Correspondent'. We were often FOSC for days at a time on great sweeps through the land, knocking off a thousand well-turned words a day on a sheep-dog trial here, a miners' gala there, the culling of grey seals in the Farne Islands, the last steam engine to be built in Doncaster. At the end of each day we'd phone in our copy, and tell Harry the strength of it, trying to make him laugh at whatever preposterous whimsy we could dig up. I recall a marzipan hippopotamus in Torquay, a constitutional crisis in the Isle of Man, a dustman who lived up a tree in Worcestershire – and the rejoicings in the office the day that David Gray, our Midlands correspondent, went to investigate why a ferry across the Severn had fallen into disrepair, and discovered that it was operated by a local estate agent called Doolittle & Dalley.

The fashionable taste in the late fifties was for the *offbeat* – oblique humour and cool jazz – and the reporter I was trying hardest to imitate by this time was not James Cameron or even Norman Shrapnel – it was John Gale, on the *Observer*. The *Observer* was the only paper that I or any of my friends at university had read. (I boasted to a girlfriend at university that my ambition was to be editor of the *Observer* by the time I was thirty – an even more ridiculous goal than chemist or photographer, not only because I had no editorial abilities but because the editor of the *Observer* in those days, David Astor, was also its millionaire proprietor, and to edit it I should have had to buy him out.) We read it mostly for Kenneth Tynan, of course, for Paul Jennings, the humorous columnist, and for the books pages. But the great draw for me was John Gale. I was captivated by the apparent innocence of his observation, the apparent naïvety of his style. He had an eye for the inconsequential detail and an ear for the oblique remark. He absented himself from his reports, but left somehow lurking behind this absence the faint ghost of a detached, wryly amused onlooker. In my early pieces for the *Guardian*, too, it was always starting to rain quietly. Pale moons rose irrelevantly behind the dying clogmakers. The redundant hedge-pleachers remarked inconsequentially on the previous evening's television. The tripe-makers' congresses ended on a dying fall.

We did some hard reporting as well, of course, when the opportunity arose – train and plane crashes, strikes and snowstorms, by-elections and visiting celebrities. I was worried before I arrived in Manchester that I had never managed to get my shorthand up to speed. It didn't turn out to be much of a problem, though, because reporters on other papers, not regarding the *Guardian* as serious professional competition, often saw it as one of their charitable obligations in life to seek you out afterwards and 'fill you in' from their own notes. We even covered the occasional murder, if it was too horrifying to ignore completely. I was sent to cover a case in which a bank manager had run amok, attacked his wife, children and mother-in-law with an axe and left them to die slowly overnight, then attempted to commit suicide by stabbing himself in the chest with a pair of rusty scissors. 'Don't do anything silly,' said the news editor anxiously.

'Don't try to get your foot in anyone's front door, or steal their wedding photographs. Just go to the police press conference, look at the *outside* of the bank, and come back to the office.' Whether a soft rain was falling in the story I subsequently wrote I can't recall.

I enjoyed almost all of it (though not the murders), and I did at any rate get to know a little about Manchester and the North of England. Among the fires and folkways I also wrote about secondary education and conditions in prisons, radio astronomy and nuclear power; and I covered Macmillan's visit to Moscow in the famous white fur hat. But when I think what the real reporters of my generation were doing I feel abashed. James Cameron himself, coming out of a party in London one night in 1963, was told by a passer-by in the street that Kennedy had been shot. Without stopping to pick up a toothbrush or any means of paying for a ticket he went straight to Heathrow and talked his way on to a flight to Dallas. My friend Nicholas Tomalin, who had been at Cambridge just ahead of me, went several times to Vietnam for the *Sunday Times*, where he wrote one of the finest pieces to come out of the war ('Zapping the Cong'), and was then killed covering the Yom Kippur War in Israel. The only war I ever got near was the Cod War, when Iceland unilaterally extended her fishery limits, and Britain sent the Royal Navy to enforce the right of British trawlers to ignore them. Not that I ever got very close even to that. I was on an ancient minesweeper that turned out to be too slow to keep up with the Icelandic gunboats. In any case its radar broke down, and on the first day of the new limits there was a fog, so that we had to anchor, and all I could do was to run from rail to rail, catching tantalising glimpses of fleeing trawlers and pursuing gunboats as they zig-zagged out of the great whiteness and vanished again. I was transferred by jackstay to a fast-moving destroyer with working radar – after which I never saw another gunboat. Only Iceland, gently rising and falling on the horizon week after week. And a great deal of satisfyingly inconsequential grey weather.

So that was how I began my professional life – as a reporter. It was also during those two years in Manchester that I wrote my first real novel. We worked alternate six- and four-day weeks. On the three-day weekends I sat in the most writerly accommodation I had been able to find – a seedy furnished 'studio' flat up under the eaves of a former mansion on the borders of Rusholme and Longsight, its ambience dismally determined by the smell of coal gas and bacon grease from the kitchenette in the corner, with my little Empire portable in front of me. Its keys waited patiently for the chance to jam together in one solid block of recalcitrant metal at any suggestion of work, while I gazed out of the single dormer window, looking for inspiration in the grey industrial haze. Sometimes, when the factories closed down for Bank Holidays or Wakes Week, the haze cleared, and you could see the mill chimneys of Oldham – though still not much in the way of material for a novel.

I was encouraged by a text that I suspect all of us in the reporters' room secretly studied – Howard Spring's autobiography. Spring had worked in the room forty years earlier, and gone on to become a best-selling novelist. It gave us all hope. Even more encouragingly, he claimed to have begun his first successful novel with nothing in his head but the opening sentence, 'The woman flamed along the road like a macaw.' It seemed so easy! I can't remember now how my own novel started, only how it ended, which was in a brown envelope at the back of a drawer, filed away on the advice of my recently acquired literary agent. She quite liked the first thirty pages, she said. It was the next three hundred that were so terrible.

Back to the clog-dancers and the still falling rain.

*

In this collection of my reporting I have not included any of the stuff I wrote in those two first years. Most of the pieces here date from a later stage in my career, when I returned to reporting as a freelance. This was after I had moved on from Manchester and the room, and spent eight years back in London writing a humorous column – three times a week for two years on the *Guardian*, once a week for six years on the *Observer*. Eight years of this kind of thing, it seemed to me, was probably enough. The example of other columnists and humorists who go on for too long was not encouraging.

By this time I was married, and one of the many improvements my wife had made to my life was to allow me to replace the terrible old Empire with her elegant and efficient Olivetti, one of the design icons of the time. With the help of this I had written a novel which had actually been published. In fact I had written four – one of them, *Towards the End of the Morning*, full of journalists telling each other how you have to get out of journalism before you're forty. I was thirty-five, and there still seemed to be possibilities in life to explore. I wanted to write . . . well . . . *what* did I want to write? More novels, certainly, more of the television plays I had just begun on – perhaps even (secretly), after mocking the theatre so comprehensively in so many of the old columns, stage plays.

I had a family to support, so to cover the bills I signed a contract with the *Observer* to write occasional longer pieces for the paper – 'review fronts', the substantial articles that opened the back half of the quality Sundays, and that readers probably got around to, if at all, only to doze over after lunch. They would consist not of my opinions and inventions, like the columns, but of straight reporting. In the characteristically back-to-front fashion in which life often seems to operate, I was becoming a reporter again just I was at last giving up regular journalism.

Actually it wasn't just a question of the money. I felt that it was time I went out and looked at the world again. Some cynics would deny the existence of any real distinction between fiction and reporting. It doesn't seem like that if you have to do it, though, and I have sometimes thought that all writers of fiction should be required by law to go out and do a bit of reporting from time to time, just to remind them how different the real world in front of their eyes is from the invented world behind them. To have a fiction in mind – whether you have laboriously created it or whether it has seemed to suggest itself – is already to have made something tractable, already to have isolated some specific characters and events, to have seen some way in which they fit together, some way in which it can all be suggested in words. Out there in the world it's very different. Nothing, for a start, is in words – nothing is the right shape to be *put* into words. Nothing has its cause or its result written upon it. Even when you find witnesses who supply you with a testimony already in verbal form, their impressions of the same things and recollections of the same event are dismayingly various. And there's so *much* of everything! All of it inextricably tangled together.

To describe is to select – and to select only a microscopic sample from this overwhelming profusion. How even, in the first place, to select a principle of selection – how to decide on a particular subject? One way is to choose aspects of the world that seem to stand out from the rest because they are untypical or extraordinary – the heroic, the despicable; the grandiose, the grotesque; the exotic, the extreme. It is difficult to describe such things, and to convey some impression of them to a reader, precisely because they *are* foreign to our normal experience. But there are also difficulties in what I decided I wanted to do, which was to describe not the extraordinary but the ordinary, the typical, the everyday. I would go to other parts of the world, equipped with little more than my wife's beautiful Olivetti and my own ignorance, and try to give some account of them as they appeared to a visiting outsider. Influenced perhaps by the memory of Norman Shrapnel's practice, I would in so far as I could avoid formal interviews, particularly ones with politicians and experts. I would simply follow up any random contacts that I happened to have and see where they led. I would use my eyes and ears. I would keep my opinions to myself.

This was the theory. In practice it didn't quite work out like that. My very first subject was Cuba – and it was impossible not to find almost everything about everyday life there extraordinary in itself. It was also impossible to give any coherent account of it without recourse to officials and experts, and their explanations and generalisations. Worse, I found that I could not remain as impartial as I had promised myself to be. Everything I saw seemed to be part of some larger picture, to be evidence either for or against the revolution and its results – and that larger picture dissolved and re-formed disconcertingly from one day to the next, from one moment to the next, with each last person I spoke to, with each change in the weather.

The same was in some degree true, I discovered, in every place I wrote about, even European cities with familiar customs and social arrangements. I should have liked to remove myself from what I was describing, to send readers on journeys without my being there myself to get between them and the sights. But I couldn't. There I indissolubly was, with my own shifting feelings. Insignificant ones, perhaps, compared with the terrors and sufferings of war-reporters and serious travellers in deserts and jungles. Impossible, though, not to be cast down by the bleakness of arriving in dreary hotel rooms in strange cities, missing wife and children as painfully as if one were a child oneself again, and nerving oneself to phone strangers with whom one has scraped some tenuous connection, asking them to interrupt their lives and waste their time meeting you. Impossible, too, waking next morning to sunshine and warm breezes, not to feel oneself soaring like a bird; to be greeted by friendly smiles or a passing flirtatious glance and not to be made a carefree honorary citizen for a day.

And, feelings apart, there I objectively was simply as a piece of optical and electronic equipment. The rays of light from the objects in front of me were being focussed through the two small lenses in the front of my head, the sounds through the two small listening-posts in the side of it. This tiny selection of photons, these extremely local variations in air-pressure, were being converted from mere physical contingency into information through the operations of my single brain, and interpreted in terms of the particular selection of experience, schoolbook knowledge, prejudice, and myth that circumstance and my own earlier choices in life had put there. There are similar constraints upon even the most supposedly objective statements about the world made by scientists, as I realised more fully later in life, when I began to explore some of the consequences of relativity and quantum mechanics. Observer and observed are inseparably bound up together.

So there I am, reluctantly but inescapably, in all these pieces. Some of the subjects were chosen by me, out of a previous interest or new curiosity; some were suggested by the *Observer*. I am indebted to the *Observer* for commissioning them, and to Alan Rusbridger, now the paper's executive editor as well as editor of the *Guardian*, for his generosity in allowing me to reproduce them here.

A few of the pieces in this collection were written in different circumstances. *Wild West Eleven* I produced for some kind of special anniversary edition of *Granta*, to which I had contributed when it was still a Cambridge student publication. *Rainbow Over the Thames* was done for *The Age of Austerity*, a collection of essays by various authors, edited by Philip French and Michael Sissons, about the years of the first Labour government after the Second World War, 1945 to 1951. *A Pilgrimage to St Trop* was written before I left the staff of the

Observer, as was *From Sea to Shining Sea*. The latter is really a series of the columns I was writing at the time. I had won the Somerset Maugham Award for my first novel, *The Tin Men*. It was a condition of the award that the recipient had to be out of Britain for at least three months, but its value then was a modest £500, so it was an expensive benefaction to receive, particularly since I had a family travelling with me, and I supplemented it by continuing with the day job.

A number of these pieces proved to be the starting-points for new ventures. Cuba became the setting for one of my early plays, *Clouds*. The articles on Berlin were particularly fruitful. It was David Astor, the editor of the *Observer*, who suggested Berlin when I told him that I had become interested in Germany but couldn't find a focus for writing about it. I was immensely taken by the city, partly because the huge destruction left from the war and the isolation of its Western districts deep inside East Germany meant that, to make sense of it, one's imagination was continuously engaged, filling in its history and its original function. When I discovered that a young television director called Dennis Marks, with whom I was doing a short film on another subject, was also obsessed with Berlin, we persuaded the BBC to let us make a ninety-minute film about the city. This led on to a series of further presented documentaries that Dennis and I did together about various places – Vienna, the suburbs of London, Jerusalem, Australia, Prague and Budapest. It was also the beginning of my long fascination with Germany, which has since fuelled various plays and novels. And I suppose that the general questions prompted by these pieces, about the relationship between observer and observed, strongly reinforced the theoretical interest that I had always had in such matters, and that later formed so much of the subject-matter of *The Human Touch*.

A lot has happened in the world since these pieces were written. Does anyone now remember what TWA or a Ford Mustang were, or who Kenny Everett was, or what 12/6d meant? Or that in 1969 Israel was still occupying the Negev, and confronting Egypt across the Suez Canal? Or even that there was once a country called Yugoslavia? Usages have changed. I shouldn't have called my black neighbours 'Negro' or 'coloured' if I had been writing now, or said that the political difficulties of 1951 made for 'a gay start to Festival year'. But I wasn't writing now, I was writing then. Sensibilities have changed in less obvious ways, too. I'm a little embarrassed now to see how unembarrassed I was then at having been at Cambridge, and having enjoyed it, and having retained intense feelings about it.

These pieces have meant a lot to me. I hope some of them also still have some kind of archaeological interest. A couple of them – about Moscow and Berlin – relate to a world that has vanished beneath the dust of history. Another couple, about Paris and Cambridge, perhaps catch something about those cities before they were quite as overwhelmed as they now are by mass tourism. Maybe all of them fix a few particular scenes at particular moments in time. Very ordinary scenes, at very ordinary moments, like the beaches and gardens in the background of snapshots in a family album.

It was my first television play, in 1968, that elicited from my father his second encouraging remark about my writing. But the series on Cuba, I'm pleased to say, moved him to a third (and final one) only a year later. 'You ought to do more of this kind of thing,' he said. Whether he realised that 'this kind of thing' was what I had been doing, on and off, for the previous dozen years, or remembered getting me started on it some twenty years before that, was one of the many things I never asked him while I still had the chance.

A Farewell to Money

Cuba, ten years on

No representation – but, then, no taxation. No bars – but then, no drunks.

No news, no institutions to protect the rights of the individual, nothing in the shops. Often no water in the pipes, occasionally no electricity in the wires. 'No liberalism whatsoever! No softening whatsoever!' (Castro). No hope of an easier life for at least ten years yet.

But then, no beggars, no barefoot children. No prostitution, no destitution, no racial discrimination. And so far, no real terror.

The tenth anniversary of the Revolution, and by common consent the end of the hardest year yet. Each year things have been just about to improve; and each year they have got worse. Almost everything you can buy is rationed, and almost everything has to be queued for. There is a feeling of greyness and weariness, as if the nation had been at war for ten years.

Havana is the saddest sight – shabby, blank, full of nothingness. The 'Revolutionary Offensive' last year put the remaining small shopkeepers out of business, leaving boarded-up fronts down every street. The State-owned shops that remain have little to sell. Many of them have nothing at all. You go into some large department store that was once full of haberdashery and notions, and it's like a scene out of a symbolist film – sales staff standing behind row upon row of showcases that contain nothing but air.

A lot of the famous nightclubs survived until last year, when they, too, were closed by the Revolutionary Offensive. The bars went at the same time. Street-corner cafés remain open to sell cane-juice, or a Coke-type drink. Once, presumably, they had some kind of superficial brightness about them. Now they are grim and bleak, providing for the input of fluid in much the same way as public lavatories provide for draining it off again at the other end.

Queues form at these cafés when word gets round that coffee may be made. Queues form everywhere as soon as some commodity is rumoured to have come into stock. In my first, somewhat stunned, walk around Havana I saw queues of over a hundred people waiting even for bread (of which there is said to be no shortage) and cigars (which are rationed, at two per day). People get up at six to queue for their rations before they go to work. They pay others to queue for them.

You can eat off the ration in a restaurant – but for these you have to queue, too. An hour or two, if you get up at six and queue for a reservation; two or three hours if you turn up without one. A Cuban friend who wanted to take me out to dinner told me that he had inside contacts, and that he could fix things so that we'd only have to wait two hours instead of three. But in the event even this modest arrangement fell through; maybe his contact was worrying about the place-ticket man at another popular Havana restaurant who got murdered recently, allegedly for this kind of favouritism. The restaurants have neon signs outside, tablecloths and intimate lighting within. In another couple of years, you can't help feeling, the immorality of eating will be discovered, and then the restaurants will go, too.

Havana is running down, no doubt about it. Most of the normal processes of renewal which characterise cities, like any other living organism, seem to have stopped ten years ago. The noise of the streets is that of ten-year-old American cars in their death agonies – loose wings rattling, worn-out engines labouring on low-octane Soviet petrol, exhausted starters struggling to coax life back into motors that die the death at every red light.

This apart, the streets are oddly quiet. Nothing's happening anywhere. No, that's a lie. Several times I went running to the window of my hotel room because I could hear things happening outside. Once it was a dozen lorries with flags flying and hooters blasting, streaming down the Malecón, the great empty highway that runs along the edge of the Atlantic, loaded with demonstrators for some manifestation downtown. Another time it was twenty new tractors, parading ceremonially with their headlights on; once a troop of tanks on transporters; once a squadron of naval patrol boats in line ahead; once a tractor towing a brightly illuminated float through the empty night, with people cha-cha-cha-ing on it. Oh, and once, in a taxi, I got stuck in a traffic jam, caused by a passing demonstration. The drivers all began to blow their horns and curse; it was a lively moment.

Havana was built for other things – for the accommodation and entertainment of the island's absentee landlords, a bourgeoisie too big for the economy to support, large numbers of expatriate and visiting Americans, 40,000 prostitutes and the practitioners of various ancillary trades such as pimps, abortionists, venereologists, and pornographic photographers. Now that these merry souls have departed, the city hangs like a discarded morning suit upon a gaunt refugee.

Vedado, where the big hotels and the best cinemas are, is built like a slice of midtown America; from the window of my room on the nineteenth floor of the Riviera, an American-style luxury hotel opened just over a year before the Revolution, and expropriated soon after it, the skyline of towers looked like a petrified forest, forever sunlit, forever empty. But, curiously enough, the shabbiness, the desuetude, and the insistently characteristic smell of the Soviet petrol made it look more Russian than American.

Down in the old town, behind the port, I thought of Graham Greene's vacuum-cleaner salesman, Wormold, who became Our Man in Havana, walking from his shop in Lamparilla Street each morning to drink daiquiris with his friend Hasselbacher in the Wonder Bar on the Prado, besieged by pimps and filthy-postcard vendors. The Wonder Bar is now just a fading sign hanging out over blind windows, with a glimpse of cobwebs and piled bar-stools in the darkness within. The idea of a vacuum-cleaner shop on Lamparilla now is ridiculous. A barber's, a lavatorial café, and nothing much else but grime and desolation, and doorways open at night on to tiny cluttered living-rooms that look like converted lobbies, lit by single dim electric bulbs. The street-boys whistled after Wormold's daughter Millie as she walked up Lamparilla on her way home from the convent each day. I can't imagine anyone whistling in Lamparilla Street now.

While I was in Cuba I met Jose Yglesias, the Spanish-speaking American author of *In the Fist of the Revolution*, a sympathetic and vivid picture of everyday life in the country. In the old days in Havana, he told me, the whores would pinch your bottom as you walked through the streets with your wife. 'Suddenly – ouf! You'd look round, and they'd put their heads back and roar with laughter.'

Cubans remain very sensual, so some of them told me. There are said to be *posadas* in Havana still, where couples can rent rooms by the hour. For the brigades of volunteers who go out to the country at the weekend to cut sugar-cane the dense jungle of the canefields fulfils a similar function. But official tolerance stops short just beyond this point. Last year a group of long-haired 'hippies' who used to meet outside the Hotel Capri were rounded up and sent to cut cane in Camagüey. They were alleged to have been involved in organising prostitution for foreign seamen, but I had the impression that their long hair was the real offence.

Homosexuals still have traditional meeting-places, on Neptuno and San Rafael, and along La Rampa, but several people I met in official positions volunteered unprompted their abhorrence of homosexuality. I met a serious young high school student one night on the Prado who said he thought he was a homosexual. The possibility filled him with anguish. In Cuba now, he said, they were regarded as worse than beasts. He had made several attempts to kill himself; he wished he had died at birth.

But then sometimes in the evening, when the brilliant

orange tropical sunsets silhouetted the towers and royal palms of Vedado, and the warm twilight hid the shabbiness, my dubious feelings about the place would come to seem grotesque. The streets would fill up with sharply dressed young couples strolling and decorously courting, laughing in the dark. You could walk round and feel easy, reasonably certain that you wouldn't be robbed or stabbed, or clubbed by the police.

All right, there were shortages and queues. But had I, in point of fact, seen anyone who didn't look decently fed and decently dressed – one single, solitary person? And wasn't that astonishing, in one of the world's less-developed countries? In fact, had I ever been in any country before, rich or poor, where I could say that? Not America, certainly – not Russia – not Britain.

Anyway, once you get outside Havana things don't look quite so bad; the countryside never was rich. The 'People's farms' are said to be inefficient and unpopular (though one of the foreign agricultural experts I spoke to was sure that their size would make the policy pay off eventually), and production of sugar, which accounts for over 80 per cent of Cuba's exports, is still thought to be running below pre-revolutionary level. Cuba is kept afloat by massive Soviet aid. But it's the rural poor who have benefited from the Revolution, undoubtedly. The government has provided schools and medical services, and forced teachers and doctors out into the country to staff them. To the cane-cutters and sugar-mill workers who had work only during the two months of the sugar harvest it has brought employment throughout the year. To a great many poor peasants who were rack-rented by absentee landlords and who lived in fear of eviction it has brought an undoubted security.

The English delegation (as I was officially designated in documents by Minrex, the Ministry of External Relations) travelled from one end of the island to the other in considerable style, chauffeur-driven, with accompanying interpreter-guide from Minrex, in a vast black 1959 Cadillac. I felt bad about this. When Yglesias was here in 1966 to write his book, he'd simply taken the bus down to Oriente; but after looking at the queues in the bus-station in Havana I weakened. I felt rather better when I met Yglesias in the motel in Santa Clara, coming back from Camagüey on a mission for the *New York Times*, travelling in a large black Minrex Cadillac himself. You had to move around by government car now, he said, the buses had become impossible.

My guide, Carlos Sanchez, was a sleepy, likeable man, a lot franker and more straightforward than various Soviet counterparts I have come across. He had previously been showing Edna O'Brien round for the *Sunday Times*. Everywhere we went I would ask anxiously, like a second wife, if he had taken Edna there. (After a few days of this I felt I knew her well enough to get on first-name terms.) No? Well, how many other delegations had he brought to this particular sugar-mill? Only six? Oh, that was all right, then . . .

Ridiculous to think of us all, really, zooming back and forth in our ancient Cadillacs, gazing earnestly at the inscrutable countryside beyond the power-operated windows, and trying to catch our guides out with the same smart questions. In each town you're greeted by the local representative of ICAP, the Cuban Institute of Friendship with the Peoples, and put up wherever possible at one of the elegant new motels and tourist centres which the government is building. A private and specialised Cuba all of their own, these, peopled by foreign delegations, foreign advisors and engineers, foreign businessmen, and Cuban honeymoon couples. They have bars, for heaven's sake, where white-coated barmen wait before pyramids of illuminated bottles, like Satan's ministers in front of the flames of hell, to mix foreign delegations a daiquiri, or sell them a whole box of cigars. There is a considerable choice of dishes in the restaurants, with little items like butter (for children only, in the shops) and cheese (not on the market at all) taken for granted, and steaks that come in American sizes – perhaps 3/4 lb at a time, a whole week's meat ration.

So we drove, westwards past the blue sugarloaf mountains of Pinar del Río, framed by tall royal palms just as they are in the little pictures on the cigar-boxes, eastwards across the flat canefields of Camagüey, where Guevara's men dragged themselves barefoot through the mud when they at last broke out of Oriente to attack Santa Clara and end the war. Armadas of complex tropical cumulus drift in from the Atlantic on the Trades. Buzzards wheel endlessly round in the wind, congregating together in slow-turning whirlwinds at the approach of rain. By each grazing cow a bird like an alert Aylesbury duck stands on guard, waiting for worms to be turned up. Peasants trot by on horseback, hand on hip, straw hat on the back of head, cigar in mouth.

From the car radio comes a non-stop mixture of ye-ye and go-go music, interspersed by indigenous cha-cha-chas, and occasional hybrids in the go-go-cha and cha-go-ye range, some of them accompanied by words which

Carlos says advocate armed revolutionary struggle in Bolivia. Down in Pinar del Río, WDVS in Miami comes in strong, with snippets of news paid for by a local supermarket chain – armed hold-ups, 65-cent chicken offers, assorted slayings, and a chuckling deejay who is giving away free sewing-kits to anyone who writes in explaining 'I need a sewing-kit like I need a . . .' (e.g., hole in the head). Fifteen minutes of this, and I'm the third most dedicated revolutionary in the island.

*

Vast radical ideals hang over Cuba, as pure and fabulous as the tropical clouds. Some day, says Castro, they will eliminate money. Already its uses have sharply diminished. There are no taxes of any sort, and no money relationship between government organisations. Most public services are cheap, and a number are free. No rent is charged for houses built since 1945, and the low rents now payable on older houses are due to be abolished in 1970.

The Constitution lays down a minimum wage of 85 pesos a month and a maximum of 450 (the peso is maintained, improbably, at parity with the dollar), but even this comparatively small differential is not as important as it looks because almost everything that money can still buy is rationed: food, drink, clothes, petrol, electrical goods, toys, cigars, the more popular sort of cigarettes. People have money to spare. The townspeople try to use it by going out into the country and buying food direct from the peasants to supplement the rations. This is technically illegal, but overlooked provided that the quantities are not big enough to suggest any form of distribution. But the peasants are becoming more and more reluctant to accept money for their food. They produce thick rolls of bills that they cannot spend and insist on barter.

Nor, on the other side of the social exchange, does money have much direct relation to labour any more. Cuba rejects the idea of material incentives as degrading, and looks down upon the Russians for employing them. (Yugoslavia, Carlos told me seriously, was officially regarded as 'a classic case of capitalism'.) Faith backed by exhortation seems to be the Cuban method, and if that fails, the Labour Courts – tribunals of workers which can order salary cuts, transfers and suspensions of up to two months.

The standard work-week in Cuba is forty-eight hours, but large numbers of workers volunteer to do unpaid overtime, sometimes another two hours a day, in certain circumstances as much as four. They also volunteer to spend their hours off performing unpaid militia duties, and their days off on unpaid agricultural work. The decisions to work unpaid overtime always seem to be unanimous; while I was there all 59,610 workers in Cuban light industry unanimously volunteered to renounce overtime pay. I was told of a meeting at one factory where the workers had expressed their unanimous approval of unpaid overtime by shouting 'No, no!' at the party official who put the resolution: he understood immediately.

The local party officials are under pressure from above to get results, and the results are measured in terms of hours worked. I often had the impression that the effort put into things was regarded as important in itself – more important than the result it produced. For instance, the voluntary agricultural work – sowing or cutting cane, usually, or planting coffee. One can see that it's good for townspeople to share in the labours of the countryside, but whether it's much good for the countryside, or the country, seems dubious. The amateur cane-cutters cut the cane too high, leaving behind the part with the highest concentration of sugar, and where the professional *macheteros* of the past completed the harvest in two months, it takes this much vaster labour force four, starting in December before the cane is properly ripe. When they go for the weekend they tend to take Monday off work to recover; when they go during the working week – as they often do, for several weeks at a time – they continue to draw their pay, often of course at skilled urban and professional rates, and the country loses the services they normally perform.

I submitted a question to 'Juceplan', the Junta Central de Planificación, asking what contribution voluntary work made to the economy, but could get no reply. It may well be that no one has ever calculated it; I was told that labour costs for new projects were often scarcely estimated. I asked Carlos if methods like these were really conducive to productivity. He told me that I was thinking in terms of highly developed economies. In an economy like Cuba's it was sheer production that counted, not productivity; and in any case the significance of all this extra work was chiefly the political attitude that it expressed.

Maybe. But while the State as employer can go on getting labour for nothing (or apparently for nothing), it's difficult to see what incentive there can be to economise on it, or what end there is in sight to longer and longer hours of work. Money is undoubtedly a bad master, but there may be worse.

*

Authority in England often seems intolerably remote and impersonal, dispensing order, help, punishment and redress as if from another world. In Cuba, Authority lives next door and round the corner and in the ground-floor flat – in the local CDR, the Committee for the Defence of the Revolution.

They exercise the visiting observer, these omnipresent committees. Are they just a corporate Big Brother, the dictatorship of the proletariat refined down to the dictatorship of one's neighbours? Or do they represent the kind of participation and communal responsibility which our own society so notoriously lacks?

Each block in the city, each cluster of houses in the countryside, has its own CDR. Any resident in the block may join; something over a quarter of the population belongs to the movement, which is controlled through a hierarchy of levels leading up to a National Directorate appointed by the party. The function of the committees is to act as links between the State and the individual. The State wants blood, old iron, empty bottles; the local CDR collects them. The State wishes everyone, even old Mrs Hernandez at No. 14, to know about the iniquities of American imperialism in Vietnam and the benefits of cervical smear testing; the CDR calls a meeting and tells them. At night the CDR patrols the block, maintaining 'revolutionary vigilance' against counter-revolutionary saboteurs, and reporting any suspicious activity to Orden Público, the police department of the Ministry of the Interior.

When Mr and Mrs Bermudez, in the room over the barber's, apply for more living space, their neighbours in the CDR go round to see how bad their home conditions really are. When Mr Martinez applies to join his son in exile in the United States, his good friends in the CDR come round and make a complete inventory of his possessions, so that he doesn't have a chance to appear generous by giving them away before the State expropriates them at the time of his departure. When Mrs Hernandez's son-in-law Roderigo smuggles a side of pork into her house from the countryside it's the president of the CDR who shops them both . . .

One is liable not only to be accused by one's neighbours, but judged by them, too. Most petty cases are now heard by Popular Tribunals, informal courts held in the evenings, each presided over by three public-spirited citizens from the district who have done a five-week training course, and who can impose sentences ranging from admonishment, through confinement to one's house, up to six months in a work-camp.

More serious criminal cases are still heard by the old *audiencias*, courts presided over by professional judges as before the Revolution, but I was told at the Ministry of Justice that the intention was to replace these in time with Popular Tribunals of a higher level. There are in addition Revolutionary Tribunals which sit from time to time to try certain offences considered to be of a serious counter-revolutionary nature – sabotage, misappropriation of public funds, robbery committed in uniform, and others – and which can award sentences of up to thirty years, or death.

I watched a session of a Popular Tribunal one evening in

the town of Camagüey. It was being held in a workers'
recreation club; the judges' table was set on the dais where
the band played for dances, with illustrations of drums and
maracas brightening the walls behind it. My interpreter-
guide, Carlos, and I arrived a quarter of an hour before
proceedings were due to commence, and already the best
seats – a row of battered metal rocking-chairs – were occupied by women who all seemed to know one another, and
who looked as if they came every night the Tribunal was
sitting, like the *tricoteuses* around the guillotine.

The impression was strengthened when the only man
among them came over to chat to us. We should have
been there the night before, he told us. They'd had to try
the case outside in the street, so many people had wanted
to watch! It had started at eight, and gone on until nearly
midnight – it had been as good as one of those courtroom
films on the television. A couple had accused their landlady of slandering them. But as the trial had gone on, the
accused had become accuser, the accusers accused – it
really had been just like a movie! – and it came out that
the couple had moved into the old woman's house and
then declared she was dead, in order to collect all the
money that was due to her.

One by one the judges drifted in, and came over to join
the conversation. There were five of them – an employee
in a milk enterprise, a man who worked for the local
authority, someone in the Ministry of External Trade,
and a couple of railwaymen – though only three out of
the five would sit on each case, taking it in turns to be
president and secretary. We really should have been there
the night before, they all said, laughing and shaking their
heads reminiscently.

Eventually they all withdrew to the judges' chambers – the warm starlit night outside. Importantly, a man mounted the dais and placed five metal cups and an orange plastic water-jug on the table. One of the two men sprawled in chairs immediately in front of the dais – militiamen, apparently – shouted 'Stand up!' and the first three judges filed up on to the platform.

The president for the first case was the External Trade official, a sandy-haired, reliable-looking man, like a local Dag Hammarskjöld, in a bright blue open-necked shirt. Two chairs waited in front of the judges' table. At a word from the president they were occupied by the accuser, a brisk young man wearing what seems to be the fashionable footwear for young activists, ammunition boots laced up only as far as shoes would be, and the accused, a strongly built man in his sixties, with iron-grey hair and grim, set features.

With a formality which contrasted oddly with the open-necked shirt and the maracas, the president asked the accused if he wished to challenge any of the judges, or to be legally represented (he could have retained a private lawyer at his own expense; in a higher court he could have had one from the State for nothing). Then, with no less formality, the secretary read the charge: that the accused had threatened to murder the accuser.

The two of them took it in turn to give their evidence, standing in front of the tribunal with their hands behind their backs, strictly disallowed from gesturing. The young man, it turned out, had been in love with the old man's daughter. According to the young man, he had broken the affair off, whereupon the girl's father had insisted that he had seduced her and would have to marry her. He had brought the young man before the tribunal at an earlier session, accusing him of making 'scandals', but the charge had been dismissed. It was after this that he had been overheard to say how he would break the young man's neck if he ever got his hands on him.

According to the old man, the boy had upset not only his daughter but the whole family by blowing alternately hot and cold – and had also, incidentally, raped the girl. Sensation in court! The young man was recalled to the stand to comment upon this. His explanation greatly amused the few men in the audience. 'He says,' whispered Carlos to me, grinning, 'that the old man thought his daughter was a virgin, but really all the young men in this town make love to her. This is very sad news for the old man, I think.'

The judges all smoked furiously. A dog trotted about the room, sniffing at accuser and accused impartially. Through a window at the side of the dais a crowd of children leaned in, as if from a stage box. Eventually the tribunal retired to deliberate. When it returned, five minutes later, the president announced that the sentence was a public admonishment for both parties. Raising his voice suddenly to the pitch and passion of an orator on some remote spotlit balcony, he moved from passing the sentence to executing it. They were both good revolutionaries, he thundered – the boy was a Young Communist, the old man the president of his CDR – and they ought to know better than to waste everyone's time and energy with stupid quarrels when they should be standing shoulder to shoulder against American imperialism. The counter-charge of rape he would refer to a higher court, the local *audiencia*.

For the second case, the only other one which the tribunal heard that night, the milk worker moved into the chair. The accused was a delinquent-looking girl of about twenty; her accuser, another large, grey-haired, solid man (wearing suit and tie, though, of all odd rig-outs) was also president of his CDR, and as such had been entrusted with supervising a sentence of confinement to house passed on the girl at an earlier hearing for abandoning her two children. He now accused her of disobeying the order, saying that one Sunday she had been out of her house all day and all night, and that on another occasion she had been seen giving a party in her home where she had smoked marijuana, taken other drugs, and kissed men in front of her children.

With the girl the tribunal were stern and headmasterly. One of the judges had made personal investigations, as the members of tribunals apparently often do. He knew the way she lived, he said – one long succession of men. What was the name of the current one? She didn't know his name, she said.

But they were stern with the accuser, too. I felt for him, coming home from work only to spend the evening organising the collection of old bottles and the denunciation of Venezuela, breaking off in the middle of that to run up to No. 43 and see what the local trollop was up to. And now to spend all evening in court, being told sharply not to wave his arms about when he spoke, and asked coldly why he had delayed for a month before reporting the girl's absence on the Sunday.

I couldn't stay to hear what happened to the girl. When I left, the president of the CDR was explaining that he hadn't wanted to be hard on her; it was the marijuana party that had made him put his foot down. 'I don't permit immoral behaviour in my block,' he said.

Is this how it is, then, a healthy society that cares? Do these tired men, working on through the evening for nothing after their shift has ended, knocking on the door to investigate when they hear the sounds of a party, represent the kind of close communal responsibility which our society must develop if its wounds are to be healed?

Cuban officials described the CDRs to me as an extension of the family. Jose Yglesias in his book enthuses about the life one leads under the surveillance of one's fellows, calling it 'the life of the open book'.

Or is it the life of the universal YMCA?

*

The general aim of penal policy, I was told at the Ministry of Justice, was so far as possible to close down the prisons, and to get prisoners into the agricultural work-camps, where they could be rehabilitated by performing useful labour. This, I was told, they did for the same hours and the same pay as ordinary workers, qualifying for a weekend at home every fortnight or so.

This seems to me to be admirable, if true, and true it may possibly be. However, in spite of making a formal application in writing to the Ministry of the Interior, I could not get permission to visit one of these penal work-camps. I asked the official at the Ministry of Justice what the total prison population was, and how many of them were serving their sentences in work-camps. He said he didn't know. He didn't even know how many people had been executed in the past year. I submitted the same questions, in writing this time, to the Ministry of the Interior, and after much prodding managed to get the reply that this information was not published.

I also asked how many political prisoners there were, and could get no answer to that, either, apart from a vague guess hazarded by the man at the Ministry of Justice that there could be 'only a few thousand'. In 1965 Castro gave the figure as 20,000, though others at that time put it as high as 75,000.

It is true that the UMAPs were closed down two years ago. These, the Military Units for Aid to Production, were the notorious agricultural work-camps to which people were sent without any form of trial, to have unsatisfactory political, social or sexual proclivities ironed out by an indefinite period of therapeutic labour, and which were condemned by many observers of Cuban affairs, including Graham Greene and Fidel Castro.

In theory now there is no way in which citizens can be deprived of their liberty without being tried first. In practice, I gather, ways exist. One can be called up for military service with the reserves, and sent to an Army unit engaged on agricultural work, or arrested and held 'under investigation' for weeks or months at a time, without ever being brought before a court. I talked to an Englishman whose travelling companion on the plane out of Havana had been a Canadian just released from La Cabaña, the old dungeon in Havana, after being held (so he had said) in solitary detention there for sixty days without charge or trial – only one of many, he had said, in the same situation. He had seen no physical brutality, but a number of the prisoners doing long spells of solitary had gone berserk; the guards just let them scream it out, and then, when they calmed down, pushed some more food round the door.

The Army is everywhere; so are armed militia, guarding everything, down to the car park at the Havana Libre Hotel, against counter-revolutionary saboteurs. I was told that there had been more counter-revolutionary activity last year than at any time since the Bay of Pigs, in 1961, when it reached its height. In a speech at the end of September, Castro listed eighteen major acts of sabotage committed during the year, mainly fires started in factories and warehouses, together with another twenty-five lesser incidents, and thirty-six fires in school buildings.

This is not a complete list of counter-revolutionary activity, even to my own knowledge. While I was walking in the Sierra Maestra, the mountains in Oriente where the Revolution was born, the local man who was acting as my guide told me that in September a complete counter-revolutionary guerrilla of more than thirty men had been operating in the area, though they had quickly been betrayed by a loyalist spy in their ranks. I was also told – though this only at second hand – that there were guerrillas operating in the Sierra Cristal, up in Northern Oriente, and in the hills behind Baracoa; and that air force exercises reported in the Baracoa area may in fact have been part of a counter-insurgency operation. Oriente and Camagüey, the two most easterly provinces, are said to be the ones most affected by counter-revolutionary activity.

I could find no suggestion that the various counter-revolutionary groups had any unified organisation, and no doubt many of the incidents are entirely isolated acts of frustration. But counter-revolutionary organisations do exist, though to what extent they're supported from

Miami is difficult to know. Shortly after Castro's September speech the State Security Department announced that it had arrested six men on charges connected with one of the biggest of the fires he had listed, in a textile warehouse in Camagüey, which had destroyed clothing worth $1.5 million; they were described as belonging to a group called the National Liberation Front.

The guerrillas I heard about in the Sierra had borne a political name, too, the '13th of March', the date in 1957 on which. student revolutionaries unconnected with Castro made a suicidal attempt to assassinate Batista in the Presidential Palace.

*

The only other way of voting against the regime is to go into exile. About half a million people have left Cuba since the Revolution, according to American sources. They continue to pour out on the ten 'freedom flights' each week operated by the US Government between Varadero and Miami, and for those with relatives abroad to pay the fare, on the handful of scheduled services out of Havana to destinations in the West – Mexico City and Madrid. According to the Cuban Government, there is a waiting-list of 200,000 who have applied to leave.

A few return, of course; a faint cheer went up in the lounge of the hotel I was staying at in Santiago when the television announced the arrival of yet another hijacked airliner, the twentieth or so that year. The fact remains that about 700,000 Cubans are either in exile or waiting to go into exile. A lot, certainly, from a country whose present population is under eight million – but it is not, as some people tend to imagine, by any means the whole of the old middle class, which was estimated to account for between a fifth and a third of the population.

Exile is not an easy option. As soon as you submit your application to leave you lose your job, and unless you have private means – there are still people living on the compensation they received when their businesses were expropriated – you have to work in an agricultural labour camp until you go. With 200,000 waiting, and only a thousand or so leaving each week, you must presumably expect to wait for the best part of four years. Conditions in the camps for *gusanos* ('worms' – the government's name for those who choose to leave) are said to be bad. I applied for permission to visit one; it was not granted.

When you go you forfeit all your possessions. I watched the Customs men at the airport searching the thirty *gusanos* who left on the same plane as I did for Madrid, confiscating handfuls of small change, riffling through the photographs and old letters in family Bibles. After about ten minutes my presence was noticed by officials, and I was ordered to leave. I'm not sure why they try to make a secret of it; there's no secret about the rules, and so far as I could see the officials were enforcing them with great correctness, even with a suggestion of amiability. 'These people are not important,' said Carlos, when I protested at my exclusion. 'They are only a minority.'

As they climbed the aircraft steps, one woman crossing herself, one man almost too senile to get up them at all, everyone of course in his best clothes, they looked irredeemably middle class; *byvshiye lyudi*, in the sad Russian phrase, 'former people'. They didn't rejoice, they didn't weep; their faces remained consciously expressionless. But there was something about almost all of them that struck me with a shock; they looked guilty. They had that air of slightly shamefaced defiance that people have when they are doing something which they think is entirely justified, but somehow immoral all the same; a living demonstration of the wrongness of minorities.

*

One day in Havana I was taken out to see the National School of Art, built in the grounds of the former Country Club that Millie Wormold, in *Our Man in Havana*, almost bankrupted her father to join. In the old clubhouse itself, beyond the formal drawing-room with its elegant period furnishings and its portraits of the wealthy landowners who founded the club, was a dining-room with tables laid as if for a Lord Mayor's banquet. I asked the director if some important foreign delegation was expected. No delegation, she replied; groups of students from the school were brought in here to have their meals with this surgically complex array of cutlery and glasses, instead of eating off trays in the canteen, in order to teach them etiquette. They had three special etiquette instructors; soon it would be a compulsory subject in all Cuban schools.

Well, well – everything gets back to normal in time. Even Fidel changes his uniform to go to parties, the director said. I suppose, in fact, that Castro is exactly the kind of leader whom the sociologist Weber had in mind when he formulated his theory of charisma, one who overthrows the pre-definitions of society on the basis of his own personal authority. Inevitably, as Weber shows, this charisma becomes 'routinised', and rarely survives beyond one generation.

One feels this process of congealment going on around one everywhere in Cuba, faster in some spheres than in others. In Castro himself, for example, to judge from his speeches. Perhaps the astonishing thing is that he has avoided so many of the corruptions of power. All the same, one's heart sinks slightly when one turns from his famous 'History Will Absolve Me' speech, made at his trial after the abortive attack on the Moncada barracks in Santiago in 1953, with its magnificently passionate account of the sufferings of the Cuban people, to his speech last year justifying the invasion of Czechoslovakia, or to some of the speeches lecturing the rest of Latin America on how to achieve the Revolution, which sound a little like those books on how to succeed in life written by self-made millionaires.

Castro seems to grow increasingly preoccupied with denouncing and threatening the regime's enemies. 'Before the Revolution ceases to be, not one single counter-revolutionary will remain with his head on his shoulders in this country,' he declared last September, in a fairly typical outburst. 'These are the rules of the game, these are the rules of the game! Before they can destroy the Revolution, the heads of all those who wish to destroy it will roll. Anything else is nothing but hogwash.'

There is something sad and ridiculous, too, in his attack last year upon the hot-dog-stand proprietors of Havana during the 'Revolutionary Offensive', the government's campaign to close down all the bars and the remaining small businesses, when he read out a kind of sociological study prepared by 'party militants'.

'The data gathered on hot-dog stands and similar vending stands,' he told his audience, 'showed that a great number of people who intend to leave the country are engaged in this type of business, which not only yields high profits but permits them to be in constant contact with lumpen and other anti-social counter-revolutionary elements . . . The greatest percentage of those not integrated into the Revolution was among owners of hot-dog stands; of forty-one individuals who answered this item, thirty-nine, or 95.1 per cent, were counter-revolutionary . . . The moral and social conduct that goes together with a revolutionary attitude was taken into consideration in the survey of the proprietors of stands, where, of the eighteen individuals who answered this point, all eighteen were anti-social amoral elements.'

This is so absurd that it's almost endearing – like Don Quixote charging the flock of sheep. All the same, Quixote at the head of a government, and an absolute government at that, is not an entirely humorous concept. Is this what it was all for? All the suffering, all the deaths, all the long hours worked for nothing? So that the great knight-errant could at last ride forth and lift the scourge of hot-dog stands from the nation?

I saw Castro speak one night on television. He skilfully warmed his audience with ad lib jokes, then, leaning his elbow informally on the lectern, and playing unceasingly with his beard, he gave his favourite demonstration of navigating single-handed across a limitless ocean of statistics. In the middle of it he threw out one of those astonishing radical ideas that time and again in Cuba force one to stop and think deeply about all one's presuppositions. This time it was the suggestion that the development of the universities in Cuba would lead to their disappearance, because eventually the numbers coming forward for higher education would be so vast that the universities would have as it were to dissolve into the life of the community, and educate all school-leavers as they went about their jobs.

After an hour or so the television set – it was in the lobby of an hotel in Holguín – abruptly ceased to function. About twenty people had been watching it, with passing interest but no sign of reverence. Some of them made vague attempts to call the breakdown to the attention of the management, but no one troubled to get out of his armchair to fix it. I wandered out into the town's central square, where the speech was being relayed over a loudspeaker. It was Sunday night, and the square was full of people. They were not there to listen to Fidel, however; they were performing the ritual Sunday evening *paseo*, strolling round and round in their best clothes.

Families greeted one another; children showed off. The boys eyed the girls; the girls chattered and laughed ostentatiously among themselves. It was a beautiful sight; they are such a beautiful people, and in the warm winter night, beneath the lamps of the square, they looked well dressed, prosperous and relaxed. It might have been any other Latin country, except that there was nowhere to get a drink, or even a cup of coffee. In the background the rather high, familiar voice lectured on, as unheeded as it would have been anywhere else.

*

But the mythology remains; the story, above all, of the two years that Castro and his companions spent in the

Sierra Maestra. I was very struck by the behaviour of a weedy young party official who showed me round a new agricultural project in Pinar del Rio, looking rather like David Frost in cowboy boots. He kept throwing colossal bone-cracking handshakes and spine-jarring slaps on the back to anyone who came within range, and from time to time doubling up over an imaginary sub-machine gun and spraying imaginary bullets into the surrounding undergrowth. He was twenty-five, and he was playing *guerrilleros*.

There is a sense of religious purification in the privations that Castro and his men suffered, particularly in the weeks immediately after their ill-managed landing from Mexico in the yacht *Granma*; and a sense of moral initiation in the betrayals they experienced, and the death sentences which they passed and carried out in return. The magnificent account of that time given by Che Guevara in his *Reminiscences* has the simplicity and strangeness of a legend.

Castro has always deprecated the religious characteristics of Communism. It's said that he also discouraged naïvely enthusiastic portraitists in the early days of the Revolution who attempted to depict him as Christ, and that he has expressly forbidden icons of himself, in the Stalinist manner, in the offices of government organisations.

The mythology has its religious aspects, none the less. The stories of the Sierra are still told and retold in the Press, and commemorated in the celebrations of the State. Schools, shops, factories – every sort of institution – are named after dead revolutionaries, as after patron saints, or bear names sanctified by association, like

'Granma' and 'Moncada'. Schoolchildren learn little devotional songs in which they pledge themselves to 'be like Che'; his icon is everywhere, now that he is dead; a national commission has been set up to ration out the use of his name.

I caught part of an extraordinary radio programme broadcast on the national day of mourning for the martyrs of the Revolution. 'What is the meaning of this word "Che"?' asked the speaker officiating, in that special sacred tone of voice that priests use. Some kind of congregation began to chant 'Che! Che! Che!' over and over again, in a low, keening tone. 'Che,' explained one of the two officials I happened to be with, reverently. 'Che,' confirmed the other, in a similar manner. They both looked at me expectantly. 'Che,' I responded solemnly. It seemed to satisfy them.

The importance of these events from the past as legend is that they offer an interpretation of the present and a guide to the future. The austerity of life in the Sierra lends significance and purpose to the austerity of life today. The constant watchfulness which a guerrilla band must maintain against ambush and treachery explains the constant 'revolutionary vigilance' which is urged now. The concreteness of the enemy in the Sierra makes concrete the notion of a present counter-revolutionary enemy.

The ambiguity in the concept of 'the Revolution' reinforces these parallels. In one sense 'the triumph of the Revolution' occurred in January 1959; in another, scarcely differentiated, sense the Revolution is something which is still in the process of being 'made'. Perhaps the most important suggestion of the myth is that some reward as satisfyingly definite and total as the one gained by the struggle in the mountains will somehow crown the sufferings of the present.

The whole economy is really being waged like a war, on a death or glory basis. Particularly agriculture. Vast campaigns are launched, to clear scrub, to plant coffee, to make a particular province self-sufficient in lettuce, as if in an attempt to deliver one final hammer-blow which will bring Nature to her knees, offering unconditional surrender. Castro himself rushes from place to place in the battle, offering inspired intervention at all levels down to company and platoon. Divisions of tractors are hurled into battle. Monumental balls-ups occur. Whole campaigns are written off as strategic ideas change. Weaknesses in the front are suddenly spotted – no onions! – and men and materials are poured in to secure them, regardless of cost.

The various foreign advisors who have been brought in watch this wild blitzkrieg rather gloomily. Productivity on the 'people's farms', created by the expropriation of the large and medium-sized holdings, is said still to be lower than on the small peasant holdings, though the most sympathetic of the foreign experts I spoke to thought that the size of the larger units was bound to make them more efficient in the long run.

The key to the economy is sugar, which accounts for 85 per cent of Cuba's exports. The industry was deliberately allowed to run down after the Revolution, so that its output declined from 6,800,000 tons in 1961 to 3,800,000 tons in 1963. The intention was to free the country from what was seen as the curse of monoculture, dependence upon one crop. But at the end of 1963 Castro abruptly reversed this policy, and announced that economic development would henceforth be pinned to sugar, and to raising output to ten million tons by the harvest of 1970. Now sugar is not just a monoculture but a monomania; you can scarcely go a hundred yards in Cuba without some exhortation on the subject being thrust at you on a hoarding: 'What are you doing towards the ten million?' 'The ten million – an obligation of honour.' Cuba celebrated the tenth anniversary of the Revolution by putting sugar on the ration.

Perhaps, suggested some of the foreign advisors I spoke to, all the effort and resources being invested in the economy now would start to show some return in ten years' time. In the meanwhile the country survives on Soviet aid. I asked how much this amounted to, but could get no answer. The figure given traditionally by outside observers is a million dollars a day. Expensive things, wars.

*

I got to the Sierra Maestra finally myself. Like many another visitor I was taken up to the teachers' training centre at Minas del Frío, a horrible muddle of standard shedding and squalid shacks sprawling like a gold-rush town 3,000 feet up on the crest of the Sierra Maestra. Castro's headquarters were here in the early days of the war. Now all the student teachers of Oriente have to spend a year of their training in Minas, just to remind them. An expensive reminder, I should think, since all the necessities of life, including visiting delegations, have to be hauled up twelve kilometres from the road-head at Las Mercedes in rugged six-wheel-drive Soviet trucks, their engines screaming in low gear on the precipitous mud gradients.

The clouds were down on it the evening I arrived. It was the first time in Cuba that I managed to feel cold. The grim shed designated as the visitors' lodging certainly made a change from the elegant tourist centres one stays in most of the time. It had stopped-up lavatories with excrement on the floor, rain blowing in through the open louvres of the dormitory and collecting in pools on the floor, and bedding as clammy as the grave. It was like some kind of nightmare youth hostel. I went to bed fully clothed, under all the blankets I could find, and shivered all night, the damp seizing up my joints. A delegation of Russian writers arrived as I left; they told me when I met them later in Santiago that they'd had rats running over them all night.

Next day I borrowed a former mule-driver and *guerrillero* as guide, and followed him along precipitous mule-tracks to some of the little villages lost among the steep, wooded hillsides round about. Coffee and bananas grew half-wild among the trees. These are the money crops of the Sierra. The mule trains take them down to Las Mercedes and the other road-heads, and bring back the few manufactured goods the peasants need; clothing, household utensils, salt – not much else. The rest of their food they raise themselves around their cabins. A simple life, its form not much changed so far by the Revolution. But I had the impression that the peasants I saw were definitely less poverty-stricken than they had been before. Oriente is traditionally the most backward province of Cuba, and the Sierra Maestra the most backward corner of Oriente. Guevara described the people who were brought to him for treatment during the Sierra campaign as 'all more or less the same: prematurely aged and toothless women, children with distended bellies, parasitism, rickets, general avitaminosis – these were the marks of the Sierra Maestra.' There is a photograph in his book of a Sierra peasant family outside their palm-leaf cabin. The women and children are shoeless and in rags; the whole family has the haunted look of grinding poverty.

In my day's march I saw no one who looked under-nourished, no one without decent clothes and decent footwear. The women were often dressed much like townswomen – as peasant women were all over Cuba, to my surprise – in, for example, brilliantly coloured skin-tight trousers. The people I saw were undoubtedly poor; but I saw no one who looked, as those really oppressed by poverty do, like an outcast from the human race.

On the open hillside above a little village called Magdalena we sat down to rest. In front of us, a triangle of deep blue nestling between the mountains: the Caribbean at La Plata, where Castro's men scored their first victory in an attack on a small barracks. Behind us, Caracas mountain, where the whole Revolution was almost aborted when one of Castro's men betrayed their position to the government air force.

It was about four in the afternoon, and we'd had no lunch. My guide cut *naranjas agrias* from a tree – sour oranges – and we sucked the unbelievably acid juice out of them. It felt good to be there, as it always does walk-ing in the mountains; even the searing tartness of the oranges was good. At that particular moment of that par-ticular day, in that hard corner of the island where the *guerrilleros* had suffered and fought, it seemed to me that maybe the astringencies of the Revolution were not so intolerable after all. If ever I came back to Cuba, I thought, I'd bring a rucksack and a pair of boots, and walk right through the Sierra, from Santiago to Cape Cruz, sucking a sour orange for lunch every day.

But I don't know. Just east of Santiago, three weeks after I left, a group of eighty people shot their way out of Cuba, and across into the American naval base at Guantánamo, leaving another seventy or more dead, wounded, or captured by the Cuban guards on the way. Perhaps ten years of sour oranges is more than anyone can be expected to stand.

(1969)

That First Taste of Abroad

Spring again, Paris again

What a pleasure still, in spite of everything, to run round to Victoria after breakfast and take the ten o'clock train to Paris! To ride out through the rain past the stares of people waiting on suburban platforms for trains to Petts Wood and Clapham Junction; to set the grimy docks of Dover behind, and the antique dingy saloons of SS *Invicta* (the very boat, I bet, that transported Mrs Melrose Ape, Miles Malpractice and the rest across the Channel in *Vile Bodies*) . . . and in the mellow, moist late afternoon sunlight to step out at the Gare du Nord into a world so astonishingly different.

I hadn't been for nine years. But nothing seemed to have changed at all. Not in nine years – not in the eighteen years since I first hitch-hiked here with a schoolfriend, carrying six pounds' worth of francs in my pocket to last a fortnight, and living largely on bread and a pot of British jam. It was my first taste of Abroad, as it must be for most English people – the symbol and essence of the great outside world into which one bursts forth at the end of winter (or always means to), and from which as children we had all been cut off by the war.

We were dropped then by a van-driver, on an afternoon of sunshine and rain, in some undistinguished boulevard in the north of Paris. Even before we had got as far as the nearest Metro I knew that the world was more spacious, more brilliant, more ordered, more charged with possibility than I had ever imagined. The vividness of that first moment of arrival was almost as strong this time. I left my bag at my hotel, in a neat little square, all elegant urban greys – pale grey washed walls, dove-grey shutters, dark grey slates and leads beneath a delicate mackerel sky – and walked round.

The terraces of the cafés around St Germain-des-Près were already packed. The pavements were crowded with strollers – impossibly worldly men with neat grizzled hair promenading impossibly polished stainless-steel girls – and the warm evening air was filled with talk and laughter. I walked across the river and back, along the *quais*, through the gardens of Notre Dame, moved to find that the whole central machinery of Abroad was still there in perfect order, waiting only for my arrival. A warm wind stirred the horse-chestnuts in the Vert Galant, the little green after-deck of the Ile de la Cité. Groups of young people sat out on the point, as they had on fine evenings eighteen years ago, dangling their feet over the water, listening to guitars being played very softly. It was all just as I had left it!

Or so it seemed. In the suburbs whole new districts have sprung up – the old youth hostel I used to stay in at the Porte de Châtillon has been knocked down to make room for the *périphérique*, the ring road. But in the centre new building has been surprisingly discreet. There is a fashion for 'drugstores', like the one in the King's Road, and 'pubs'. A few experimental new double-decker buses, looking rather like old Sheffield Corporation tramcars, jar slightly upon the eye, and on two of the Metro lines now you ride with an unfamiliar soft swooshing on pneumatic tyres. But when you get out of the rubber-tyred train, and in the *correspondance* pass the familiar beggars holding babies or exposing a deformed foot, the blind lottery-ticket sellers, the same men with accordions and ancient foot-pumped melodicas playing the same heart-breaking old tunes, it seems almost as if the city has been preserved like a king's court in a fairy story, by being asleep.

It was the first anniversary of last year's near-revolution, and the first month without the General. There were police everywhere; half the population of Paris seemed to be in the police. They came in pairs, in half-dozens, in scores; waiting at road junctions with a string of squad cars drawn up on the pavement; waiting in buses with screened windows in the Avenue Gabriel, behind the Elysée Palace. I didn't know there were so many policemen in the world. Another six buses – doors open on a hot afternoon, but the full complement of police inside each, at the ready – wait in reserve beside the Panthéon. They are already out in strength at the Philosophy Faculty, the Rue de l'Abbé de l'Epée, and a number of other centres where postgraduate students are boycotting the *agrégation* exam.

Behind the Sorbonne, more bus-loads of police wait outside Louis-le-Grand, the most famous of the great French *lycées*, to supervise the phased return of pupils after a nine-day closure. The situation at Louis-le-Grand, and at the other 'hot' (disrupted) *lycées* in the neighbourhood, has gone from anarchy to violence, like the children's island in *Lord of the Flies*. Louis-le-Grand was closed after an extreme-right 'commando' some forty strong, helmeted and carrying clubs, broke into the school, and a grenade was thrown which blew the right hand off a nineteen-year-old boy called Gabriel Rebourcet. *'Gabriel, tu seras vengé!'* say the slogans pencilled up in the Metro. At Henri-IV, another of the 'hot' *lycées*, 'death sentences' were subsequently reported to have been passed on alleged 'Fascists', one of whom was said to have been clubbed into insensibility.

There are revolutionary slogans up everywhere still, particularly scribbled on advertisements. *'La démocratie c'est la merde'* – *'Achète, tais-toi, et crève'* ('Buy, keep silent, and die.') An unfortunate poster for somebody's beer, which shows a rather camp male model with a bottle of the stuff hung round his neck like the *légion d'honneur*, and which has a lot of white space left for writing, is a regular target. 'I am prostituting myself to earn money. How about you?' he smiles on one Metro station.

*

Wherever I went we talked about politics – about the election, about May. Like old times, it seemed to me, before politics were replaced by de Gaulle. No one talked about *him*; there's no one so thoroughly forgotten as the newly departed.

I had lunch with a friend of mine who teaches in the Law Faculty. When I last saw him, three years ago, he was a great admirer of de Gaulle – had in fact written his doctoral thesis on 'de Gaulle and the Structure of Europe'. Now, to my astonishment, he was a *gauchiste*, a *contestataire*. 'You should have been here in May,' he said. 'Everyone was transformed by this same feeling of sheer joy. Even the girls you passed in the streets seemed more beautiful.'

He had been moved to boycott his *agrégation* last year, and he took me on a rapid tour of university establishments to see how this year's boycott was developing. We went to the intelligence centre of the *contestataires* in the courtyard of the Sorbonne, where groups of students and teachers stood exchanging the latest news, and reading bulletins from the various examination centres written on sheets of brown paper pinned up on screens. 'Complete strike at Ste. Geneviève . . .' 'At Rue de l'Abbé de l'Epée the *flics* in control, with closed circuit cameras . . .' 'Brétigny: 140 candidates sitting out of 300 . . .'

Tracts and handbills lay scattered on the ground. My friend darted about picking them up and examining them. He was making a collection of them – since May he had amassed a stack about so high, he said, indicating a point some three feet above ground level – with the intention of making his next book a history of the period.

We walked rapidly across the Latin Quarter, he keeping the earpiece of a miniature Soviet transistor plugged into his ear to catch the latest from the *agrégation* front. Inside the new university complex in the Rue Censier the walls were smothered with painted and scribbled slogans. 'Down with electoralism' – 'Destroy the University' – 'The teachers are inept idiots' – my friend had collected them all already. Only one fresh one caught his attention – 'Act and be silent. International of the Invisible Ones.'

'I believe that France is going through a crisis similar to the cultural revolution in China,' said my friend. 'The bourgeoisie hasn't really been touched by it yet, but the working class has. Nothing's been settled. Nothing was settled by de Gaulle's departure – nothing will be settled by the election. There is a force abroad now that no president, whoever he is, will be able to hold down.'

*

Odd how every great city has its characteristic range of smells, which place it in one's mind more solidly than anything else. One of the smells in Paris at this time of year is house-painting, being done with oil paint that smells exactly like the sort that artists use. It mingles with the smell of all those canvases being painted for the tourist trade around the Place du Tertre, so that one has the impression sometimes that the whole city is being painted into existence like a picture.

And the smell of the Metro, particularly that sudden acrid whiff you get overlaying the regular ground bass. I've only just placed it after all these years; it's the smell of the brake-linings running hot as a train stops. The mere names of the Metro stations are evocative enough in themselves: Sèvres-Babylone, Réaumur-Sébastopol, Denfert-Rochereau, Barbès-Rochechouart – more like entries in the *Almanach de Gotha* than stops on the Tube. Can one imagine a Frenchman trying to evoke London by pronouncing Tottenham Court Road, Clapham North and Leicester Square?

I walked and walked, finding it difficult to remember that I could afford now to sit down on a café terrace for an occasional cup of coffee, until I had that familiar crushed feeling in the stomach and the small of the back that comes from walking in cities (but not from walking even all day in the country). The soft spring weather was suddenly replaced by a heatwave; the city of delicate greys against pale blue skies became one of a brilliant white, where the light beat up into one's eyes off cleaned white stone, white gravel walks, dazzling water. Then the weather broke and the rain washed the streets and roofs a new range of dark luminous greys, filling the air with the scent of growing grass and fresh green leaves.

Glad of the excuse, I bought a Maigret story for old times' sake, and sat reading it in a café on the Boulevard St Germain while the rain swept in silver clouds along the street outside. Even the rain seemed comfortably familiar, perhaps because it's so often raining in Paris in Simenon stories. A lot of the Paris that seems most familiar comes out of Simenon – the barges on the Seine, the sleazy back-street hotels, obscure streets with names like Rue de Picpus. So do half the people one sees. And if not from Simenon, then from *Sous les Toits de Paris*, and some of them, still, from Lautrec and Flaubert. No city has ever been so thoroughly and intimately made over to the world through art and films and literature. Nineteenth-century Paris seems almost more real and more familiar to us, from Monet, and Pissarro, and Sisley, than our own back-garden, particularly in those pictures of rural scenes which were then just outside the city, but where the city's presence somehow lurks as powerfully and poignantly as a memory or a dream one cannot quite recall.

One worrying thing about my Maigret, though – an English police officer called Monsieur Pyke who is sent over to study Maigret's methods. M. Pyke is everything an Englishman should be in French eyes: correct in dress, correct in manners – even his French is so correct that it makes Maigret feel uneasy. Not half as uneasy as it makes me feel.

Who is this blackleg? How can any Englishman ever hope to be as correct as the Parisians I come across, who remain cool in their impeccable dark suits and discreet ties even on the hottest day, refusing, by unimaginable powers of self-control, to move a muscle as I grind their language to shreds? It's terrible to think of them reading about Pyke, then looking up to see me running in twenty minutes late, with no jacket or tie, sweat pouring down my face, gasping out '*J'ai pris le train de Métro incorrect!* No, I mean, *le train incorrect de Métro!* No – *le train pas juste – non juste – injuste . . .* Well, anyway, *le train pour la Gare d'Orléans* instead of the *Porte d'Orléans . . .'*

One of the great pleasures of cities is knowing your way about the complexities of its geography and manners. You think you're not doing too badly – better than some fellow-countrymen you've seen making fools of themselves, anyway, asking for beer and getting Byrrh, telling the waiter '*Mon thé sur la table*', and all the rest of it. Then this bastard Pyke turns up and raises the stakes, and you might just as well be making the waiter climb on to the table with a pint of Byrrh after all.

*

A sign (in English) outside a nightclub called the Pussy Cat ('Danger!! Charge your battery at Pussy Cat. The Parisianest show with the prettiest "Mademoiselles". Giggle . . . laugh . . . and explode!') suddenly reminded me of an even Parisianer show where I was once taken for what seemed to me to be a uniquely French giggle. I couldn't believe that the Cabaret Le Néant would still be going – but it was. I was first brought to this 'cabaret philosophique', as it calls itself, among the strip clubs of the Boulevard de Clichy, by a commercial traveller who had given my friend and myself a lift into Paris from somewhere out along the Dieppe road, and who could scarcely wait to let us in on the joke, late as it was. The black paint is flaking off the facade now, but the joke inside the Nothingness Cabaret remains the same: death.

You sit at coffins instead of tables, drinking unnaturally expensive beer, in a room hung with various skeletal remains, and various serious texts on the nature of death (e.g., 'Neither the sun nor death can be contemplated unblinkingly.' – La Rochefoucauld), while a master of ceremonies dressed as a priest makes various rib-tickling remarks about the inevitability and possible proximity of death, and goes round from coffin to coffin teasing the customers individually about the alarming pallor of their complexions and lividness of their tongues beneath the sickly lighting.

He then operates a number of decaying trick tableaux round the walls, so that the clothes and flesh appear to fall away from the figures in them and reveal the skeletons within, moralising as he does so on the shortness and vanity of life. The customers, in a fairly hilarious frame of mind by this time, adjourn to a neighbouring room laid out as a chapel. One of them is persuaded to get into a coffin and be wrapped up to the neck in a shroud. A scratched record of funereal organ music plays, and by a Pepper's Ghost effect the flesh of the lucky customer's face appears to decay down to the skull beneath.

The whole entertainment is a kind of low-comedy version of Baudelaire. The rest of the audience – all French, even in Pigalle, mostly young men out with their girls – pretty well died laughing, if that's the phrase. I wasn't quite so entertained – the French sense of humour has depths and subtleties where a foreigner cannot easily follow. In a joke shop behind the Quai St Michel I once saw a packet of powder which you were supposed to put into someone's drink. 'The victim,' explained the instructions, 'will at once have an irresistible desire to piss! What is more, he will be panic-stricken to discover that the pipi is completely blue!'

I wonder how M. Pyke would cope if his good friend Maigret slipped him a dose of that in his *bock*? With unshakable correctness, no doubt. Enter into the spirit of the thing, and borrow a corpse from the morgue to put in the *commissaire*'s bed in return.

*

Anyway, there are other interests which form an indissoluble bond between our two peoples. 'MARGARET JEALOUS OF PRINCESS ANNE,' said *Ici Paris*, my reserve reading matter for rainstorms. '"After all, Margaret, I don't understand you," the Queen said to her. "It's natural that Anne should replace you . . . And frankly, I thought I was doing you a favour by relieving you of these official chores . . . Everywhere you represent me, everyone reports that you smile only when you leave."

'Margaret hung her head and did not deny it . . . "You're right," she admitted. "It's better that way. And then, Anne is young and pretty. Much more so than me anyway . . ." '

Giggle, laugh and explode.

Or possibly, *achète, tais-toi, et crève*.

(1969)

59

Anticlockwise is Best

Israel, inch by inch

'From the *Observer*? Then tell me something, please. Why is the *Observer* so anti-Israeli? And how could *The Times* publish that terrible Arab advertisement? Why does the BBC tell lies about us? Why is everyone against us?'

The start of many conversations. Sitting outside someone's house, at night usually, with jugs of fruit squash on the table against the heat, crisp white shirts gleaming beneath the terrace light. From somewhere close at hand, the steady, drenching pulse of the sprinklers sustaining the fragile green superstructure of life upon the arid earth; and never very far away, perhaps a few miles, perhaps only a few hundred yards, the edge of the green. Beyond it, nothing but enemies; the troops and the terrorists, the defeated and the refugees; and behind them, the hostile or indifferent Great Powers, the unfriendly friends.

'It's so unfair, that's what maddens me. Just because we won the war, everyone thinks, "Of course! Naturally! How could you expect a few poor peace-loving Arabs to stand up to this invincible military machine?" But, look, nobody thought we were an invincible military machine before we happened to win! We went into that war in desperation! We thought we were finished! You can't imagine how we felt when suddenly it was all over and we'd survived . . . !'

Somebody remembers it's time for the news. Somebody always does. They relay the bulletins on the buses – coming down from Upper Galilee to Jerusalem I heard four, every hour on the hour. You see older people walking about the streets with transistors to their ears like teenagers; they have sons or grandsons on the Canal. In Tel Aviv I passed a beggar with a transistor beside him on the pavement.

I asked what the news was this time. Oh, nothing much. Another exchange of artillery fire on the Canal – the soldier who was shot by the Syrians in the Golan on Monday night has died of his wounds.

The sprinklers pulse, the cicadas whirr. The darkness is full of those hot resinous and vermouth scents which to North Europeans mean the Mediterranean and holidays.

'You remember Peretz's cousin?' says someone. 'The one who was staying with us last summer? He's wounded – he was on the Canal. Lungs punctured by shrapnel. They think he's going to be all right. They don't know yet.'

'Yaakov's boy's in that unit that took a beating when the Egyptians attacked at Lake Timsah on Monday night. Yaakov's going grey with worry.'

One afternoon I was being driven through the dusty outskirts of a development town in the Negev by a Government press officer. He switched the car radio on for the news, and as soon as he heard the first item his foot came up off the accelerator. One hand went to his forehead; the other rested dramatically on my forearm. The car wandered off the road and drifted to a halt in the dust. I gazed at him, frozen with alarm, unable to guess the sense of the Hebrew.

'We've shot down seven MiG 21s over the Golan!' he reported at last, in a low, awestruck voice. 'Seven! For none! What will those Jews do next?'

*

'*Nu?*' said everyone sharply, when they weren't complaining about the British Press. 'Well? You've been here for a week now. What do you think of the place?'

'Well, I'm finding it very . . .'

'I envy you, you know, seeing it all for the first time. It's a marvellous experience.'

'Yes, well, I . . .'

'The point is, you see, that Israel isn't like other countries. It's something entirely new – something completely different . . .'

It certainly is – it's the only country with over two million people working in government public relations. You can't live in Israel without being totally committed to it, said a friend of mine, giving up the attempt after five years. Even as a visitor you can't remain neutral. It's not a country, I read somewhere – it's a faith.

Of course the world is full of places consisting chiefly of faith, where grandiose futures are just on the point of emerging from seas of mud and oceans of statistics. Looking at the raw new fringes of development in Israel – the newly established towns and settlements in the dust of the desert – you can imagine how notional this country was twenty years ago. But now here it is, actually happening; the tangible structure of a modern State, in all its sophistication and complexity, has actually come into being. Without natural resources, or cheap native labour, an egalitarian, democratic, and dynamic society has taken shape and established a livelihood for itself. Things work.

I'm not sure quite how. The economy is highly directed; taxes are astronomical; far too much power, both political and economic, is in the hands of the party machines, which were the effective government before independence, and of the trade union organisation, the Histadrut, which not only represents its members to the employers, but is itself the biggest of the employers. The task of holding down the conquered Arabs and holding off the rest exhausts resources, coarsens feeling, and numbs logic. All the same, it seemed to me to be a place where it was possible to live and breathe, to argue and extend oneself, to shout and whisper and even to laugh.

Right little, tight little Israel. You can't get out of it by land to north, east or south, and with a foreign travel tax which adds, for instance, £50 to the already expensive air fare to London, they don't make it easy for themselves to escape to the west, either. After the Six Day War, people poured into the West Bank to stare at it. Now few go – though you see plenty in East Jerusalem and the Golan, which are regarded unequivocally as parts of Israel. When I asked if they ever felt claustrophobic, people looked surprised. Many of them, particularly the older ones, seemed to know every inch of the country by heart, and to have watched each brick laid.

'Look, there's an old house! Seventy years old, at least – First Aliya – you can tell by the iron railings . . . Late fifties, this estate here – built for the big Polish immigration in Gomulka's liberal period . . .

'. . . Look at these flats – full of Oriental immigrants. Anywhere else this place would be a slum. But our women's organisations went in and taught them how to live in modern society – how to use the toilet, when to change their underclothes . . . .

'And this is the playroom. We did all this ourselves, of course. You see these screws that the cupboard door-handles are fixed with? Well, they're a special sort, which we only got hold of after a terrible struggle . . .'

*

In the older kibbutzim the shade trees have had time to grow, the lawns to mature. Twenty years, and a settled, venerable air hangs over them, as over Finchingfield or Upper Slaughter. A friend of a friend of a friend invited me (this is how it goes in Israel) to spend a few days on his kibbutz – one in the Huleh Valley, in Upper Galilee, which was established just before independence. It was a bit like a cross between a very select holiday camp and a small university. The members' houses were lost in shade and flowers. There was a swimming-pool, in idyllic pastoral surroundings, and tennis courts. People cycled slowly along the winding paths, in and out of the dappling sunlight, as if on the way to lectures or tutorials.

I went out to the orchards to join the apple-pickers at five in the morning, riding on the mudguard of a tractor, and flinching as we drove through the chill douches of artificial rainstorms pouring down here and there upon the trees. Already, as the sun came up from behind the Golan, the sprinklers were turning above the cotton like a well-rehearsed *corps de ballet*. A crop-spraying plane was diving repeatedly at the next field, and the apple orchards were loud with the roar of the hydraulic lifts on which the pickers moved among the tops of the trees. Every inch of the ground seemed to be under scrupulous modern scientific management.

In the early years of independence, said my host, the food situation had been worse than in occupied Europe. His wife said they had spent the first three years of their married life in a tent shared with someone else, and furnished with two beds and three orangeboxes. A hard life, I remarked.

'Not at all,' she replied. 'My life was never hard. In the first place we were unceasingly thankful to be alive, and then we were free of the cares that householders have. We had no choice! Now the children are faced with making choices; my children are finding it very difficult to make up their minds about what they want to do and where they want to live. It's not so easy for the young people who go out to found new settlements now, either. After all, they've got an alternative – they've got homes to go back to. We didn't have anywhere else we could possibly go.'

The kibbutzim account for only 28 per cent of the country's agricultural production now. The commonest form of settlement is the *moshav*, the co-operative village where each member works his own land and leads his own life, and which has proved more comprehensible and congenial to the great mass of immigrants who have come in since independence. The kibbutzim still exert a disproportionate influence on the political life of the nation; they still have a certain moral aura. 'Every time I visit a kibbutz,' two separate urban intellectuals told me, 'I feel so guilty. I feel this is the way I ought to be living, too.'

They are changing, none the less. Because the home market for farm produce has been saturated, and also because they want to create less strenuous and more sheltered jobs for their older members, they have started to industrialise – fruit-juice bottling and shoes on the kibbutz I was visiting, everything down to soap flakes and electronics on others.

They have found it necessary to employ outside labour – a fundamental departure from the ideology of the movement, for which my host's kibbutz was regularly berated by the central organisation to which it was affiliated. 'But what could we do?' said one member. 'We needed more hands – and there just down the road was a new development town full of immigrants with no jobs.' There is a movement the other way, too – some of the young kibbutzniki go into town to work each day.

Originally there was no pay – distribution was to each according to his needs. You went into the store and said 'I need another tube of toothpaste,' and you were given one. Then there were complaints, particularly about the issue of clothing, and it was changed to a ration system – to each exactly the same. But this didn't work well, either, and now members are given tokens, marked with a face value the same as currency, and exchangeable for currency. 'Some people', said one of the members gloomily, 'are saying that the next step will be to introduce work norms. But I think this would break the back of the kibbutz system.'

Families are tending to eat in their homes in the

evening, instead of in the communal dining-room. Some of the young mothers are keeping their children with them at night, instead of letting them sleep in the children's house. 'What will happen if this goes on I don't know,' said my hostess. 'The houses weren't designed to provide bedrooms for the children – we'll have to rebuild them all.'

As the old frontier conditions recede, so life becomes more private, more based on the family, more like life in the rest of the community. And more torpid, more institutionalised, according to a group of rather disillusioned overseas volunteers I met one night in the dining-hall. 'It's like being back at school,' said one from England. 'They're so set in their ways, and intolerant of outsiders. If you scour a pot clockwise, someone's sure to come up and tell you that the way they do it here is anticlockwise.'

They sat at a table apart from the rest – though some of them had been on the kibbutz for the best part of a year – a little nucleus of disaffection, sustained by a private bolshie humour, of a sort very familiar from other institutions like the Army. 'I got told off for laughing out loud at a book of cartoons,' said one. And just at that moment one of the members on dining-hall duty came over and told us all we were making too much noise.

'I was put in the packing plant for a week when I first came, to get acclimatised,' said the first man. 'I told the man who's supposed to be in charge of the volunteers that I was bored and wanted a change. "Bored?" he said. "Of course you're bored! What about me, a qualified architect running an alfalfa meal plant? Don't you think I'm bored? What about the PhD who's working as a storekeeper in the garage – isn't he bored? We're all bored! That's life!"

'People come for a month or two, and stay for years. Time just somehow slips by here. You do your eight hours a day, and then sleep for the rest of the time. People vegetate. No one wants to do the responsible jobs – the same old lot have to run everything.'

I repeated these remarks to a girl I met in Jerusalem who had recently immigrated, and spent some time on a kibbutz. She reacted sharply. 'If a kibbutznik tells you that the way to scour a pan is anticlockwise, then you can be sure that's because they've found out after years of experience that anticlockwise is best.'

*

When I arrived at the Knesset to meet Uri Avnery he was in the middle of a speech, opposing a Bill which he said would give the government powers to close down any Arab school on the grounds of subversive activity. A former Irgun terrorist, Avnery has become famous abroad (and notorious in Israel) for his persistent questioning of the government's policy towards the Arabs, and for urging the renunciation of Zionism. He sits in the Knesset as the sole member of the This World Party; it takes its name from the weekly news magazine he runs, which has a reputation for political muckraking in the *Private Eye* style.

Everybody had warned me against Avnery. 'Foreigners always let themselves be impressed by him,' they said, 'because he looks so romantic with that beard, and because he goes in for the kind of wide-eyed liberal ideas they can understand. That magazine of his is disgusting. Did you see that photomontage they did recently which made it look as if a rabbi was talking to a girl with no clothes on? It was in the worst possible taste.'

He does cut a rather romantic figure, with his beard, and his famous white Mustang. He took me to an Arab coffee-house in the Old City, and ordered a water-pipe, which he sucked at while he talked about some of the new Israeli settlements I had been visiting in the occupied areas.

'I can feel nothing but disgust,' he said, 'for people who settle land they know to be stolen, whose real owners are still alive – probably only a few kilometres away across the border. Some of my friends in Jerusalem have moved into Arab houses. I often wonder about them. Don't they ever wake up at night and think about the man who built the place?'

He thought that the atmosphere in Israel had deteriorated terribly during the past two years. 'All this cheap militarism – all these popular songs about how we've come to Nablus and we'll never leave. We missed a great opportunity after the war. For the victor to be magnanimous on the field of battle – this is something that would have been understood.'

In the book he has recently published, *Israel Without Zionists*, he urges the unilateral resettlement or compensation of the refugees, and the creation in the West Bank of an independent Palestinian State which would be federated with Israel in a Semitic Union. He said he hoped to increase his party's representation from one seat to two at the elections. All the same, he seems a rather lonely voice. He says in his book that there have been three bomb attacks on the *This World* offices, and that his hands were injured in a night attack on the editors.

All the other customers in the coffee-house were Arabs; the streets of the Old City outside were deserted. I had the impression that we were the only non-Arabs in the whole of East Jerusalem. Over the endless monotony of cards and sheshbesh around us, a voice on the radio ran on and on in Arabic, hypnotically, like the unceasing flow of a stream. Radio Cairo, said Avnery. 'Propaganda from first word to last – and even more effective now, because there's even less for the men to do in the evenings, except sit smoking their pipes, and sipping their coffee, and letting the words wash over them.'

*

There have been some unofficial contacts between prominent Israelis and their Arab counterparts. They do not seem to have been very encouraging. *Israel Magazine* managed to persuade half a dozen Arabs who were generally thought to be of ministerial standing to take part in an exchange of views with Israeli politicians and intellectuals, the text of which it published. The result, as a member of the magazine's staff said gloomily, looking out the issue for me, was yet another blow on the head for the classic liberal faith that everything would be all right if you could just get the two parties to a dispute around a table. Few of the participants on either side could resist rising to every bait offered. One of them told me that the discussions had been continuing, without publicity, but that it was now felt they should be abandoned.

The chasm of mutual incomprehension sometimes seems beyond all possibility of bridging. I had a long talk one night with a wealthy Arab landowner, of impeccable English upper-class style and manners, who didn't want

to be identified for fear of reprisals. He listed many griev-
ances against the Israelis – priceless buildings demolished, houses confiscated with inadequate compensation
or none at all, families ruined.

But there was one incident which stuck in his mind
above all others. He had been detained for questioning
one night after a bomb incident, and held for four hours
before being released. He had no quarrel about his detention – when he had been an Army officer he would have
ordered exactly the same kind of round-up – and he had
been treated correctly. What had hurt him was that a
colonel in the Israeli intelligence who happened to be a
personal acquaintance had come into the room where he
was waiting among the crowd of Arabs who had been
detained – and cut him dead.

'That I shall never forget or forgive. Would you, if I
were, let us say, military governor of Jerusalem, and I did
the same to you?'

I suppose not; but I can imagine what went through
the Israeli colonel's mind, in the moment when he
realised he knew one of the detainees and decided that it
would be unforgivable to treat him any differently from
the others.

My informant thought that some Israeli peace formula
would emerge this year after the elections. 'If it doesn't,
there will certainly be war. If the Arab governments have
not launched that war by the end of the following year
there will be such a bloody revolution in the Arab countries as you have never seen, with sons turning their hand
against their fathers.'

Our conversation got off to a curious start, incidentally. 'I have read some of your writings,' he said, 'and I

know that you are a Jew.' 'Well, partly,' I heard myself reply. Partly! One thirty-second, so far as I know, and hardly the moment to start boasting about it. Oddly enough, except for one occasion when an over-enthusiastic rabbi started to strap a phylactery on to my forehead in a synagogue next to the Western Wall, this was the only time during the whole of my visit to Israel that this quite fundamental question came up.

*

Israel's peace policy is simple. In General Dayan's celebrated phrase, she is waiting for the Arab governments to ring her telephone. An event unlikely to occur much before the Day of Judgement, one would have thought. Talking to some Israeli government officials in Jerusalem, however, one gets the impression that it might happen at any moment.

'If only the big Powers wouldn't keep poking their noses in,' people explained to me, over and over again, 'and making the Arabs think they might be given their territories back without negotiating, they'd soon see reason. If everyone would just leave us and the Arabs to get on with it we could settle things in a matter of weeks.'

The Arabs were gradually becoming accustomed to the idea that Israel was here to stay, said the official; one more round and they would be completely convinced. Some of the young people I spoke to stoically envisaged a state of war continuing for twenty or thirty years – fifty years – indefinitely. 'Well,' said a lady I met at a party in Jerusalem with philosophic calm (a Gentile, incidentally, like several other particularly Israeli Israelis I came across), 'it's always difficult to settle an argument, when you're right and the other person's wrong.'

'This eternal rightness of the Israelis!' cried a foreign diplomat at the same reception, exasperated. 'I was very pro-Israeli when I came out here, but all this rightness wears you down.'

The official position of the government until recently has been that nothing affecting the terms of a settlement would even be discussed until the Arabs agreed to negotiate. This rigid stand has now in effect been modified with the publication of an election platform by the Maarach, the alignment of Labour Parties which has dominated the wall-to-wall coalition governing Israel since the war. The platform calls for the retention of the Golan Heights, the Gaza Strip and a belt giving land access to Sharm-el-Sheikh; and for the permanent establishment of Israel's eastern security frontier along the River Jordan.

This last provision is in essence the Allon Plan (named after its creator, the Deputy Prime Minister), which envisages the settlement by the Israelis of the western side of the Jordan Valley, so that apart from a narrow connecting corridor across the valley in the middle, the West Bank would be physically separated from Jordan proper. When I was in Jerusalem, before the publication of the Labour platform, this was still officially not even being discussed. But in fact it was already being implemented. Three military-agricultural (Nahal) settlements had already been started in the valley, and Mrs Golda Meir, the Prime Minister, was promising the Knesset that they would shortly hear about new outposts in the occupied areas, where the government felt that security required them.

There is no secret about these settlements, and with the Army's permission I visited two of them. They are run by young men and women doing a somewhat extended version of their military service, who divide their time between agriculture and military duties. It's not an easy option. Down here on the floor of the Rift, a thousand feet below sea-level, you feel as if you're submerged in hot treacle. The soil is saline, and impossible to work without long and expensive washing. The whole valley is dead. Driving north from Jericho through the brown emptiness, the only signs of life you pass are occasional Army outposts, and one or two abandoned Arab villages and refugee camps.

At Mehola, the most northerly settlement (a religious one), they already have air-conditioned huts, and an air-conditioned dining-room with a synagogue corner where they study the Torah in the evening. Further south, in the Argaman settlement, they are still living in tents, while Arab labourers build the huts. Through the binoculars of the sentry on look-out you can see a Jordanian gun-emplacement on the other side of the valley, an abandoned hut where they have seen El Fatah terrorists living, and precious little else but dust and scrub. Impossible to believe that this could ever be turned into green Israel; but this is how it was all done.

This is the classical tradition of Zionist colonisation. As the old slogan goes, 'dunam after dunam, goat after goat' (a dunam is a quarter-acre); a process also known in Zionist phraseology as 'creating facts'.

When I asked officials in Jerusalem about these settlements they dismissed them lightly. 'A mere three,' they said; 'that's neither here nor there. If you want to see what we do when we're serious about colonisation, take a look at the Golan.' The impression which they were anxious I should take away at that time was that 'everything' (i.e. the whole of the West Bank) would be 'given back'. But as a sceptical journalist friend told me, 'What counts in Israel is not what is said, but what is done. Things are done first, without any announcement, and justified afterwards.' Uri Avnery, the most persistent Israeli critic of the government's policy, told me that the Arabs would regard the colonisation of the Jordan Valley as an act of war. A prominent Arab moderate to whom I spoke agreed that it would jeopardise all chance of agreement.

'Dunam after dunam, goat after goat . . .' Isn't this insidious, creeping 'creation of facts' exactly what the Arabs fear about Israel? As Mrs Meir put it with great succinctness recently, addressing members of one of the youth organisations which form nuclei for new Nahal settlements: 'Outsiders have never, and will never, determine our borders. Wherever we settle, that's where our borders will be.'

*

Jerusalem, said a letter in the *Jerusalem Post* one day while I was there, 'was given to the Jewish people by a force much higher than that wielded by the world Powers . . . In spite of this the so-called Security Council has the audacity to arrogate to itself the power to decide the future of all Israel. If they are foolhardy enough to try to enforce their decisions without first meeting the prerequisite of Jeremiah 31: 36, 37, they are heading for a direct and disastrous confrontation with the Almighty (Zechariah, 12: 8, 9; 14 : 12, 13).'

Even the most secular and religionless of the Israelis I met became rather mystical about Jerusalem. 'You must understand,' they said, 'we thought we'd never see the Old City in our lifetime. For nineteen years not a single Jew was allowed to pray at the Wailing Wall!' Now the city authorities have briskly bulldozed a large empty space in front of the Wall, to add to the bitterness of the Arabs. Down at Hebron, in front of the mosque, which is also a Jewish shrine because according to tradition it houses the tombs of Abraham and his family, another great swathe has been bulldozed, and planted out as a rather insipid municipal garden. 'Doesn't that look more like a proper Holy Place?' asked my Israeli guide, with quiet satisfaction. Troops with sub-machine guns waited on a roof opposite the entrance to the mosque – the walls were pitted by shrapnel from a grenade which had been thrown there some time back. Arab boys got under our feet as we went up to pay our respects, offering tourist whatnots and begging. 'Look what they teach them, when they're kids already!' said my guide.

The Israelis have tried out a variety of terms to describe the territories they captured in 1967. 'The occupied areas' – but that sounded a little blunt; 'the liberated areas' – only nobody could say it with a straight face; 'the administered areas' – an agreeably bland formula which seems to be the commonest official designation now; and, in ordinary conversation, just 'the areas', or 'the territories', which conveniently avoids the whole question.

The military government of the 'areas' tries to be discreet; the whole machinery of administration is still operated by the Arabs, with fewer than 300 Israelis holding the strings in the background. Israelis tell you how

Nablus has called its main square after General Riad, the Egyptian Chief of Staff who was killed on the Canal in March, and now Dayan refused to intervene to stop it.

They boast that you can travel right through the areas and never see an Israeli soldier. This isn't quite true. I saw a number of armed patrols – and Gaza was alive with troops. By June this year 140 people had been killed by terrorists in 'the war after the war', and more than 2,000 people are now detained for terrorist activities, many of them without trial, under the old British emergency regulations. Most of this terrorism seems to be both indiscriminate and inept. Any really determined resistance movement, one would have thought, could have caused chaos. The real success of the terrorists – and perhaps this is all they hoped for – has been to call down suspicion upon the whole Arab community. Wherever you drive in Israel you come upon police road-blocks. The police glance in at your face and wave you on – the cars they stop and search for bombs are the ones driven by people who look like Arabs. I was told about a young Arab headmaster who had driven down to Eilat in a car with West Bank number-plates. He had been stopped repeatedly, not only by the police, but by civilian busybodies who wanted to know what an Arab could possibly be doing down there.

*

Will the whole of the West Bank go the same way as the Jordan Valley, and subside, dunam by dunam, into Israel? A lot of people I spoke to, particularly the younger ones, were in favour of outright annexation, and no nonsense.

The trouble is, those who are most attracted to the idea

of the 'Greater Israel' which this would create are usually
also the ones most deeply committed to the idea of a
Jewish State. How, then, to absorb another million
Arabs, with a higher rate of natural increase than the
Jewish Israelis? An industrial chemist told a friend of
mine that the present inhabitants of the West Bank
should be offered money 'to make their homes elsewhere'.

The more usual solution among Greater Israel supporters, however, is faith in increasing the Jewish population
by immigration. A goal of five or six million was usually
mentioned. The present Jewish population is under
2,500,000, and immigration is running at about 30,000
a year, after sinking to half that in 1966 and 1967.
General Narkiss, the director of the Jewish Agency's
immigration department, told me that if this new rate
could be maintained, they could with natural increase
reach five or six million by the end of the century.

Where could all these immigrants come from? There
are perhaps three million Jews in Russia. No one knows
exactly, and no one knows how many of them would
want to leave if they were allowed to. Some guess half a
million; Narkiss was confident that it would be far more.
(As a matter of fact, a trickle is coming out now, but
nobody will talk about it for fear the Russians will stop
it.)

Then there are six million in North America. The
Israelis have great hopes of the United States, as violence
and racial conflict there grow. Last year 4,000 American
Jews came; this year they expect 6,000. 'Whoever would
have predicted that a few years ago?' people tell you opti-
mistically. 'It just shows you – anything's possible.'

Most moderate Israelis see the solution as being the creation in the West Bank of some kind of independent, neutral State of Palestine, as Uri Avnery suggests, perhaps federated with Israel in a Semitic Union, with Jerusalem as the federal capital. 'But how could Palestine ever be economically viable on its own?' objected one prominent Arab I spoke to. 'We should just be a puppet of Israel.'

'Of course we could be economically viable!' retorted another Arab, active in the cause of independence. 'Who told you we couldn't . . . ? Oh, well, naturally – he's drawing a Jordanian salary. How do you think Jordan survives? By getting aid from abroad. If we had a share of that aid we could survive perfectly well. After independence we might federate with Jordan – later, perhaps, with Israel, too. But that would be a long time off.'

A Palestinian State federated with Jordan would scarcely offer the Israelis much reassurance. One senior Israeli official I spoke to thought the whole idea of independence was a dream. 'We can't *impose* independence upon them. Who should we deal with? Most of the local officials, who were appointed by the Jordanians, want the West Bank to remain part of Jordan. We can't impose an election upon them to get new, more amenable officials. In any case, the Jordanians would never accept the situation. Can you imagine them agreeing to half the kingdom disappearing permanently? The Jordanian terrorist organisations would turn on an independent Palestine at once.'

An Arab Israel? A permanent Arab prison-colony? An Arab army back within twelve miles of Tel Aviv? The choice is impossible, and will no doubt never be consciously made. People take refuge in various forms of double-think. 'They talk federation and think annexation,' said Avnery. And in wishful thinking, which is what his opponents accuse Avnery of. A lot retreat into simply not thinking. When you ask them what they think should be done, they produce ideas on the spur of the moment, almost at random, which lead immediately into self-contradiction.

*

I did take a look at the Golan, in fact, as the officials in Jerusalem suggested. Ten new Israeli settlements have been started there since the Syrians were driven out in 1967, according to Colonel Yaakov Stern, the local military commander. 'We believe in the settlement of the area, and we are doing all the other things necessary to turn the Golan into a part of Israel.' This has included the demolition of every village 'of military significance'.

I was taken to visit what must be the oddest settlement in the Golan – Ramat Shalom, up on the slopes of Mount Hermon, four kilometres from the Lebanon border. Like all dangerous border settlements it was surrounded by a barbed-wire perimeter fence which was floodlit at night. Inside the wire there was not a kibbutz or a *moshav*, but a holiday centre being hacked out of the mountainside by a group of people who had formed themselves into a limited company – an anomaly which seemed to have put them beyond the help of all the established agencies for supporting settlement.

I was shown round by a former French photographer called Philippe Bonneau, a Gentile who had come out to Israel as a volunteer for the Army at the time of the Six-Day War. He was a man transfigured by energy and purpose. 'There were fifty of us,' he explained, 'sitting around in an *ulpan* [a Hebrew course for new immigrants], bored, bored, bored. We didn't want to go on a kibbutz and just stand in a line picking fruit. We wanted something where we could all use our initiative, and see our own ideas being put into practice. We came up here on a trip, saw this site – and it was a *coup de foudre*.'

It was in fact the site of a Syrian village called Joubbata ez Zaite, one of the villages which had been demolished by the Army. It was difficult to find out exactly what had happened. According to Bonneau, it was a reprisal for the murder of two Israeli officers. According to Colonel Stern, the story of the two murdered officers was legend. He couldn't explain exactly why the village had been demolished; I had the impression that it had perhaps been a mistake, or unauthorised.

Anyway, demolished it had been. And now this likeable and enterprising Frenchman and his friends were turning it, by imagination and energy and their own sheer back-breaking labour, into a restaurant, a children's riding school and a ski-resort. I asked Bonneau what he would do if one day, through some unforeseen concession in a peace settlement, he found the Arab population of Joubbata ez Zaite standing outside the wire, waiting to claim its village back. He scuffed his foot back and forth in the dust thoughtfully, then gave a short laugh. 'I don't know,' he said, with frank and charming helplessness. 'What can I answer you?'

*

One day while I was in the Negev I went out to have a look at Masada, the extraordinary fortress which was excavated by Professor Yadin five years ago.

It stands in the shattered and broken desert at the lip of the Rift, looking out over fold upon fold of burnt brown nothingness, and far below, sunk deep beneath the level of the world, the appalling deadness of the Dead Sea. Cliffs drop away on all sides from the flat top of the rock, which was rimmed by Herod with a wall and thirty-seven watch-towers; a place to retreat to each time Jerusalem was taken.

It was here that the Zealots retired, after the sack of Jerusalem by Titus, and eventually committed mass suicide rather than surrender to the Romans. In the past few years Masada has become a national symbol – of defiance, of resistance to the death. The day before I visited it, the remains of twenty-seven skeletons found on the site, and thought to have belonged to the Zealots, were buried with full military honours. The guide leading the party I went with – a relaxed, rather humorous man – became suddenly emotional when he spoke of what Masada meant to Israelis today.

The Army, which was partly responsible for excavating Masada, retains a close connection. An Army unit was already on top when we got there, moving steadily with packs and radios and automatic weapons. It was 105 in the shade – or would have been, if there had been any shade. Under the vertical noon-day sun another line of tiny figures – more soldiers, or mad dogs and Englishmen – was just starting to toil up the long ascent from the east. 'They have races up here,' said an American girl. 'I was talking to someone in the Army the other day. They run up.' The guide said that the armoured troops came out here for a very emotional ceremony at the end of their basic training. They hear the Masada story, take the oath of loyalty, and cry out in unison, 'Masada shall not fall again!'

It must have been a kind of little Israel up here, certainly. There was a water collection and storage system which enabled them to cultivate the mountaintop, and provide ritual baths and even a swimming-pool. Outside the walls – the desert and the encircling enemies.

An alarming symbol, though. The Romans had to build a line of fortifications all round, and a ramp of earth and stone 450 feet high, before they could breach these walls; but breach them they eventually did. I couldn't help thinking of something a friend of mine in Jerusalem said: 'We have only about twenty years before the massive education programme in Egypt produces its effect, and we begin to lose the one advantage which has enabled us to hold them off.' Twenty years, if he is right, to find what the Zealots couldn't: an alternative to walls.

(1969)

Capital of Nowhere

Summer in the gardens of Berlin

Berlin is *enormous*; it had never occurred to me. East and West together, it's twenty miles across – from Greenwich to London Airport, say; as big as Munich, Frankfurt and Stuttgart put together; twice as big as Paris.

Thinking about it as just one more international problem you forget what it is – one of the world's greatest capitals. It grew because it was a capital, at the centre of trade and political power. Now, its shabbier eastern boroughs apart, it is capital of nowhere and centre of nothing. Cut off from their raw materials and markets, the industries of West Berlin – the huge Siemens electrical complex, Borsig engineering, ready-made clothes, foodstuffs, pharmaceuticals – are not viable. The city's stranded – a great house with its estates gone, a whale with the tide out.

And yet it is still maintained with much of the magnificence and luxury of a capital. The Federal Government preserves it from subsiding into East Germany, like Venice into the sea, by an elaborate structure of subsidies in the form of help to its industry, and large tax concessions and direct payments to its citizens. The cost is staggering. In the current year it will amount to £400 million;

getting on for twice as much as the grants in aid which the United States gives to the whole of Latin America and India combined.

But what the money buys! All the surplus-value luxuries which make life in a great capital deep and complex and sweet; the machinery of pleasure, cultures and counter-cultures. The rebuilt areas in the centre are mostly not very distinguished, but somehow they seem to work. On a summer evening the Kurfürstendamm is as alive as the Boulevard St Germain with strollers and people talking at café tables. Like some museum of costly religious art, the pavement is lined with free-standing showcases displaying the highly wrought products of industrial civilisation, from inconceivably complex cameras to elegantly produced leftist books advocating the overthrow of this whole society. Prostitutes smile. Beyond them, at the kerb, people look over cars which their owners have left parked with signs in the window offering them for sale.

And in the streets off the Kurfürstendamm a solid bourgeois calm reigns beneath the trees, among the nine-teenth-century apartment blocks full of high, cool rooms, and the gaps between which serve as parking-lots and car-washes. Even the working-class districts of Wedding and Neukölln look neat and prosperous – not at all bad by English standards. Westwards the city dissolves into placid green suburbs – Dahlem and Zehlendorf and Nikolassee – mile after mile of the twenties and thirties, drowning in trees and the scent of flowers, to all appear-ances scarcely touched by the war or its aftermath. Then, beyond the suburbs, like a back-garden, forests and a chain of lakes studded with islands and sailing-boats; and beyond that, as at the bottom of all proper gardens, the

Wall. An enclosed world, secure and limited.

My Marxist friends – most of the people I met seemed to be Marxists of one sort or another – tried to open my eyes to the city they saw; an old, cold city of workers manipulated by the Springer Press, of relationships corrupted by money – a geriatric ward of war-widows and dispossessed old people, who felt that their lives had been destroyed and couldn't understand why, barely suppressing a frustrated authoritarianism which burst forth violently against the students at the time of the 1968 demonstrations.

Nearly a third of the city's inhabitants are over sixty. With no access to the Central European hinterland which supplied it with new blood in the past (and gave it in the process its New York sharpness of style and humour), the population is slowly ebbing away as the older generation die, and younger people drift off. The suicide rate is the highest in the world – twice as high as in West Germany – though none of the explanations about age or 'the pre-suicidal syndrome' of the walled-in city quite fits.

But I couldn't help feeling that the underpopulation was a unique charm in a great city. Think of it – two million people in the West, one million in the East, rattling around in a city that once housed four million. I scarcely saw a traffic-jam. I never got caught in a crowd. You can walk in the Grunewald on a Sunday morning, and five minutes after you've left the last suburban street you're on your own.

Can it all go on? Will the taxpayers of grimy cities in the Ruhr continue indefinitely to keep it in state? With the signing of the Berlin Settlement in June, the role created for Berlin as the 'outpost' and the 'showcase' of the

West came to an end. (Jobs for the superannuated great – compare Britain as 'Head of the Commonwealth'.) What's Berlin going to be *for*?

None of the businessmen and city officials I spoke to seemed to be worried. As relations with East Germany and the rest of Eastern Europe improved, they suggested, hopefully, the subsidy might be needed less. They foresaw a future for the city as a great trading-post with the East; a key air-traffic centre, like Chicago; a teeming cultural exchange. When East Germany had been recognised, a Berlin senator pointed out to a journalist I met, East Berlin would be full of lonely diplomats and tired businessmen, so that West Berlin would have a chance to become 'the Reeperbahn of Central Europe'.

Capitals of lost empires! Who'd live anywhere else? Why doesn't everyone in the Federal Republic crowd in while the bonanza lasts? Cost of travel and removal paid – 30 per cent off their income tax – 8 per cent bonus on top of their wages – no conscription . . . They must be crazy!

*

The Left (the leftist Left, the revolutionary Left) is a bit like Berlin itself – a head without a body; a complicated middle-class institution to liberate the working class, but lacking a working class ready to be liberated. The demonstrators in 1968 were met with open hostility in Wedding – the 'Red Wedding' of the twenties. Students who subsequently sacrificed their university places to take factory jobs and make contact with the workers were greeted with antipathy or indifference.

As a result the Left has splintered into impotence – as

everyone on the Left tells you at once – and its gestures have become formalised. 'Everything's going downhill,' said Sarah Haffner, a painter and teacher who was deeply involved in the 1968 events. 'Everyone's either going SEW or smoking pot and privatising.' The SEW is the Western counterpart of the East German SED (Socialist Unity Party), and their discipline and organisation have become increasingly attractive as the multiplicity of Maoist, Trotskyist and Stalinist splinter-groups fight amongst themselves.

'Most students aren't radical,' a young Marxist professor at the university told me. 'They're either SEW, which is left conservative, or they're anarchist, which isn't anything.' He'd just been in a meeting to appoint a new lecturer. There had been two candidates, one SEW and one a Maoist, and the meeting had gone on for seven hours before the SEW faction withdrew and got instructions by telephone to accept the Maoist. Other meetings had lasted twelve hours. 'Academic work suffers,' he said wryly, hurrying off to another confrontation.

The effect of the Left has been above all on middle-class manners and fashions (I quickly stopped wearing a tie in Berlin). Being Left has become a kind of lifestyle, one of those rather general allegiances like being artistic, or ex-public school, by which people orient themselves and locate congenial friends.

Here, in the small ads in *Konkret*, the leftist magazine with the *Playboy*-style nudes, for which Ulrike Meinhof used to write, is a 'leftist market-researcher and amateur photographer, 40 yrs, 178 cm', who is looking for 'an attractive flatterer with knowledge of English and typing, for lasting friendship'. Perhaps he could try the 'leftist

Lufthansa stewardess, 25 yrs, 170 cm', in the next column, who 'can't stand pilots and managerial types any longer'. They could move in with the 'wild married couple, 28/30', who 'seek leftist but not necessarily like-minded pair for spare time and holidays. No offence taken if the couple have followed the petit-bourgeois trail to the registry office.'

A lot of the advertisers in leftist publications want to join communes or *Wohngemeinschaften*, shared flats or houses run as common households. A man in *Konkret* seeks one 'which will give me the possibility of self-liberation, but also concrete political work. Am left-oriented, but undogmatic and with no party affiliations.' In *Extradienst* someone wants 'a friendly and attentive communal life, with people talking about more than just the weather – at the same time without exaggeratedly idealistic yearnings for psycho-terror'.

These social arrangements shade over into business ones. A café advertises warm cakes until 5.0 a.m. at 'comrades prices'. A dressmaker offers to sew red flags. A commune in West Germany announces that 'in order to give Berlin comrades the possibility of relaxing a little from the strain of daily life in the city, and to fill out our sometimes monotonous rural existence, and to improve our financial situation, we have hit upon the idea of letting rooms to comrades . . .'

They are not the first comrades to have discovered the novel idea of exchanging goods and services for money. All over Berlin leftists have been opening small businesses – handicraft galleries, antique shops and, above all, *Kneipen*, pubs – usually offering food as well as drink. A publisher and his wife who were connoisseurs of these places took me to one down in Kreuzberg, a clearance area full of artists and foreign 'guest workers', where we had one of the best meals I've ever eaten. The waiter, who looked like Brecht, with a shaven head and small round spectacles, urged aperitifs and liqueurs with improbable urbanity. 'He's playing the part of an Austrian waiter,' whispered my friends. 'They're all playing parts – as waiters, restaurateurs, businessmen. After a few months the game will be over, and they'll go away.' All around us young people in cord Levi battledress greeted each other and talked seriously and ate stuffed vine leaves and smoked oysters at about £3 a head, unless they were getting special comrades' prices that we weren't. 'You see that man standing at the counter?' whispered my friends. 'The one who's just drinking a glass of beer? He's simply an ordinary worker from the neighbourhood.'

There are signs that the next generation may be reacting against this prevailing leftist style. Wolf Lepenies, the sociology professor I met at the university, told me: 'Now for the first time I have students coming to me – *students*, coming to *me* (and I don't have the reputation of being one of the most left-oriented teachers in the department) – and saying: "Maybe we ought to study more what Weber, for instance, actually says, before we apply Marxist criticism to it to dismiss it."' Sarah Haffner was appalled at some of the new generation of students she had come across. 'Either they're on pot or they're fascists. They really are. They want to go back to capital punishment. In public.'

*

The central European summer set in – days of solid mid-continental heat, when the children were sent home from school on *Hitzefrei*, heat holiday. At night the thunder rolled. All day more great explosions shook the city – Russian fighters breaking the sound-barrier. A luxury flat near the Europa Centre was blown up, after Baader's arrest, in an unsuccessful attempt to destroy the consignment of arms hidden in it. The people I knew were rather embarrassed by Gudrun Ensslin's capture, after she took off her jacket in a boutique to try on a dress, and left a gun sticking out of the pocket. 'Poor Gudrun!' said everyone. 'In a boutique! Oh God!'

I went to stay with friends, in a semi-detached house in a quiet suburban street on the northern edge of the Grunewald. (The international conspiracy of the middle classes, who always know someone to go and stay with.) It was an actor called Mac Unterzaucher and his wife – he also studying at the university, she working in a hospital as a preliminary to studying medicine. They'd formed a small *Wohngemeinschaft* – they called it an enlarged family – with another actor and his wife, sharing the budget and the house-work and the child-minding, talking over their problems in the evening.

There was a dreamlike sense of familiarity about the house. It was the outer suburban street of my childhood in London. Yet not quite. The houses were less gawky, the gardens less prim. It was a representation of a London suburb in another medium, like a painting; and, as with a painting, this translation distanced the familiarity of the scene, and made it visible.

So with the household. It was the life of all my friends in London over the last fifteen years! A certain sort of middle-class ease; disorder deftly shaped by all kinds of unnoticed skills, with children running in and out, and tennis-rackets and oilskins crammed away on top of the coat cupboard in the hall; and room for everyone to sit round the kitchen table, eating great salads from a wooden bowl; and under the confusion of toys in the front room, where the children were supposed to play, a Bechstein grand piano; all strangely heightened by being two families instead of one, and spoken in German – or, more often, for my benefit, in a marvellously accurate and naturalistic representation of English conversation.

The garden was full of ancient basket chairs, grey with age, which Mac had found in the street – thrown out, under a scheme they have in Berlin, for anyone to help themselves before the refuse truck comes round. You could furnish a house for nothing. I'd sit out in the sunshine reading the paper (university senate meeting halted by Maoists with a loudhailer, more bombs found in Hamburg), surrounded by the complex comings and goings of the household. Mac off to the university. Christian, the other actor, repairing the tiles they'd cracked on the back porch the week before trying to barbecue a pig in the rain. Gabrielle, Mac's wife, back from the early shift at the hospital. Christian off for another performance of *Offending the Public*, the Peter Handke play on the Kurfürstendamm. Dog walking through Christian's wet cement into house. Children I'd never seen before, and young wives with serious spectacles, wandering through the garden, nodding gravely at me, and disappearing through the gap in the hedge into the next garden, where everyone in the neighbourhood seemed to be playing volleyball.

How sweet life can be, living in the cracks and on the fringes of a wealthy society! This is real riches, voluptuous to the touch – to sit on old basket chairs someone threw out, to work late and early, to run out to the super-market and buy a two-litre bottle of wine for 40p and fall asleep after lunch, to know the children have just disap-peared into somebody else's garden with five of their friends, and with any luck won't be back until bedtime. You think Rockefeller had such a life?

*

Sunday. We sailed on the Wannsee with a friend of Mac's, then came back and cooked spiced meatballs over a fire in the garden, underneath the pines. After lunch we went off to see some more friends, a couple Mac and Gabrielle knew through their younger son's nursery school, who had a weekend cottage on one of the islands at the south-ern end of the Tegeler See.

We crossed on a little ferry from Spandau, through the dense traffic of yachts and power-boats, with the cap-tain's transistor playing Wagner; followed a path through deep woods, past the quiet music and laughter of the weekenders you couldn't quite see through the trees; and crept doubled-up through a small gap in the bushes. We were in a tiny overgrown clearing in the woods, with a couple of rotting boats in the long grass and, lost in the bushes, a one-roomed wooden cottage. The Wall in the centre of the city was about six miles to the east, the wall at the back of the estate about four miles to the west.

Around a table in front of the cottage sat a large fam-ily party, somnolent with sun and Sunday and rich cake. We sat down, and it quickly became clear that the domi-nant figure in the company was a visiting uncle sitting at the head. He was a big man in the prime of life, wearing nothing but shorts, and smoking a large cigar. One look at that powerful, handsome face clamped round the cigar, and you knew immediately that here was God's arche-type of the thrusting West German businessman. But he was not a businessman at all, it turned out; by profession he was an architect, and by vocation and deep conviction a member of the KPD (Communist Party of Germany), a small 'cadre' party of extreme ideological puritanism, founded to restore the true traditions of the old KP of the twenties.

He gave up the rest of the afternoon to explaining to me how Russia was reintroducing capitalism, and how East Germany was merely Russia's agent. It was Russia's renascent capitalism which had made the Eastern treaties possible; Russia and the West were getting together to carve up the East European market between them, and to generate in it the needs and desires of the consumer soci-ety. It was the 'clear duty' of workers in both Germanies to rise up and make a revolution. When I asked if he saw any immediate prospect of this happening, he laughed and agreed that it was very remote.

I realised, after his wife had urged him away to dress and drive back to Düsseldorf, where the party had sent him, and where he had got a job building hotels for busi-nessmen, that he had given me almost his only free hour in the week. His sister-in-law told me after he had gone that he worked from nine to six in the architect's office, then drove all over the Ruhr in the evening on party work. 'If he gets home by eleven, that's early, and he'll say to his wife, "Come on – let's drink a little wine! Let's go to the cinema!" I've never seen a man so able to con-centrate and enjoy what's in front of him, whatever it is

– food and drink, work, talking to someone. He comes to the island and he has only an hour or two here. But in that time he relaxes completely.'

I thought of one or two Christians I'd met, light-heartedly enjoying a world which they valued as nothing against the new world they glimpsed inside their head. Later in the twilight, I strolled round the island with a friend of the family, a girl studying at the College of Fine Arts. She was hesitating on the brink of committing herself to the KPD, she told me, trying to work out exactly what her position was. Ghosts passed us, of long-dead girls of good family, out walking on other summer Sunday evenings, talking to visiting Englishmen about whether they had a vocation for the religious life. On some other island across the still water a radio was playing more Wagner. Frogs gargled in the reeds. A nightingale sang.

*

And everywhere, like a trick of the light, the odd, disturbing glimpse of an obliterated and inconceivable past. In the paintings of the twenties, as modern as Matisse, but depicting a city as vanished as Troy. In calm green Nikolassee, when a half-Jewish friend pointed out the surroundings of his precarious wartime boyhood.

This, said my host one evening over in East Berlin, as he showed me out of the courtyard of his block of flats into the Friedrichstrasse, is where the central administration of the concentration camps was. Martin Bormann was last reliably seen running behind a German tank along the Friedrichstrasse over there, just before the tank was hit . . .

Not far away, in the Grosse Hamburger Strasse, is a little public garden that was once a Jewish cemetery and old people's home. The cemetery was obliterated by the Nazis, and the home used as a collecting-point for Jews being transported to the camps. Now there are Christian graves there. 'Our dear Papa', say the headstones, 'My deeply beloved husband'. They were dug desperately in the summer of 1945 to bury the corpses littering the streets around; a scratch unit of hard-core Nazis from Berlin police headquarters, who died defending the Stock Exchange.

In another cemetery in East Berlin I happened to notice a headstone which seemed to sum up all those years in this one spare and desolating cryptogram:

Frieda Scholz, nee Sauerwald
* 10.12.1895
† 1.5.1945

Ursula Claassen, nee Scholz
* 22.1.1917
† 1.5.1945

Werner Claassen
* 14.4.1907
† 1.5.1945

Karin Claassen
* 19.6.1939
† 1.5.1945

Doris Claassen
* 11.3.1942
† 1.5.1945

*

'Tell people you've been to China,' said a businessman I met in West Berlin, 'and they say politely, oh yes? Tell them you've been to the DDR, to East Germany, and at once they're interested. It's a funny thing – it's as if we were all secretly rather proud of it. "Well, what do you think of it?" we all say to each other casually when we get back. "Not too bad, is it?"'

Nearly 700,000 West Berliners went across at Whitsun, when the visiting arrangements which came into full force in June were tried out – a third of the population (netting, incidentally, the best part of a million pounds for the East Germans in visa charges alone). When the Springer papers talk about 'the Zone' and 'the other part of our city' now, it sounds as desperate as the Beaverbrook Press going on about 'the Empire'.

I was very struck by how much the people I met in West Berlin wanted me to like East Berlin. 'You must remember,' they prepared me anxiously, 'that they were the ones who paid for the lost war . . . Their health service is much better than ours . . . People over there are more relaxed and friendly . . . Family life has an old-fashioned *Gemütlichkeit* that we've lost . . .' The old waiter in the restaurant where I was lunching with a friend one day had just been over, to see his sister, for the first time in twenty-five years. 'He went to see if she was managing to survive,' reported my friend, laughing significantly, 'and he discovered that she'd got a car and a yacht, and three people working for her.'

But what really catches people's imagination is how little everything has changed. 'It's like visiting a museum of the old Germany,' they told me. 'Like a trip into the past' – 'Like revisiting one's childhood.' The businessman who

commented on the West Berliners' secret pride in their fel-
low-Germans' achievements had just taken a holiday in
Hiddensee, the little Baltic resort where he'd gone every
year with his parents as a child. 'Nothing in Hiddensee had
changed since 1939,' he said. 'But nothing! Not a nail! A
little more dust had settled, that's all. I went back to the
hotel I last stayed in twenty-five years ago. There were the
same people running it, in the same way. I sat down and
drank the cup of tea I left twenty-five years ago . . . As we
were driving back to Berlin the sun came out, and I
thought, this is me, Joachim Severin, coming back from a
holiday in Hiddensee! I never expected to see it again in my
lifetime! Really, this was one of the most surprising things
that has ever happened to me.'

*

I needed the preparation people gave me, I must admit.
Because of an error in the dates on my hotel reservation,
which no amount of tramping round from office to office
in East Berlin could put right, I had to spend several days
commuting in from the West. Each day I'd ride in on the
S-Bahn from the green suburbs out on the edge of the
Grunewald, where I was staying; and each day, as the Wall
came in sight out of the train window, my spirits sank.

There's something almost embarrassing about the
naked desperation of those gimcrack concrete slabs; the
poor shooting one another to stop themselves running
away to join the rich. In the centre here life seems to have
shrivelled away on either side of it. On the western side,
odd enclaves of eastern territory lie derelict behind
barbed wire, and rabbits dodge away into the long grass
as you approach. (The East Germans have just sold one

bit to West Berlin for nearly £4 million.) On the eastern side is a broad free-fire zone of raked sand, the roads beyond blocked off with forests of 'Spanish riders', three-legged obstacles massed to halt – what? – defecting armoured divisions?

Armed guards stir in the watch-towers. Armed guards wait on each of the dimly lit disused stations of the two Western underground lines which pass beneath East Berlin, drearily watching the trains go by. Armed guards patrol the last kilometre of overhead S-Bahn track from the Wall to the Friedrichstrasse terminus and controls, and gaze down from the gantries high up under the vault of the station roof.

When you get beyond this grisly mantrap the sheer ordinariness of East Berlin comes as rather an anti-climax. It was always the seedy end of the city, and seedy its pre-war inner districts remain. The post-war Soviet baroque of the Stalinallee (now Karl-Marxallee) must be almost due for discovery as an example of High Camp. But the rest of the new building is plain honest Borough Council Perpendicular (the view out of my hotel room, when I eventually got into it, consisted of thrity-seven blocks of the stuff, of varying heights, some arranged parallel with the hotel, some at right-angles to it). The new city centre, the Alexanderplatz, might have been conceived by Cotton and Clore – enormous pedestrian piazzas surrounded by high-rise office-blocks and parking-lots, with S-Bahn trains running through a glass cloche overhead, and the Television Tower dominating it all like a drum-majorette's baton; a vision of the future off some ancient pinball machine, I felt sourly, as I trudged back and forth across those paved plains on my way from almost everywhere to almost everywhere else. All that was missing was an airship coming in to moor at the tower.

West Berlin, which is the capital of nowhere, felt like a capital; East Berlin, which (as they remind you anxiously on every possible public sign) actually is one, felt like a large provincial town. A decent place, I had the impression, if obstinately unlovable. Rents are extremely low – £5 a month for a typical small flat, reckoning at the official exchange rate of parity with the West German mark (which seems reasonable, on the basis of prices in the shops), against an average wage of £94 a month. Fares are cheap, utilities pegged at pre-war prices. There are some good restaurants, and an adequate provision of espresso bars, ice-cream parlours, and beer-halls. Plenty of food in the shops, with few queues. Plenty of consumer goods, at reasonable prices, with a reasonable choice – such comparative plenty, in fact, by East European standards, that the Poles and the Czechs come across the new open frontiers on organised shopping expeditions.

There's a certain amount of ill-feeling about the Poles. They are said to come by the busload, whole villages at a time, to buy up items which the Polish economy has somehow overlooked. One old man I talked to claimed to have seen a Pole buying sixty pairs of children's shoes. East Berlin's becoming a city of Polish jokes, like Chicago. 'I don't like to hear that kind of thing,' say people. 'But do you know the one about why there's no grass on the Alexanderplatz? – Because the Poles would bring their cows to graze on it.'

'You want TV – we build high aerials,' advertises a firm called J. Baron on the underground. In the small ads in the *Berliner Zeitung* Schimmelpfennig, the estate agents, are offering suburban houses for sale; Oehmcke's want weekend plots 'urgently, for cash purchasers'. A lot of the shops are privately owned, and in streets like the Schönhauserallee you pass blocks of small tenement workshops with boards at the door announcing Siebert and Hellman, Neon Signs . . . the Max Pretz Hand Loom . . . Filtz and Co., Venetian blinds. About 10 per cent of the economy remains in private hands, I was told – mostly shops and services. Many doctors are still in private practice. Until this year there were a number of private industrial companies making goods like clothes and toys, and 'craft co-operatives', which had started as repair and service organisations, but found it more profitable to go into large-scale production. Many of them were very successful – too successful, it's said, and the government has now taken them into public ownership, to prevent 'the recapitalisation of the economy'.

But still the material exuberance of the West casts its spell. Western brassieres are in demand, and Levi's with the genuine Levi label. People come up to you outside the Friedrichstrasse station and ask you out of the corner of their mouth if you want to sell any Deutschmarks. 'All the kids on the Alex have got a hundred Deutschmarks in their pocket,' said John Peet, the former Reuters man who now edits a propaganda sheet for the East German Government, and is called upon by all visiting correspondents and television crews. 'I was talking to a policeman up there the other day. He said they only picked them up if they were dealing – they get some innocent from the West and offer him one for one then resell at three to one.'

'I don't want to be a cold warrior,' said one foreign journalist apologetically, 'but there's nothing much for people to do here except watch television, and what they watch mostly is Western television.' I couldn't help wondering how many of the goods in the shops would have been on the market if they hadn't been produced in the West first, and seen on television. Would anyone have bothered to make dishwashers? Or those little wheels for rolling on the floor to get your weight down? Or the cocktail bar and six stools I saw in one shop for just under £1,000, in red plastic and wrought iron?

*

Perhaps they don't need the Wall any more; nobody knows. People are still escaping, and dying or being arrested in the attempt. But friends with West German passports, who have always been able to visit their relatives in the East, told me that there had been a change in the last two or three years, and that even the older generation no longer wanted to leave.

The East German government plainly aren't so sure. They are now allowing out small numbers who have urgent family reasons, and it's generally thought that if most of these return there'll be a further cautious easing of the restrictions. Stefan Heym, the East German novelist, told me that people didn't know themselves how they would behave if they were allowed to leave; they were really schizophrenic in their feelings about the West.

'If the Wall had never been built, it wouldn't now be necessary,' said John Peet. 'But because it's there it has a powerful psychological effect. If the government said, "On such-and-such a date anyone can go and visit his relations in the West," three-quarters of the country would disappear. Not necessarily because they really wanted to go, but just in case they did, and it was the only chance they got.'

Wolf Biermann, the East German poet, who lives in the Chausseestrasse not far from the Wall, has a good poem about it. The ghost of François Villon, he says, lives in this apartment, struggling to read *Neues Deutschland*, the party paper, and when Biermann has a girl in, discreetly goes out to take a stroll on top of the Wall, where he is shot up by the frontier guards. When he gets back to Biermann's place in the morning he coughs up three pounds of bullet lead, and is 'full of understanding for both of us.'

Biermann himself fled the other way, from Hamburg, at the age of seventeen, out of political conviction, and has remained, loyally, to vex the Democratic Republic with the tender, coarse, raging, funny poems that he sets to music and sings himself. Like 'The Ballad of the Man* (*who with his own hands hacked off both his feet)' which is about a man who is disgusted to see that he has stepped in a heap of excrement, and tries to clean up by chopping his foot off – but by an unfortunate error chops off the wrong foot first. 'Many a good foot,' says Biermann, 'the party chopped off like this.' Germany is a rats' nest, he sings, in his 'Balance-sheet-ballad in My Thirtieth Year'. 'If you let yourself be bought, my friend, no matter whether for East money or for West, you'll be eaten . . . digested . . . and before next morning forgotten.'

Biermann is one of half a dozen leading writers whose work is banned in East Germany. But they are allowed to receive their royalties from publication abroad, to see foreign visitors, and even, in some cases, to make trips to the West. Friends of Biermann's in the West told me that his telephone was tapped. Possibly, shrugged people in the East who knew him, and maybe everything he says is going into some great file somewhere. But there it would remain. No one, I was assured by several different people, East and West, whose views I should have been inclined to accept, is now thought to be in prison for political offences. Amnesty International disagree, however, and list a variety of political offences for which they say people are currently serving sentence.

But people in the public eye seem to be fairly confident; once again the proximity of West Berlin may have a moderating effect. Stefan Heym, whose last three books have been banned, told me that after he published the first of them in the West without permission he was fined – 300 marks (£37), the maximum that could be imposed without a court case, and all its attendant publicity. 'I call it pipi-Stalinism,' he said.

*

I met Heym at his home in Grünau, in the outer suburbs – a comfortable detached house with a well-mown lawn before it and trees around it, full of pictures and good furniture; we might almost have been in some half-rural suburban lane near Leatherhead or Stoke Poges. I went out to the suburbs again, to Köpenick, with someone I knew in West Berlin, to meet various relations of hers. Solid upper-working-class people, these – serious, responsible Party members. It was a different style of suburb, of a kind I saw all round the eastern edges of Berlin; a neat grid of unsurfaced roads, along which small bungalows retired into the privacy of tidy, respectable gardens. Roses bloomed. Hedges of macrocarpa screened vegetable-patches and little bright green lawns peopled with gnomes, and aspiring here and there to a striped 'Hollywood' swing-seat.

We sat with her uncle, a retired printing worker, under his fruit-trees, beside the neat rows of lettuces and carrots in his vegetable-garden, talking about how he'd had his bungalow built twelve years earlier. He'd asked his union for permission, and been given it because he was a Party member and a good worker. He'd bought the quarter-acre plot off an old lady for £440, and paid £4,000 for the building, with the help of a twenty-five-year government loan. There was a plan now to clear the district for a high-rise scheme. He reckoned that with the general improvements in the district's amenities, and the additions he'd made to the bungalow, it would cost the authorities £6,000 to buy him out.

We went indoors for coffee and cakes. Three rooms, and a verandah he'd added himself: fitted carpets, a barometer on the wall, pot plants; neat ornaments placed with absolute precision upon lovingly polished veneers; order, tranquillity, pride of possession; everything reminiscent of Ken Loach's portrayal of the destructiveness of the bourgeois home in his film *Family Life*.

Out there in those quiet suburban streets I began to feel this odd hallucinatory sense of revisiting the past that so affected my West Berlin friends when they came over. Only for me it was the more recent past – the late fifties say, under Macmillan, the Age of Affluence; the first taste of the apple, when you could still notice the flavour.

'Now he believes in progress,' says the girl in a magazine advertisement, of the young man beside her. She is wearing a blonde wig and long dark artificial eyelashes, and is holding up a bottle of pre-shave lotion, 'the astringent blessing'. In Boutique 70, the more exclusive section of the gents' outfitting in the Centrum department store, offering the 'Exquisit' range of suits at around £60 a time, I picked up a brochure which began with a quotation from Marx about how art objects created for themselves an informed public ('Thus production produces not only an object for the subject, but also a subject for the object'), then went on to declare that the staff of the boutique wanted to 'assist the customer to shopping pleasure . . . with fashionable clothes to fit the occasion and create a good impression . . .'

Für Dich, the women's magazine, and the best read I could find among the pallid selection on the news-stands, listed the fifty different categories of household equipment a young couple need when they get married (. . . 2 cake-servers, 1 sauce-spoon, 1 ladle, 1 small ladle, 1 skimming ladle . . .). In the next issue a reader described how her marriage had declined into silent evenings in front of the television, until in desperation she pretended that the set was broken – which drove her husband to drink instead. They'd bought their house, she explained, the children were at school, and 'we'd got everything that we'd longed for. Often with difficulty, often with a struggle but in the end we were always a little bit further on.'

'Always a little bit further on.' I can imagine what my liberal and leftist friends in West Berlin would think of that as a lifestyle, if there weren't a ten-foot wall separating them from it. Or what they'd think about the problems of the East Berlin rich. 'I spent my first month's salary on a car,' a scientist newly promoted to a job paying £20,000 a year told John Peet. 'Then I spent the second month's salary on a boat, and the third month's on a dacha. What on earth am I going to do with the fourth month's?'

Odd to think of all the *Genossen*, the comrades over in West Berlin, sitting open-necked in the informality of their own pubs, making a point of calling each other *du* instead of *Sie*, as they did in the old KP before Hitler. Here in East Berlin only Party members are *Genossen*. Everyone else is *Frau* and *Herr*, and they stopped calling strangers *du* back in the fifties. I started wearing a tie again, and wished, as uniformed waiters arranged napkins over their arms, and string trios played, that I'd brought a darker suit.

No, everything's very nice and quiet. There are a few drunks around, it's true, and according to the journal of the Supreme Court, young *Rowdygruppen* who go round committing *Rowdytum* under the influence of alcohol and imperialist ideology. I didn't see them; though someone had pencilled the word 'sex', very small and faint, and in English, on the name-boards of Friedrichshagen S-Bahn station. But at the theatre they're playing *My Fair Lady*, *Hello, Dolly!*, *The Merry Widow*, and *Der Fiedler auf dem Dach*, and if your Auntie Win from Southsea is thinking of emigrating I believe she should consider this place.

Or will it all start happening here, too, as the moss thickens on the garden gnomes, and contact with the West increases? Simulated intercourse at the Maxim-Gorki-theater? Students turning their backs in disgust upon the wrought-iron cocktail bars, and yearning for the simpler older life lived in cities farther east – in Wroclaw, in Szczecin – where they slosh the sauce out with the skimming-ladle, and think nothing of it . . .?

(1972)

Avalon Again

Cambridge revisited

Every time I go back to Cambridge I'm surprised by the strength and constancy of my feelings for the place. It's ten years this summer since I came down, and it still seems to me a sort of Avalon – one of those magic islands and secret gardens which recur in mythology as a perpetual source of refreshment and strength – a symbol, I suppose, of that Primal Good Object, as psychologists call it, from which we are separated by weaning, and to which we try to reunite ourselves by comfort and drink and religious experience.

Undergraduates are used to the sight of us separated brethren returning, often with the excuse of writing articles about them, or lecturing to them, or offering them jobs. Some of them are curious about our condition; several asked me with polite sympathy if I suffered at all from nostalgia, as it might have been neuralgia, or possibly some rather more geriatric complaint.

Perhaps it *is* just nostalgia. A great feeling of being at home in the place, certainly, of knowing with unsurprised intimacy every inch of this complicated maze of alleys, courts, paths, staircases, waterways, and bridges – a feeling that every street and building is part of what I once was, and am still.

Cambridge has changed a little, certainly – and I like it still more the way it is now. There has been a great burst of new building, some of it exhilarating, some of it grandly eccentric, with (for instance) split-level rooms from the upper deck of which people fall six feet or so and break their limbs – but all of it visibly modern, and far removed from the neo-Georgian and neo-Gothic nonsense which was being put up in my time.

The undergraduate population has gone up from 7,000 to 8,000. There are more pretty girls about, and the combination of the bicycle and the mini-skirt has had an astonishing impact on the Cambridge street scene.

I rented an ancient upright bicycle myself and cycled slowly round those familiar streets, starting to feel that Marshall McLuhan was right after all, and that the Medium was the Message. All around me, information was percolating down unseen, like the rainwater through the subsoil – about Sidney's *Arcadia*, the dramas of Kleist, the papacy from Gregory VII to Boniface VIII. But the message was Cambridge. And the message of Cambridge, I'm afraid, is that the rich and the clever shall inherit the sweet places of the earth, and lavish their loving care upon them, and draw serenity and strength from them in return.

But how satisfying to be riding a bicycle again! Weaving through the traffic, negotiating the tricky iron posts put up to keep bicycles out of all the fine cycling on the pedestrian ways of the city. Best of all, the narrow escape-route from the centre of the town out to the University Library on the other side of the Backs – down Senate House Passage (across which the night-climbers jump, high up in the dark, from Caius to the roof of the Senate House), out through the echoing brick canyon between Trinity and Trinity Hall – then up on to Garret Hostel Bridge, with a flash of river and punts on either side, and across the Backs through a tunnel of blossom and fresh green leaves. It's even more agreeable when you don't have to go into the University Library at the end of it.

I caught myself one evening admiring the perfection of the oilstains on the roadway in Peas Hill, and thinking how essential they were to the appearance and function of the University. Really, my attitude to Cambridge is ridiculous.

*

I enjoyed my time as an undergraduate here intensely. Some deep and continuous pleasure bore me up over dull lectures, unhappy love affairs, disastrous contributions to magazines and revues – even over a strong, perhaps parricidal, dislike of my own particular college.

I think the truth is that I was deeply impressed by the sheer glamour of being an undergraduate. A naïve attitude, and probably a discreditable one; far from rich and not particularly clever, I felt a vague aura of riches and cleverness adhering to me by association.

I'm not sure I've shaken the feeling off even now. Part of the pleasure I get from visiting Cambridge comes from the sense of belonging to a privileged minority. It's not a very exclusive minority, of course. At a rough calculation there must be something like 100,000 Cambridge graduates in the world – enough to fill the Wembley Stadium. Suppose all 100,000 of them turned up to moon about the place at once!

*

Seen from outside, Cambridge has the irresistible attraction of a scale model. The diversions, commercial enterprise, and politics of the macrocosm can all be seen here in concentrated form.

Varsity, the undergraduate newspaper, for instance, continues to be more Fleet Street than Fleet Street. I worked for it once, but couldn't write headlines, and never rose above assistant features editor. Its racing correspondent this term tipped the winner of the 1,000 Guineas, and there's a familiar note about its announcement that it has acquired another publication, *Cambridge Research*, not in order to change its content, but to 'put it on a firm financial footing and to provide for possible future expansion of circulation'.

The most vigorous commercial development this year has been the growth of a pop music industry. There are half a dozen groups in business, with names like the Boston Crabs, the 117, and the Uther Pendragon. They're hired for parties, which seem to be given now by syndicates of five or six undergraduates, who pay perhaps £20 for the group and another £25 for a public room.

A group called the Pineapple Truck appear to be the most successful, or at any rate the best publicised. They have been playing about three engagements a week, and they have special lighting effects, with a go-go girl who throws sugar lumps to the audience. They also own a racehorse.

I called on Peter Rudge, one of the group's two managers, at his lodgings one morning. He had the gentle, open, demotic manner which one often meets among students now. The Truck, he said, didn't play blues and soul, like most of the other groups. 'We stay very poppy. We're not a clean group. We're more a noise group.

'When we started, we advertised the Truck as a new group up from London – and people believed it! Chris Jagger – Mick Jagger's brother – came up and sang with us, and people knew he was from London, so they somehow thought all the rest of the group must be from London too.

'Well, we went round telling everyone the group were good – and they believed it! Then people would go to hear them, and perhaps they'd say, you know, "They weren't good last night," so we'd say, "Well, a wire went in the amplifier," or "We didn't have our proper guitarist last night, but they'll be good next time." And they'd believe it!'

Now they play at the sort of parties where you see everyone – 'All the Whim-at-eleven, all the Union-at-four,' as Mr Rudge put it. The Whim is a coffee-house.

The landlady hovered anxiously as the visitors tramped up and down Mr Rudge's stairs, to interview him, or to hire his band. 'Are you up, Mr Rudge?' she called. 'Am I going to be able to get in there to do the bed? I'm sure the room's looking a real sight.'

*

The standards of competence and professionalism in undergraduate enterprises have been high ever since the revue producers, actors, and journalists began to set their sights on London in the early fifties. The standards seem to be rising all the time. I was invited to a Footlights 'smoker' – one of the private entertainments which the club gives for its own members and their guests. It was an astonishingly enjoyable evening, with much funnier turns than I remember at these occasions.

Afterwards the Idle Hour jazz band played for dancing, performing with a technical accomplishment which I don't think any of the jazz bands in my time even approached. Then again, there are women in the Footlights now – talented and beautiful women. A great improvement on the transvestites of the past, ladylike as some of them were.

Several members asked me deferentially afterwards if I felt that the club's standards had fallen very much since my day. I told them, rather regretfully, that the opposite seemed to be the case. I'm not sure they were all that pleased to hear it; the Cambridge world is sustained, not undermined, by the myth of a golden past, as by the parallel myth of a golden metropolis an hour and twenty minutes down the railway line.

My contemporaries and I gazed raptly at the golden trails left in the upper air by Mark Boxer, Jonathan Miller, Frederic Raphael, Ronald Bryden and others on their assumption into London. Our whole mythology would have been shaken if they had come zooming down again and said they were no more superhuman than ourselves. Besides, it wouldn't have been true.

*

A rubric against nostalgia for Cambridge-past: in Victorian times the river was used as a sewer, and the Backs *stank*.

Or so Gwen Raverat recalls, in *Period Piece*, her marvellously evocative but clear-eyed memoir of childhood in Cambridge at the end of the last century. When Queen Victoria was being shown over Trinity she asked the

Master, Dr Whewell, what all the pieces of paper floating down the river were.

'Those, ma'am,' replied Dr Whewell solemnly, 'are notices that bathing is forbidden.'

*

I'm remembered here!

An undergraduate from my old college tells me that my name is still in the debates book. I'm touched by this small toehold in immortality – particularly since I can't recall ever taking part in a college debate.

'Well,' he explains, 'it's about the time they threw you in the pond for an article you wrote in *Varsity*.'

Oh. That.

*

The 'secret garden' feeling of Cambridge was heightened for me by reading Isherwood's *Lions and Shadows* the year before I came up as an undergraduate, while I was learning Russian here in the Army. As he records in this almost physically delectable piece of fictionalised auto-biography, Isherwood did no work at all at Cambridge, and was sent down at the end of his second year for writing his Tripos papers in the form of pastiche, concealed verse, and witticisms at the expense of the examiners' style.

He and a friend he calls 'Chalmers' spent all their time fantasying a Metaphysical University City beneath the surface of the physical one. They called it 'The Other Town', and believed that it was entered through an old door with rusty hinges which they found set in a blank wall in Silver Street. Later, the sight of the name 'Garret

Hostel Bridge' glimpsed in flickering gaslight on a dank winter's night suggested the concept of 'The Rats' Hostel', a Gothic underworld investing The Other Town from which surrealist mythological support could be drawn against the University establishment.

They eventually transplanted the Rats' Hostel out of Cambridge, to a village 'among the enormous downs, on the edge of the Atlantic Ocean' called Mortmere, about which they projected one of the century's great unwritten novels. ('Chalmers', whose real name was Edward Upward, later did write about Mortmere.) But I still cannot walk down Silver Street, or cross Garret Hostel Bridge, without the feeling that something lurks just out of sight.

*

There were two suicides in the University the week I was there, and several of the dons I talked to were worried by the amount of unhappiness they saw among their students. There is a cruel aspect to Cambridge, certainly. Success and failure are often sharply defined. Failure destroys confidence; success in this atmosphere undermines the character. Cambridge produces in abundance talents with the ability to please, but few with that greater ability to disregard whether they please or not.

I still feel a definite uneasiness about being seen alone in restaurants and theatres; solitude seems like a badge of social failure. Particularly here in Cambridge – particularly in the Whim at eleven, or the Union at four.

*

The icon of Cambridge pop, and the current lord of the whole Cambridge manor, is Jonathan King.

Mr King, who has been reading English at Trinity in odd moments during the last three years, writes professional pop songs, and sometimes sings them. He makes a lot of money out of it. He spent the last vacation touring the United States to launch his latest record – an anti-drug song.

The secret of his success, according to the local experts, is that he's at Cambridge; people are intrigued by the idea of songs like 'Everyone's Gone to the Moon' issuing from one of the great brains of Trinity. He wears heavy horn-rimmed spectacles, and puts out publicity pictures of himself reading enormous folios bound in ageing leather. Back-numbers of *Varsity*, perhaps?

But he doesn't take any part in the Cambridge pop world at all, and is never seen at Cambridge parties (though he is apparently seen in the Whim at eleven, and did consent to pose for a *Varsity* picture recently with Lord Butler and one or two other notable Trinity figures).

When I arrived he was stretched out on his sofa reading *Bleak House*, a white telephone on the floor beside him. The telephone was a professional necessity, as he explained. 'My telephone bill's been coming to about £100 a quarter. I was telephoning America every night practically! I somehow needed to phone America – it was very comforting.'

Again, the easy, open, gentle, pop manner; the demotic pop accent (modified in this instance from Charterhouse); and the ability to talk with disarming effortlessness about himself. He showed me a Guards bearskin he had just acquired. 'I'm about 99 per cent pure exhibitionist in my cloak! Wait till I make my appearance in the bearskin as well!' He claimed to have introduced camp humour to Cambridge (in which claim he is fifteen years out to my certain knowledge, and probably something more like 700). The only subject he wouldn't talk about was pop music. Every time he wandered on to it he stopped and waved a languid, joky hand. 'I'm doing myself brain damage,' he said. 'Honestly, talking about the pop scene damages the mind.'

He dismissed most of his contemporaries with equable professional contempt. 'They're all amateurs,' he said. 'There are only two or three real professionals up here. The rest of them – the summit of their ambition is to be Editor of *Varsity*, or President of the Union. Then they go down and in a year or two they find their fame's slipping. They come back up for one last fling. Then they're never heard of again – and serve them absolutely right.

'Anyway, it's not interesting talking to exhibitionists like me. You want to go and talk to some of these people who commit suicide.'

Later a white sports car tooted at me from the midst of an impenetrable traffic jam in Trinity Street, and Mr King offered me a lift. He was on his way 400 yards up the road from his lodgings to buy envelopes.

*

I called on an old friend – someone I've known since we were in our first year at university. He was at Oxford then; we were joint editors of an inter-university magazine printed in italic type on grey paper, called *Seed*, which ceased after one issue. We walked round and round the Fellows' garden of his college, talking about how oddly everything had turned out.

He's a psychologist, and he lent me a paper he'd been brooding on, entitled 'Death and the Mid-Life Crisis', by Elliott Jaques. Sometime in one's thirties, says Jaques, one comes face to face with 'the reality and inevitability of one's own eventual personal death'. Up to now one's life has sloped endlessly upwards and over the skyline. Now one reaches the skyline, and sees that the road stops short somewhere on the way down the other side.

I sat reading the paper in the evening sunshine on the river bank. On the other side, on Laundress Green, a young man lay in the grass, while a girl with long blonde hair and a plum-coloured trouser-suit climbed on to his knees, then revolved into a perfect handstand on his braced palms.

Intimations of mortality.

(1963)

From Sea to Shining Sea

Chasing America

1. Stonington, Connecticut
The *Senator*, the *Hell Gate*, the *Yankee Clipper*, the *Gilt Edge*, the *42nd Street*; you can hear them coming miles away along the coast – the shining silver expresses of the old New York, New Haven, and Hartford, with their grand names and their huge headlights, as they race up the shoreline from New York to Boston, sirening mournfully for their lost passengers, their lost solvency, the lost days of railroad greatness.

They drum along the causeway across the harbour here – three hours out from New York, two to go to Boston – to catch a glimpse of boats at anchor, white clapboard houses lost among maples and chestnuts, a couple of small factories, quiet, shaded streets, and then disappear over the causeway across Wequelequock Cove, in the direction of Rhode Island.

They seem to bring the great distances of America with them. They have bullet-holes in their windows, from being shot up by Indians on the Great Plains, or at any rate by juvenile delinquents in the urban deserts of Brooklyn. They also bring the papers from New York, with word of all the marvellously American, sophisticated things that are going on down the line there. Electric card-shuffling machines, six-foot-long sandwiches costing £12 each, 'happenings' in Central Park which include the public washing of dirty nappies and demonstrations of eating and retching. The key word down in the metropolis seems to be 'psychedelic'. Dr Timothy Leary, the high priest of LSD, is giving 'psychedelic celebrations' in Greenwich Village which consist of re-enactments of the world's great religious myths using psychedelic methods; sensory meditation, symbol-overload, media-mix, molecular and cellular phrasing, pantomime, dance, sound-light and lecture-sermon-gospel.

Indeed, seen through the special vocabulary of headline writers and the haze of misprints in the early editions which come up this way, the whole world outside Stonington sometimes appears a little psychedelic. In the headlines politicians *slate* their plans, *score* their opponents, *roil* their supporters. By the time you get into the text they are also apparently becoming dumbfunded, possibly by the news of roits in San Francosco, or by the prediction that frought in the New York area is unlikely to azate. It sounds pretty drightful out there.

There is nothing very psychedelic in Stonington: we have no sandwiches over a foot or two in length here, and we shuffle our cards (if at all) by hand. There may yet be a happening, though: we're thought to have a skunk living under the floor of our house, which could lead to something fairly froughtful, if not downright azominable when the children finally locate him and roil him with their heavy-handed affection. I anticipate quite a lot of sensory meditation and symbol-overload, together with a fair amount of pantomime, dance, and gasp-choke-dumbfundment.

*

Of course, Stonington isn't America, as people frequently tell us. Every time I look at the map I am appalled by the sheer quantity of America left to be explored. So far, by *Senator*, *Hell Gate* and *Yankee Clipper*, and by car along turnpike, freeway, highway, thruway, expressway, parkway and beltway, we have covered about three inches of map in each direction, which leaves a stretch some three feet wide still untouched. We discuss plans of campaign with friends, gesturing broadly over the map like senior generals.

'New England isn't America, you know,' they say severely. 'You'll have to get out of New England if you really want to see America.'

Sometimes they get to hear that we've been to New York.

'Oh, God!' they cry. '*New York*'s not America!'

'What Michael should do,' says one of them, pointing about a thousand miles to the left, 'is ride a train through the Mid-West.'

'Oh, *God*!' groan the others. 'The *Mid-West* isn't America, for heaven's sake! It's just an extension of New England!'

They shift their gaze a thousand miles or so downwards. But no one thinks I shall find out much about America by taking snapshots of Williamsburg or the Vieux Carré, so we move a couple of feet to the left and contemplate California. But California is apparently nothing but retired insurance assessors from Kansas City, and we execute a strategic withdrawal upmap to the mountains, only to find them totally untypical of anything except mountains, which would give us an entirely false picture of the sort of life led by insurance assessors in Kansas City.

'Why don't you take a trip to Mexico?' say our friends. 'That's a very interesting country.'

*

Stonington is intimate, timeless, and secure, a seductively solid place to be. Showers come and go through placid autumn afternoons; women drive slowly into town to change library books; children walk home from school, scuffing the fallen leaves. Poverty, the root disease of American as of British society, is remote.

Yet poverty and hardship it was that shaped the place. The charming little houses inland were once farms, and the rolling, endless woods hiding them were stony fields which the poor Yankee farmers cleared of their primeval forest to scratch a hard living from. The delectable clapboard-and-shingle houses in town were the homes of whaling captains who were away in the Antarctic for two, three, four, and even five years at a time. When the West was opened up, the men deserted the whaling ports, and left the poor New England soil to subside into forest again, freed from the necessity to endure such a life.

Eventually the giant hand of six-foot-sandwichland will reach out and gather even Stonington into its bosom. It's predicted that the whole north-eastern seaboard will turn in time into one 400-mile-long conurbation – a Megalopolis. The trees will be cut down once again; the *Hell Gate* will be renamed the uptown local. Still, there'll be some 2,500 miles left for suburban development on the west side of town.

2. New York

Great cities are like television sets and washing machines; behind their shiny fronts are squalid backsides which by a strange convention we agree not to notice.

New York makes one realise that there is another convention on backsides which involves a more subtle form of illusion – the convention of the theatre.

The excitement of the theatre lies not in what the audience see there, but in what they don't see. The events on stage (often insufferably tedious in themselves) are given life by the audience's awareness that they are only the outward manifestations of a whole secret world behind the scenes. There would be little theatrical excitement in seeing *Hamlet* performed in Elsinore Castle; what titillates us is the knowledge that the great stone pillars are made of canvas, and that behind them are ropes, electric cables, and bored stagehands in grubby sweatshirts calculating their overtime entitlement.

No play in the whole history of drama was ever as exciting as the possibility of a play you feel in an empty theatre, when the raw working lights on stage reveal the steel ladders on the great back wall, and Fred is shouting up to George in the flies to throw down the hammer, and the leading lady is walking about without her eyelashes, coughing over a fag and looking ninety.

So with New York. A hard, nervy, exciting city – to a great extent, I think, because one can't help being aware of the squalor everywhere behind the wealth, the great mulch of slums and suburban wasteland from which the lofty urban blooms of Manhattan draw their sustenance. Not even the most casual visitor to New York can walk far without being begged for dimes, and without coming across hopeless figures huddled in doorways, collapsed across the sidewalks, sprawled against parked cars – drunk, perhaps sick, maybe both. No one stops to find out.

Mythology extends the sense of contrast. In the mythology of show-business, we like to believe in early struggles and destitute old age. We like to think of comedians arriving on stage fresh from their mother's deathbed; that actors who play baddies are really goodies; that the goodies are really baddies; that the great portrayers of sexuality are really impotent or frigid.

In the same way, New Yorkers are quick to tell you about the violence of the suburbs, and to warn you against going to Harlem, or riding the subways at night, or going into the park practically any time. Rightly or wrongly, they see the city as hard and insecure.

Wealth amid wealth and success amid success are as dull as caviar spread upon caviar; wealth and success amid poverty and failure are wealth and success indeed.

*

Politics, it occurs to me, is another prime example of the theatrical convention. The House (Chamber, Senate) is the stage; the lobbies, members' bars and dining-rooms the world behind the scenes. What is done in the House, in public, for the record, becomes more and more formalised. Like the contents of Soviet newspapers, it's interesting only if you have a sense of the world of private debate and intrigue going on below stairs.

People who really take an interest in politics are not surprised or upset to hear politicians make uncharacteristic, meaningless, or false utterances in public, any more than theatregoers shout 'Impostor!' when Sir Laurence Olivier, well known to be British and a resident of Brighton, gives himself out to be a Moor living in Venice.

Most of the political observers I've ever met would be very bored by an entirely visible politics, where men said frankly and plainly what they thought, and spent the rest of their time bicycling or playing with their children.

*

And restaurants – particularly expensive ones – are theatres pure and simple. The public section is stagily decorated – dramatic lighting, portable greenery, perhaps gilt and mirrors – or got up to look like a grotto, a riverboat, or a Turkish brothel. Programmes are brought round; music may be played. And behind the padded swing door, as we are agreeably aware, there is another world of white tiles and harsh fluorescent lighting, where sweating cooks toil with a professional disenchantment equal to any stagehand's.

Out through the swing doors hurry men in stage costume – dickeys, perhaps, or Spanish gypsy kit, or French matelot outfits. (At one restaurant in New York they wear shortie togas.) They walk in special waiter-like ways, twirl bottles of claret to show the label as if performing a sleight-of-hand, sincerely recommend whatever we are going to order anyway, care as deeply about our tastes and whims as Gary Cooper cares about the rule of law in *High Noon*.

Their wives give them canned spaghetti at home, we

know. They have bad feet – they came up from Brooklyn on the subway wearing open-necked check shirts – behind the swing doors they pick their ears and curse us.

But that's restaurant business – the heartbreak behind the dickey, the tears behind the service. One day waiters will rise as far above food in the public's estimation as actors have above plays. Crowds will wait for them outside the service entrance each night, screaming and pushing forward autograph books. The gossip columnists will get on to them, revealing to our deep, contrary satisfaction that the favourite food of the head-waiter at the Claribelle is doughnuts and soda-pop, and that the *sommelier* at the Aspidistra passes out on one dry Martini.

It'll put all the fun back into eating.

3. *Washington*

I have the Lincoln Memorial and the Jefferson Memorial safely recorded on film, and the Washington Monument and the Capitol. Can I give it a rest now, camera, and put you away for a bit?

I mean, I don't have to photograph the White House, do I? Oh, come on, now, not the *White House*! All right, I see there's something a little odd about coming all the way to Washington and taking pictures of the Lincoln Memorial, the Jefferson Memorial, the Washington Monument and the Capitol – then missing out the White House. It'll take a bit of explaining to the eager audiences around the slide projector this winter. I see that.

*

But everything about you takes some explaining, camera – I'm deeply embarrassed to be seen with you hanging about my neck. How did you get into my life in the first place? And having got there, how did you rise from being the paid travelling companion you were taken on as to leading me around by the nose like this, ordering me to point you this way and that, to wait until the sun comes out, to walk backwards and forwards and sideways with my free eye screwed up tight, an unseeing slave to my own completion neurosis?

As I understood it at the beginning, you were going to grapple the changing shadows for me, and hold them still. You were going to snatch off fragments of the passing world for me to keep, which would make it clear for ever what certain things had been like at certain particular moments. Like some powerful drug, you would recall the past, clarify perception and produce astonishing hallucinations of perspective and colour, the way they do in the colour supplements.

And what strange half-glimpsed visions are we snatching from the passing parade, camera? The Jefferson Memorial. Some drug you've turned out to be, that can produce total recall of the Jefferson Memorial at will. If I wanted total recall of the Jefferson Memorial I could buy a picture postcard for a nickel. And *have* I ever bought a picture postcard of the Jefferson Memorial, camera? Never. It's not that I've anything against the Jefferson Memorial; it's just that large marble public monuments don't play any very intimate part in my personal world. They really speak to you, do they, camera?

*

I believe you have some vague artistic aspirations. I think you nurse some muddled hope that in five or ten minutes, without skill or effort, you can arrange the Jefferson Memorial, its shadows, and a handy tree into a composition which offers mankind new insights into the nature of the world and the language of form and colour.

Well, I have news for you, camera. Cameras with really serious social and artistic purposes give the Jefferson Memorial a miss. They go out and photograph old men sitting in social clubs, young men in leather jackets leaning against the wall outside amusement arcades, girls dancing – that kind of thing. Why don't you try something along those lines?

Yes, why are there never any *people* in your pictures, camera? You're too timid to stare at them, that's why. You're frightened of embarrassing them. You're afraid they'll stare back, or come over and put their boot through you. (And the time it takes you to get yourself set up, they would, too.) So we get reduced to the Jefferson Memorial, which never yet stared back at a camera, or moved out of focus just as the button was pressed.

*

No, I'm being a little unfair. You've managed to get the backs of one or two people's heads. You caught a rear view of another photographer photographing the Lincoln Memorial – very witty. You snatched a rear view of someone fishing in the Potomac – a great human document.

But, camera, other cameras get front views! They push their way right up to the centre of the crowd, and gaze unblinkingly into faces streaked with tears, faces dissolved in laughter, faces relaxed by intimate and revealing emotions of every sort. They happen upon starving beggars sitting in front of advertisements for food, and ministers of religion standing next to life-size cutouts of bathing beauties.

If *you* saw someone weeping, you'd quickly look the other way. If you saw a starving beggar, the last thing you'd do would be to intrude upon his misery.

Supposing I got you one of those telephoto lenses – would that help? Then you could peer into the faces of any passers-by who happened to be involved in emotional scenes on the corner of Pennsylvania Avenue and 7th Street, say, while seeming to be completely absorbed in contemplating the marble columns of the National Gallery on Constitution and 6th.

Though whether I should feel that anything you saw on Pennsylvania and 7th was any very intimate part of my life, when I was stuck there with you on Constitution and 6th, I rather doubt.

Little black monkey, get off my back.

4. *Chicago*

Flurries of men wearing almost identical grey mohair suits are blown along Michigan Avenue like leaves in the pale sunlight at lunchtime, their wide trouser-bottoms and folders of publicity material flapping wildly in the wind. They are businessmen attending conventions, which blow into the Windy City – the centre of the nation's airways and the busiest airport in the world – in every cross-draught.

Indeed, all sorts of people one last saw in London or last heard of in Bangkok come sweeping and swirling through Chicago sooner or later. The city is full of ideas and possibilities – it's in a constant state of turbulence, changing its shape almost before one's eyes. Up on the

North Side luxury apartments spring up along the lake shore like armed men from dragons' teeth – whole new suburban neighbourhoods surprise the weekend motorist.

The traces of the whirling wind are everywhere. Large, ornate mansions lurk improbably among the factories of the industrial Near South Side, left over from the time when it was the most desirable residential district in town, the home of the Swifts, the Armours and the McCormicks. On the churches in the Negro districts of the West Side you can see inscriptions in Hebrew – they were the synagogues of the Jewish community which once occupied the West Side, but which has now shifted bodily, with all its delicatessens and institutions, to the northern suburbs.

Down on the South Side the urban renewal programmes are cutting great swathes through the slums. Whole neighbourhoods have disappeared off the face of the earth, laid low with astonishing energy – entire urban jungles depopulated and reduced to the plains from which they arose, with nothing but perhaps a lonely Elevated line left standing above ground to mark the spot.

Round and round the wind whirls. The intention of the national urban renewal programme was to rehouse the poor. But the effect in most cases, according to Americans who have watched the process at work with growing scepticism, is merely to replace slums with middle-income housing, so that the poor are driven to colonise other declining middle-income districts. Eventually, I suppose, these districts in their turn will become overcrowded and impoverished enough to qualify for urban renewal, and the process will start all over again.

Odd combinations and confrontations occur in these swirling currents. One of the most powerful agents for urban renewal on the South Side has been the university, which over the last few years has carved a considerable middle-class neighbourhood out of the surrounding slums, partly to provide accommodation for its staff, and partly to protect itself against crime and violence. This has brought it into conflict with the militant organisations which have grown up to protect Negro rights. But already, some people say, the wind is veering round from conflict to co-operation, because the backbone of the Negro militancy is middle class itself.

Negroes are not the only immigrants from the South. There is also a community of poor whites who have come in as the Appalachian coal industry declined, and who have settled in a district on the North Side known to its richer neighbours as 'Hillbilly Heaven'. Here again nothing is simple – poor whites are traditionally the most entrenched racists in America, but some of the young radical organisers who have moved in to work with them insist that away from the South they can be persuaded to accept Negroes and make common cause with them in a way which the middle classes find almost impossible. The only sure thing seems to be that, if present trends continue, the Negroes will one day inherit the city.

Underneath all the flux, according to Chicagoans, some things remain unchanging. The police, say people who deal with them from the underside of society, are still corrupt, in spite of Superintendent Wilson's well-publicised reforms, and can be brutal. The city is still firmly held in the interlocking grip of the Mafia and the

Democratic Party machine. In large areas of life, graft is still the established procedure, and violence the reward for anyone who rocks the boat. The latest job-selling scandal is what the papers call 'the stink in the sanitation department', and the official who first began to sniff it out found a bomb in his car.

Corruption and violence – they shock the timid British visitor, I think, in much the same way as the lethargy and bloody-mindedness of the British outrage even the most sympathetic Americans. The Ford Foundation should finance a project to standardise failings on both sides of the Atlantic.

*

My mother was born in Chicago – my grandparents lived in America for some time. I went to look for the street, far down on the South Side. Friends insisted on driving me – they wouldn't hear of my going down through the South Side alone, even by day.

We found the street now over-shadowed by the Skyway, the great elevated expressway built to connect Chicago with the transcontinental highway system, and partially obliterated by the successive approach ramps to it. Between the ramps sections of street remained, some white neighbourhoods, some black. There was an old red house with a black steeple like a witch's hat – rusting cars resting on their hubs in the gutter – gang slogans painted on the concrete piling of the Skyway – 'BEWARE THE DUKES', 'BEWARE THE ROYAL DEACONS'.

And the wind, gusting and scouring beneath the pale October sky.

5. *Santa Fe*

They're giving away money in Santa Fe. They're also giving it away in Albuquerque and Denver and El Paso. Whichever button I push on the radio of my Budget Rent-a-Car, fruitily over-excited voices from every corner of the West urge me to swing down to my nearest supermarket, car salesroom or furniture store, and there win a thousand dollars, a refrigerator, a Ford Mustang, or ten Ford Mustangs.

Outside the windows the high, empty wilderness of the New Mexico–Colorado border country drifts slowly by, burnt every possible shade of parched brown. Here it's smashed into buttes and mesas; there ridged with crests of brilliant red sandstone. Greasewood, juniper and piñon suck the ghost of moisture out of the rock. Broad stream-beds, as dry as bone, course whitely down into the Rio Grande, which Will Rogers once said was the first river he'd ever seen that needed irrigating.

It's like an extremely slow travelogue, complete with a commentary of sorts. 'Enter now, for bigger cash prizes than ever before! Would you believe *a thousand dollars*? Well, you *better* believe it – because it's true!'

Basket-light balls of dried tumbleweed roll across the road in the wind, and when you turn off the highway on to the dirt-roads of the back-country the fine white dust raised by passing vee-hickles (as some of the voices on the radio call them) coats windscreen, sunglasses, hair and the inside of nose and mouth.

The heart beats a little faster in this part of the world; the whole area is a mile or so above sea-level, and air to breathe, like water to drink, is in somewhat short supply.

My heart almost stops altogether when I think of the first men to come here, before there were roads, or cars, or motels, before there was KDEF in Albuquerque or KTRC in Santa Fe to offer free barbecue pits. Their moral as well as their physical fortitude in challenging this inhuman landscape is almost beyond my imagination. It was the hope of gold that brought Coronado and his armoured conquistadors up from Mexico in the sixteenth century, and the openings for trade which lured the first Anglos out along the Santa Fe Trail in the nineteenth; internal radios with voices even more persuasive than KDEF or KTRC.

'Enter now, and win a 1967 Ford Mustang – OR, a year's free supply of Icee, the coldest drink in town!' I turn off the damned radio, and really listen to – well, to the roar of the airconditioner. Turn off the airconditioner – open the windows. There should be a town coming up in forty miles or so. Vast gloomy doubts about the nature of man begin to roll about inside my head like tumbleweed. I start wondering what the point of it all is, just like people with a sense of metaphysics do. What's it all about, eh? What do I personally think I'm up to, um? Yes, what the devil *am* I up to, creeping about this moonstruck place so far from the gentle urban blanket of industrial air-pollution?

Sing to keep my spirits up. Voice thickens and cracks from all the dust in my throat. With astonishing earliness and suddenness the sun drops behind the horizon. The Sangre de Cristo mountains in the east show their sullen blood-red sunset tinge, then turn blue, then launch a round, frozen moon into the sky, then disappear into darkness and rising mist. Turn on the heater. Turn on the radio. A station in New Orleans, a thousand miles away, is coming through faint but clear.

They're giving away money in New Orleans, too.

*

By nine o'clock the neon 'No Vacancy' sign is showing outside my motel, and the courtyard is packed tight with jeeps, pick-ups, and station-wagons. But when I look out next morning at half-past seven – nothing but my own Budget Rent-a-Car to be seen. It's the first day of the hunting season, and no one is missing a moment.

They are shooting, according to my information, deer, bear, turkey, and each other. The last is strictly speaking illegal, of course, since *homo sapiens* is a protected species, and the hunters wear brilliant red check shirts and fluorescent red fatigue caps so that they can be seen and identified from afar – a curious inversion of hunting technique down the ages.

I talk to one or two hunters along the road, and they all seem more concerned with defence than aggression. 'I figure on staying right alongside this white pick-up of mine,' said one. 'There's Apache up there, shooting anything that moves, and Texans. The Texans shoot wilder 'n hell.'

Another hunter says he knows a man who painted his horse fluorescent the previous season – only he got shot while he was doing it. There's a piece in the paper about a man up in North Dakota who had a heart attack while he was out hunting, fell on his gun, and shot himself through the foot. Staggering away to get help, he shot himself in the head, and trying to sort *that* one out, he put a third charge through his side. How he had the presence of mind to reload after each volley the paper doesn't say.

*

In the towns, people come up to talk and offer help and advice, in the best traditions of Western legend. Many of them are tall men wearing bolo ties, with sombreros shading their spectacles.

An upstanding middle-aged woman behind the bar of one of the hotels here tells me forthrightly that she just can't stand that damned Queen Elizabeth of mine. I ask her what that damned Queen Elizabeth of mine has done to roil her so. Well, she explains somewhat obliquely, there was this English girl in the bar one day who laughed when someone told a joke about the President. 'I wasn't standing for that. I went right up to her and told her, "That's *my* President you're laughing at. What would you think if I told you that I just can't stand that Queen of yours?" Because I can't, and that's a fact. I really *hate* that Queen Elizabeth.'

In a bar in a scruffy little mainroad town called Cuba I watch with even greater uneasiness while a bantering disagreement about a pool game almost turns into a fight. One of the players is a Texan up for the hunting, wearing stetson and high-heeled riding boots, and his alleged confusion of the balls on the table calls forth a streak of anti-Texanism among the New Mexicans. 'Ah've never seen pool played that way in Texas!' growls the Texan. 'You're just colour-blind, Texan!' shouts his opponent. 'Ah ain't colour-blind!' 'You'll have to prove that on the table, Texan!'

Big hunting knives project ominously from their hip pockets. But a small man in a fluorescent fatigue cap calms them both down. Not a moment too soon, either. Another instant, and a tall stranger with a silver star and two six-guns would have kicked open the door and said quietly: 'Ah'm the law enforcement officer from Twentieth-Century Fox, and Ah'm takin' you in fo' breach o' copyright.'

6. *San Francisco*

When British voters go to the polling station and are faced with the task of putting a cross against one of three names on the ballot-paper, a terrible confusion is apt to seize them. They forget which of the three is their man; they put a tick instead of a cross; they put three crosses. And faced with selecting three names out of perhaps a dozen in the municipal elections, say tellers I have met, people are seized by total hysteria, and split their vote between Conservatives and Communists.

How they would fare in a Californian election I cannot imagine. Ballot-papers, in districts where they are used at all, are as big as newspapers – they have to be to accommodate all the various choices on offer. In San Francisco the voter finds himself face to face with not a ballot-paper but a voting machine – a bank of levers about the size of a telephone switchboard. In last week's election each machine had a choice of 114 levers to pull, plus forty little shutters to be raised for writing in additional candidates.

As in other States, the voters elect not only their Governor, their Senators and Congressmen, and their State Senators and assemblymen, but a whole list of State officers, from the Attorney-General and judges to the members of the Board of Education. The difference is that in California they also vote on a large number of specific issues in State and city politics as well.

Last week electors in San Francisco were faced with choosing twenty-four officers from a list of fifty candidates. Then they had to make up their minds about sixteen State 'propositions' – to amend the State Constitution, to alter the rules governing the investment of public retirement funds, to provide tax relief for blind veterans, and various other worthy questions of the sort that most electors pay their representatives to decide on their behalf somewhere out of earshot. Then there was an 'initiative' – a proposition (to tighten the law against obscenity) put forward not by the State but by a private group of sponsors. And then there were a further seventeen propositions sponsored by the city and county.

By this time the voter was getting down to a pretty fine focus on civic affairs. Should the fire commission be increased from three members to five? Should policemen working in other city departments be allowed to remain in the police department's pension scheme? Should the limitation of .0075 of a dollar per 100 dollars assessed valuation in deficit utility budget for capital cost expenditure be repealed?

Of course, voters don't go in to face those 114 levers entirely unprepared. They have been subjected to a barrage of advertising by interested parties on the major propositions – 'vote yea on 1A'; 'no on 2S'; 'happiness is voting yes on proposition 16'. And they have been sent by the authorities beforehand 116 closely printed pages of explanatory material, including all the arguments for and against each move in the game. Provided they've digested all this and marked up their crib-sheet in advance they're home and dry.

Takes me back to happy days canvassing in South London last March, and to all the thoughtful British voters who told me they were going to vote Liberal, in a constituency where no Liberal was standing. Give British voters 114 levers to play with and we'd move the earth. Elect Ronald Reagan, probably.

*

The Berkeley campus of the University of California at lunchtime is an astonishing sight. The central plaza is built like something out of the Festival of Britain – different levels, overhead walkways, outdoor eating-places. Men with long hair and girls with delectable knees showing through vents in their jeans sit around the fountain and on the steps of the administration building in the sunshine, while one after another firebrand speakers take the microphone at the top of the steps, and urge subtly different shades of leftist action. It's like the first Soviet of Soldiers and Peasants after the Russian Revolution.

In the crowd people argue with passion about the exact political constitution of the National Liberation Front in Vietnam. The children of married students run about laughing and shrieking. A cyclist weaves through the strollers, pursued by wildly barking dogs. On a lawn nearby a man sits cross-legged, playing strange oriental modes on a wooden pipe.

The morals and politics of Berkeley outrage everyone. There are regular indignant letters in the papers. The university authorities last week introduced further restrictions on the lunchtime demonstrations – allegedly to forestall the possibility of Governor-elect Reagan's appointing a State committee of inquiry to clean the place up.

The FBI are said to be swarming on the campus. I had lunch in the sunshine with Robert Treuhaft, a local radical lawyer, and his English wife, Jessica Mitford. They said their phone had long been tapped (and a former FBI agent writing in the current issue of the San Francisco magazine *Ramparts* says that Treuhaft was one of the people he listened in to).

We talked briefly to a local folk-hero called Mario Savio, who led the free speech sit-in in 1964. Afterwards Treuhaft pointed to a rather handsome man in a dark blazer who had been standing like some theatrical villain behind a pillar as we spoke, apparently gazing into space. He was, said Treuhaft, an FBI man, and he had been recording our conversation on a tape-recorder in the briefcase standing open at his feet. Miss Mitford went and stared first into the bag, then into the man's face. He continued to gaze raptly into the distance.

It was a moment of fragile ludicrousness. I should have been inclined to scepticism, except that an English friend of mine who was once a graduate student at Berkeley went to observe one of the early demonstrations on the campus, and was subsequently followed by two FBI men right the way across America – from San Francisco to Washington, by car.

But the most surprising thing was not the putative FBI man. It was just the sight of a public concourse with no cars – only people walking and talking to each other – and the sound of loudspeakers broadcasting not muzak or free offers or paid political advertisements, but wild demands upon the intelligence and spirit. An oasis, certainly.

7. *Los Angeles*

Humbert Humbert, driving Lolita endlessly from motel to motel, lived out one of the most fundamental of all American myths, the idea that *you can always move on.*

The feeling is one which I've heard even the most sceptical Americans express in one form or another. They mean it figuratively – that you can change jobs and even careers comparatively easily, or get a college education in middle life. But they also mean it literally – that if you don't like it where you are, there's always somewhere else.

Americans spend over $50,000 million a year getting themselves about this vast country, which comes to around £100 a head for every man, woman and child in the United States. A fifth of the population moves house each year. They move out of the country into the towns, out of the South into the North, out of the Mid-West into the East, and out of practically everywhere – Mid-West, East, North, and South alike – to the West Coast and the West.

The great westward migration since the war is said to have been headed by ex-servicemen who had experienced the climate in training camps out here. (Has anyone ever investigated the scale on which nostalgic British ex-servicemen flood back into Aldershot and Catterick?) People pack up and move on an impulse; one of the first people I spoke to here had left Buffalo because there was a snowstorm on, driven 1,000 miles with his family to Memphis, Tennessee, got stuck in a traffic jam there, and decided somewhere in the jam to turn right and continue the odd 1,800 miles out to the Coast.

The drawback to the Moving On philosophy which Humbert Humbert's travels suggested was that everywhere turned out to be much the same as everywhere else. This thesis is not accepted by many Americans, who have a strongly romantic feeling for the regionalism of the country, and find the most profound differences between one part of America and another – particularly between the West and everywhere else.

You can enjoy a quality of life in California unattainable anywhere else, Californians assure me. The ordinary man, insisted one ordinary man earnestly, could have a better life here than a millionaire could on the French Riviera. Well, maybe; I'm not sure I know enough about the lives of millionaires on the French Riviera to express an opinion.

At times I've felt the magic of the place; particularly one evening, having dinner on the terrace of a house projecting on struts from the side of an elegant residential precipice in the Santa Monica Mountains. The air was very warm and perfectly still. Way below us the lights of the endless suburbs in the San Fernando Valley twinkled and shimmered as restlessly as the ocean. Gradually the black mass of the San Gabriel Mountains in the east detached itself from the night as the moon rose from behind it. Then suddenly the Santa Susanas loomed out of the north against a wavering blood-red glow in the sky like some portent of the Apocalypse; a space-rocket on ground-test, burning out on its gantry.

Do people continue to feel that they can always move on even after they've reached California? A lot, said one of my informants, felt that California was the end of the line, and if they didn't like it here turned to religion, or to drugs, or shot themselves. But there seem to be plenty who keep circulating – from one part of California to another, from California to Arizona, from Arizona back to California, and perhaps out to Florida for their holidays. And just as the poorly paid itinerant fruit-pickers follow the crop from district to district, so a great many of the highly skilled and highly paid workers in the aerospace industry follow the government contracts from Los Angeles to Seattle, from San Diego to Tucson. Sometimes the whole American nation seems as nomadic as the Mongols.

*

Actors, producers and musicians are nomads, of course. So, increasingly, are university teachers. An academic who has established his celebrity on a national basis may become what show-business people call 'hot'. Universities compete for the prestige of employing him, offering not only straightforward financial inducements, but often immense grants of free time; one sabbatical year in three – one in two. A really white-hot figure, I should imagine, might be able to negotiate a contract by which he was on permanent sabbatical, and sold nothing but the use of his name on the university's prospectus, like an actress endorsing soap.

There is often more to this than prestige alone, and sometimes other interested parties behind the university. In one city I visited in the West various prominent citizens wanted to help attract big names to the local university by setting up an art-gallery and a local symphony orchestra for them. The presence of hot dons on campus, they reckoned, would encourage endowments and attract able students, which would in turn draw industrialists with plants needing a constant supply of graduate labour. So that a small outlay on Bach and borrowed Botticellis would bring in a big return in new business.

*

The frontier of free land in the West closed over sixty years ago, but the Moving On outlook is in the direct tradition of the mythology which sustained the drive to open the continent up in the nineteenth century.

The mythology of the West, as Henry Nash Smith showed in his book *Virgin Land*, was successively sylvan, pastoral and agrarian as the need arose, and the ideals it embodied eventually solidified into a widely held historical theory, the 'frontier hypothesis', which attempted to explain American development entirely in terms of the availability of free land. Smith demonstrated the subjunctive nature of the myth. Many things about America, however, can be explained by the fact of the myth's existence.

The faith in the potentialities of Moving On springs from the optimism which is such an attractive and humanistic attribute of the American character, and nourishes the sense of liberty which Americans undoubtedly feel. Like the hope of heaven, it makes the shortcomings of the here and now endurable; but I suspect that it also helps to perpetuate the shortcomings – to encourage the impermanent, makeshift atmosphere which renders some places in America so ripe to be Moved On from.

And imagine Moving On to heaven, and finding that it

was after all only a temporary, improvised heaven, made tolerable only by the hope of eventually Moving On again – to another temporary heaven a thousand miles down the road . . .

8. *New York*

'What hath God wrought!' cabled Samuel Morse thoughtfully from Washington to Baltimore in 1844, after God had invented the electric telegraph. A rather bigger revolution in human communications than even Mr Morse guessed, I think.

Western Union, who operate the telegraph network in America, have lighted upon a characteristic of the system which has not been fully appreciated or exploited elsewhere; that since telegrams are not identified by voice or handwriting, they need not be composed by the apparent sender. They can be made up of units prefabricated by the telegraph company, at a great saving in time, imagination, and literary effort for everyone involved.

For instance, Western Union offer a special Happy Birthday telegram, to be sent to people who are having birthdays. You can certainly write your own message on it if you want to – but who'd want to, when you can just put a tick against any one of the twenty-eight messages which Western Union have written for you already?

'A simple greeting, short and snappy, to hope your birthday will be happy' – are you honestly going to do better than that? Or: 'This cheery greeting by Western Union is the next best thing to a real reunion.'

For a nominal extra service charge Western Union will call up your old mother and *sing* 'Happy Birthday' to her. If she's going away you can send her a Bon Voyage telegram, perhaps inscribing a heartfelt tick against 'A good journey and don't forget we'll be thinking of you every mile of the way.' Then the company has a Congratulatory Telegram which offers messages suitable for congratulating those near and dear to you on a wide variety of successes, from Promotion or Election, to the Opening of a New Store or Business – 'You deserve every success and I (we) know you will have it.'

A tick in box 34 of the Congratulatory Telegram form, and Bobby Kennedy gets a cable telling him: 'Well done! Your excellent speech was convincing and to the point.' Put the tick in box 33, and you have him down as 'eloquent and convincing'; in box 35, and his little effort was 'a masterly presentation of the facts'.

There is no formula listed for telling someone that his speech was a load of drivelling humbug, or inaudible at the back of the hall. Nor is there any suggested form of words for celebrating the Sack, Bankruptcy, or Impeachment of those who mean much to you. There is a Storkgram to announce a birth, but no Reapergram to announce a death.

Well, why should Western Union help you spread gloom and despondency? There's enough in the world already. 'Mother and child/son/daughter doing fine,' declares the Storkgram – irrefutably, so far as I can see, with no option for minor modifications like 'in oxygen tent' or 'sinking fast'. But you're perfectly free to choose a 'suggested added sentiment' such as: 'Has all the earmarks of a future president (first lady)' or 'We never won prizes in arithmetic but we're good at addition.'

I can imagine Mom and Pop back in Cincinnati opening the Storkgram from their son-in-law out East.

They're pretty relieved to hear that mother and child are doing fine, of course, since there's always the risk in these cases that they would be doing fine, or even doing fine; and they have quite a chuckle over the bit about not winning prizes in arithmetic but being good at addition. They've never got on too well with their son-in-law, if the truth be told, not much liking his literary pretensions and fancy Harvard ways. But as they read his telegram they suddenly feel he's human after all.

So they call up Western Union and send back a Candygram, which is the world's sweetest message – a delicious one- or two-pound box of fine chocolates delivered kitchen-fresh with the sender's personal message attached. The one they select is:

'Huzzah! Huzzah! You're Ma and Pa! Eat up. Keep up your strength!'

Their son-in-law is curiously moved by this warm and impulsive reaction. He'd always thought that Charlene's parents were a couple of old sticks, incapable of human emotion. What deep chords childbirth touches in the human heart, he reflects, almost unable to swallow his candy for the strange lump in his throat. He wants to make it clear to them how moved he is. He grabs a Western Union Dollygram form from the desk, and with simple eloquence puts a tick against 'Thank you.'

But there's so much more he wants to say! As if his heart has been unlocked after a long silence, he ticks 'Have a happy day' and 'Seasonal greetings', thinking to hell with the expense, a thing like this doesn't happen every week. He takes another candy. 'Please cheer up' he ticks, his pen flying over the paper in his tremendous yearning uprush of emotion. 'Good luck.' 'Hello.'

When the Dollygram Desk in Cincinnati deliver the simpering little figurine which has this message attached to it, Mom cries unashamedly. 'He can certainly write, that young feller,' concedes Pop. 'Write? I'll say he can write!' says Mom, sniffling. 'Yep, he certainly knows how to write,' says Pop. 'I'll say he knows how to write,' says Mom.

So they send back a Congratulatory Telegram, Success of Artist division. 'Tremendously thrilled by your great performance,' they tick, and: 'Your performance magnificent. I shall never forget it. Congratulations and thanks for a wonderful treat.' Plus: 'I (we) enjoyed your work beyond words. The very best of good wishes.'

They are just about to put another tick in the space at the bottom where it says (Signed), when they notice underneath: 'For only a few cents additional the word "LOVE" can be added to any of the above texts.'

Love! That's the word they've been searching for all this time! And at only a few cents additional it's a real human relations bargain.

9. *New York*

On the thin northernmost tip of Manhattan, where the Bronx crowds in upon the island from north and east, the ground rises steeply to the craggy heights of Fort Tryon Park. A curious medieval citadel crowns the heights, as if commanding the river crossings against barbarians from the outer boroughs – The Cloisters. It is the Architect's Digest of the Middle Ages; European building from the twelfth to the fifteenth century, from Reims to Madrid, compressed into one compact corner of space and time.

The Cloisters is a department of the Metropolitan

Museum, and it houses a collection of medieval art. But the fabric of the building is designed as a museum in itself, to incorporate bits and pieces of disused ecclesiastical architecture from all over Western Europe. They were mostly collected by George Grey Barnard, the American sculptor, who housed them in a brick building down the road. But between the wars John D. Rockefeller Jr paid for the stuff to be taken out, fitted together, and supplemented where necessary with appropriate period additions to make a single structure.

What they have most of at The Cloisters is cloisters – four of them, built out of pieces of cloister from four separate monasteries in south-west France. They include a catholic selection of parts from other kits, too. The cloister from St Michel-de-Cuxa, near Prades, for example, incorporates an arch from Narbonne and a doorway from Burgos. The cloister from Saint-Guilhem-le-Désert, near Montpellier, contains ten humorous corbels from the Notre-Dame-de-la-Grande-Sauve, near Bordeaux; an angel from Burgundy; a relief from Reims and another from Florence; two marble figures from Lucca; and a fountain which was once a capital in Saint-Sauveur at Figeac. The cloister from Bonnefont offers a magnificent vista of the George Washington suspension bridge.

We pass (as the guides say) from the Saint-Guilhem cloister to the St Michel-de-Cuxa by way of the Romanesque church of Notre-Dame-du-Bourg, which hails from Langon near Bordeaux (with stained-glass windows believed to have come from Troyes), and a twelfth-century chapter house taken complete and entire from the former abbey of Notre-Dame-de-Pontaut in Gascony. We note a Florentine fresco above the door of the Early Gothic Hall, and in the Gothic Chapel pay our respects at the tombs of the Counts of Urgel, which were at Lérida, in north-east Spain, when the counts went abroad around the end of the thirteenth century.

Passing on into the Romanesque Hall, we note with scarcely a tremor of surprise that one of the doorways comes from Reugny on the Loire, another from Moutiers-Saint-Jean in Burgundy and a third from . . . oh . . . 'We do not know the provenance of this doorway,' says the guidebook.

Well, it happens to all of us – it's happened to me. You pick little oddments up on holiday, and when you get home you can't remember where the devil you got them, or what the devil you got them for. I can imagine George Grey Barnard's surprise when he came back from France and found this spare Romanesque doorway in his bag. He probably discovered it in the customs.

'Any stained glass to declare?' asks the customs man. 'Any tombs? Romanesque doorways?'

'Yes,' says Barnard. 'Two Romanesque doorways.'

'Sure it's only two, now? I get an awful lot of wise guys trying to slip the odd doorway past me. Let's have a look.'

So they open the bags – and there are the three doorways.

'I swear I only bought two!' protests Barnard. 'It was in a little Romanesque doorway shop just behind Notre Dame . . . I have the receipt somewhere . . . Someone must have planted it on me – unless that little man in Chartres slipped me a doorway instead of a cloister! Let me see – how many cloisters do I have . . .?'

On into the Fuentidueña Chapel. A comparatively

recent acquisition, this – a complete apse, about a third of a church, brought stone by stone from the diocese of Segovia in 1961, but already looking as though it was born and bred in New York.

But hold on! The apse is only *on loan*. Any day the Spanish government may call up and ask for it back! It's going to take some time to chip it off the rest of the building when they do, though – it's mortared awfully firmly in. If I lent someone an apse and I found they'd got it attached to their property as solidly as this I'd start getting a little worried. I have a feeling that the Spanish government may live to regret its soft-heartedness in doling out apses to people who were too improvident to have tucked one or two away for a rainy day when apses were in season.

True, the Metropolitan lent Spain six Spanish frescoes in exchange, but I'm not entirely sure that six frescoes to the apse is a fair rate. Frescoes are very bearish these days. In Zurich, as I understand it, apses are fetching up to eight or nine doorways apiece. The apse/cloister rate eased off a little last week, however, as speculators against the cloister tried to cover themselves.

Anyway, The Cloisters is a brilliant collection, superbly displayed, and I am thinking of doing the same thing for American art in Britain. I've been collecting unwanted floors from various obsolete skyscrapers as I've gone about the country, and I'm in touch with an agent who swears he can get me a considerable portion of the Pennsylvania Station back from where they threw it when they knocked it down.

I'd like to see it all fitted together on Hampstead Heath somewhere – we could call it The Scrapers. If we could

just temporarily borrow the spire off the Chrysler
Building to top the whole thing off we'd be almost there.
I told the Mayor we'd be happy to lend them the left half
of Tower Bridge in exchange.

10. *New York*

I'm not sure that I ever did find the *real* America, or the
real Americans, that the unreal Americans I met in the
unreal America were always so anxious I should see. I
hurried from place to place, but at the end of the rainbow
all I ever found were more unreal Americans – people
rather like oneself – who had it on good authority that
the real America was 374 miles up the road.

Some of these unreal Americans were so much like real
Englishmen that communication became rather a problem.
I'd speak to them in plain enough American – cookies,
candy, riding the subway, and all the rest of it (or rather a
dialect of it which goes more like biscImeancookies,
sweetsorIshouldsaycandy), and they'd come back at me
with a lot of stuff about *petrol* and *lifts*, or at any rate
gasserpetrol and elevatorasyousaylift.

'Jeez, baby,' I'd cry in the vernacular, 'if that ain't just
the darndest thing I ever heard, man, and that's for sure,
kiddo, by golly gosh.'

Well, they'd just stare at me. 'Oh, I say, what?' they'd
murmur uneasily. 'Steady on, old chap, by George, and
all that.' Sounded as if they'd got a plum in their mouth,
some of them.

Still, the trip wasn't wasted. I've found out a lot about
the real *England* while I've been over here – really stood
back and got it in perspective. Found out all sorts of
things about the country that I never knew, largely by

reading the advertisements in the American press.

We're awfully smartly dressed in England, one can't help noticing for a start. We have a certain 'British flair and swagger' which shows in the 'sturdy corduroy trench-coats' our men wear. And in our berets, of course. ('Quite properly British', as the importers explain – particularly when worn with a half-smoked Gauloise and a string of onions.)

Indeed, Englishmen are scarcely ever out of rainwear of one sort or another, as I understand it. Not surprising, really; everyone here knows it rains continuously in England. Well, not in *London*, of course, since London is wrapped perpetually in London fog, an exhalation of such evocative fairy charm that there is even a brand of American raincoats called after it. London Fog raincoats do sterling service protecting their wearers against the filthy New York smog which everyone loathes so much.

We take off our raincoats sometimes, of course, if we're absolutely sure the room we're in is dry – and reveal scarlet waistcoats, as stocked in the midtown English boutiques here. Or else we stand rather correctly about after the day's shooting with our left hands in our pockets, sipping Scotch, and wearing military moustaches, loud green check suits, and Onyx for Men, 'the bracing, buoyant scent that Englishmen created for Englishmen'.

Exactly who pours the Scotch in these circumstances, I'm not too sure; it's becoming very difficult to get real English butlers in England, I read about once a week in various American papers. This must make life rather hard – we're notable drinkers, with about five thousand different brands of Scotch to choose between, each of which we enjoy with more quiet, reflective, British pleasure than all the rest. A good butler is a simple necessity of life in these conditions.

We're notable eaters as well as notable drinkers. In fact, eating and drinking are just about the only activities we *have* been noted performing, and we seem to be bravely undeterred by the sight of one another's scarlet waistcoats, loud green check suits, and bracing, buoyant smell.

We start the day off with a traditional breakfast of English muffins ('A British and grape jelly, Jeeves,' as those of us lucky enough to retain our butlers murmur aristocratically through our moustaches). Our traditional food on most other occasions, if Keen's English Chop House on 36th Street has got it right, is roast beef and Yorkshire popover.

The British Travel office on Fifth Avenue, however, disputes the narrowness of this diet. It has devoted a whole window display to our eating habits, in the hope of persuading Americans to come over and observe them from close to. According to British Travel we eat plastic – plastic finnan haddie, plastic kidneys, plastic cockles and mussels, plastic haggis, plastic strawberries in plastic cream, and many other plastic delicacies.

'Eat Like a Native in Britain', a sign over this formidable collection challenges New Yorkers, who gaze back awe-struck, their faces swiftly going as green as English check suits. When it comes to pale pink plastic kidneys, I believe we definitely have the Americans beaten.

Eat like a native and drink like a fish, in a typical English pub. I'd almost forgotten just what a typical English pub was like, I must admit, until I saw some of

the typical English pubs which have sprung up all over
New York in the last few years. The Roman Pub in the
New York Hilton, for instance, 'where you can enjoy the
sophistication of an "American Bar" in a smart
Continental setting'.

Anyway, that's England, when you really get it into
focus. One slight drawback – there don't seem to be any
women there. A great imperial destiny, I think one can
deduce, reading between the lines; a sound currency; a
magnificent ability to hold our liquor. But no women.

I am hastening back to investigate.

(1966)

The Music of Radishes

Japan at close quarters

It was the season of the summer rains, and stepping outside into the streets was like going inside the Palm House
at Kew; the air palpably enclosed the body – hot, moist,
saturated with the dank smell of sub-tropical greenery.

In little trains squeezing between the backs of the
houses in muddled old wooden towns, and labouring up
through humid sunlight into the densely green mountains, heads sank under the weight of the air, and rolled
and swayed like shaken berries. Between Shimoda and
Ito three old women sitting with their feet tucked up
beneath them, and the wind from the open window
blowing over their faces, sang strange, ancient songs
together, very quietly so as not to disturb the other passengers, tapping out the rhythm on their knees.

In certain quarters of Tokyo the streets were full of
small businesses. Inside each doorway – a tiny work area
with a grey steel desk, or industrial protective clothing
hanging up; and beyond, like a miniature stage-set, the
raised floor of the living quarters, with the inner world of
sliding screens, and straw-matted floors upon which no
shoe is ever set.

In certain suburbs the streets and alleys were not much

wider than the walkways of a conservatory. You could reach out and touch the bamboo fence on either side; when it rained, passing umbrellas clashed and tangled. Only inches behind the fence and the screen of miniature trees, only inches from one another, the houses looked inwards upon themselves, every house of different design from every other. From this one came the heartbroken plunking of a koto, the ancient Japanese zither; from that the sound of someone practising Chopin. Resinous fragrances of building timber hung in the air, and the stench of cess-pits.

One of the things I remember most clearly in Japan I saw within minutes of steeping off the plane. The monorail in from the airport weaved among a densely packed world of neat modern industrial plant, polluted commercial waterways, and high-stacked expressways, then, just before its terminal at Hamamatsu-cho, it zoomed up to cross the New Tokaido Line, along which the famous aerodynamic expresses streak out to the rest of industrial Japan at 130 m.p.h. And there below, trapped between the two tiers of the main line and the monorail on one side, and the traffic jams on the double elevated decks of the expressway on the other, was an old palace garden.

I caught another glimpse of it as I left, its archaic formalised serenity still stranded among the reinforced concrete and moving steel – perhaps the point of it all, the somewhere to which the expensive transportation towering all around it eventually led. Or perhaps just a picturesque antique to glimpse out of the window.

*

I stayed for a few days with some people in a new dormitory town outside Osaka. They lived in a block of concrete flats which from the outside could have been in Cumbernauld or Rotterdam. But inside their front door was a traditional Japanese interior. You left your shoes in the little concrete vestibule, and stepped up into slippers waiting on the raised wooden floor beyond. The slippers took you some four or five feet to the door of the living-room, where you kicked them off to step on to the straw mats, the tatami, in your socks.

It was a $4^1/_2$-mat room – about nine feet square – just big enough to accommodate Mr and Mrs Okamoto and myself sitting on cushions around a low table to eat, or at night, with the cushions piled in the corner and the table upended, the bedding for me to sleep on. Around the walls were the colour television, the big speakers of the stereo, and Mr Okamoto's library of philosophy in four European languages (he was a lecturer in aesthetics). The walls were decorated with a collection of model air-craft he had assembled from kits. One of them was the white-painted bomber in which the Japanese leaders flew to offer their surrender in 1945.

Every time I moved I had to think about my extremi-ties. Was my head sufficiently retracted to avoid door frames and hanging curtains? The lintel over the lavatory doorway in one hotel where I stayed had been knocked halfway out of its frame, presumably by some lofty Western head – probably one thinking about whether its feet were in the right footwear. Concentrating on my head, I'd suddenly realise that my feet had done some-thing terrible. Stepped off the tatami on to the (scrupu-lously clean) wooden corridor in their socks, perhaps. Or, having put the slippers on, then changed into the special slippers kept for contact with the (scrupulously clean) lavatory floor, and then changed back again to traverse the corridor, taken two steps into the living-room in the corridor-slippers! A hurried, guiltily slippered leap backwards, and crack! – head again.

I watched, enviously, the way Japanese stepped in and out of footwear without thinking about it, revolving as they approached the tatami to step out of their slippers backwards and leave them facing the right way for when they returned. On trains women sometimes slipped their shoes off and folded their legs away beneath them, like a retractable undercarriage. Occasionally men would kick the right shoe off and cross left leg over right, then put the right shoe back and air the left foot. In the first-class coaches of the trains on the New Tokaido Line there were elaborate foot-rests which were faced in rubber to support shoes, but which could be turned over to produce a tiny, personal area of raised carpet where your stockinged feet would feel at home.

I met some people who still made a point of folding away their Western suits when they got home in the evening and, after the ritual soak in a hot bath, changing into a kimono. Mr Okamoto told me he liked to see his wife in a kimono, but she would put one on only for New Year's Day and for friends' weddings. (It took about an hour to get into the whole outfit, she told me.) She liked to see him in a kimono, too – but he absolutely refused to wear one at any time.

He was an endlessly thoughtful and attentive host – polite, smiling, anxious . . . inscrutable. (I'm sorry!) And she was beautiful, diminutive . . . like a delicately animated doll. (I can't help it!) She had a little silvery voice and a little silvery laugh – was always gay, unflustered, interested in everyone around her, modestly flirtatious. She did everything. Worked (she taught Japanese to foreigners). Was up early to prepare me complex traditional breakfasts. Did all the driving – slowly, sedately, safely, while the insane provincial traffic overtook on both sides of us, and cut wildly across in front of us, racing ruthlessly for every foot of the road and never giving way – and while odd little high-pitched cries of complaint came from her husband in the back at her having missed the opportunity to shoot into some fast-moving gap not much longer than the car.

At traffic-lights she would take a fan out of a glass-fronted box by the gearshift and fan herself. As she drove I would have to lean across to catch her tiny voice, almost inaudible against the hot wind through the open windows, and the squeal of violently over-accelerated tyres scrabbling at the roadway. 'Would you like to go to a hot-springs resort where men and women all take the bath together without any clothes?' she would be asking demurely, or, 'Have you had many love-affairs since you were married?'

In restaurants it was she who handled the money and settled the bill. When someone had to run half a mile to persuade a temple to let us in to see its Zen stone-garden after it had closed for the night, she ran, and persuaded, and ran half a mile back (with the thermometer around 90, and the air humid enough to be wrung out), and reappeared unflustered and delicate and smiling.

And when her husband, in the back seat, told her to avoid a traffic-jam on the expressway by turning round and driving the wrong way down the ramp, in the face of traffic coming up it at 40 or 50 miles an hour, she turned round and drove the wrong way down the ramp, still smiling and calm as ever.

*

On the television (nine channels, mostly running from early in the morning until late at night) there were costume serials in which good samurai remained apparently unaware of bad samurai creeping up behind to kill them, but who turned at the last moment and did for them with one colossal blow of the sword. One of the series was about a blind samurai – a kind of medieval Ironside.

One Sunday in Tokyo, Hidé Ishiguro, who teaches philosophy at London University and who was back in Japan for a conference, took me to a programme of kabuki plays. The huge theatre was completely full, and the traditional shouts with which each actor's supporters in the audience 'called forth' their man on to the stage, and acclaimed the extraordinary stylisations of his performance (the forcings of the voice, the vibrations of the eyebrows) were violent, as if for boxers or wrestlers. The star was Ennosuke, the third generation of a famous kabuki family, and as the curtain fell on his last long tragic monologue an old man in the audience, deeply moved, called out: 'I think of your grandfather!' There was a sympathetic murmur from the whole house.

The only distraction from the intensity of this highly stylised ritual was the sniffing and nose-blowing all round us. I remarked to Miss Ishiguro in the interval that a lot of people seemed to be suffering from hay fever. 'Hay fever?' she said. 'They were weeping!' (Who in Europe – honestly – goes to the theatre and weeps at some 250-year-old classic?) We were eating fried eels in one of the theatre restaurants. She pointed out the groups of middle-aged women around us wearing kimonos. The kimonos were dark blue on brown, or patterns of dark blue on white. These were 'downtown' styles, she said, worn by women in the districts where the small merchants and craftsmen traditionally lived, and quite unlike the pastel shades and flower-patterns of kimonos in the 'uptown' district, traditionally where the nobles lived around the Imperial Palace, and by extension the suburbs.

'Kabuki is their whole world,' said Miss Ishiguro. 'People talk about the Japanese being the Prussians of Asia. This is absolute nonsense. They're terribly sentimental. The historical figures they admire are not the cunning, successful ones, but the people like Shunkan in the play today, who get carried away by their feelings, and in the heat of the moment kill someone, or make a romantic gesture of despair by killing themselves. This is what these people live for – a warm bath of emotion.'

*

I learnt to use a toothpick behind a concealing hand, and to take a public bath while holding the special little towel as if by accident in front of my private parts. I ate raw fish, raw chicken, jellyfish, sea urchins, various forms of seaweed, and whale fat with plum sauce washed down by saké with salt. I failed to convince, however. As I sat with the Okamotos over dinner one night in a hot-springs resort (a segregated one, sadly), wrapped in a long cotton yukata after the scalding medicinal bath, the delectable Mrs Okamoto was suddenly overcome with uncontrollable silvery laughter at my funny foreign ways.

'I'm sorry,' she said when she could speak. 'It's your efforts not to make a noise as you eat! Why do Europeans behave like that? Why don't you let us all hear that you're enjoying the food? We particularly like to hear the radishes being crunched.' (We were eating pickled radishes and rice with tea poured over it.) She crunched a radish to show me, with deafening delicacy. 'And we very much enjoy the sound of rice and tea being sucked up.' She vacuumed up rice and tea, with an exquisite slurping noise.

'Though what we like most of all,' said Mr Okamoto, 'is the sound of someone sucking noodles up.'

I managed to produce a few muffled sound effects with the radishes. But long years of Western inhibition, I discovered, had forever destroyed the possibility of sustaining any very expressive coloratura with the wet rice and noodles.

*

For many Japanese, though, the old lifestyle is beginning to slip away rather like a garden seen from a train window. The first time I slept on the tatami was in a *ryokan*, a traditional Japanese inn – all mats and sliding screens and a kind of incense burning to keep the mosquitoes off. *Ryokan* are reluctant to accept unaccompanied foreigners, in case they put their hobnailed boots on the tatami, or do unspeakable Occidental things in the bathroom, so I had to get myself taken by a Japanese friend. But she – a sociologist with a metropolitan lifestyle – had never stayed in a *ryokan* before, and knew almost as little about it as I did. We had to get a Swedish woman she knew to take us both.

This particular inn, the Chrysanthemum Plum, was in the 'gay quarters' – the geisha district – of Kyoto, the old Imperial capital (the *first-class* geisha district, the local people assured me). In Tokyo, said Kiyoko Kusakabe, the sociologist, the Prime Minister even held meetings of Ministers in one of the better-known geisha houses. But this archaic world of expense-account tea and sympathy, where an apprentice might still complete her training by selling her virginity to a patron for several thousand pounds, was as closed to her as it was to me – she'd tried to do some research on it, and been forced to give up by its tradition of secretiveness.

The *ryokan* (the owner of another one, near Shimoda, told me) would all in the end have to give place to Western-style hotels; they needed too much labour to run. And television, said Miss Tetsuko Kuroyanagi, who has a daily talk show on one of the TV channels, was transforming the appearance of the Japanese home. All over Japan, she said – particularly in the countryside, among farmers made rich by the heavily subsidised prices which the Government pays for the whole rice crop, and by the soaring inflation in land value – people were ripping out the old traditional interiors, and installing the Western decors they'd seen in the 'home dramas', the afternoon soap-operas for housewives: fitted kitchens, French windows, carpets and sofas. The only thing they preserved was the earth-closet out at the back – because the lavatory was the one room that the home dramas never showed.

In most of the middle-class homes I visited a compromise had been arrived at. You left your shoes inside the front door, and stepped up (in slippers) on to fitted carpets, with Western armchairs to sit in. Often, though, a single last tatami room would have been left as a final stronghold, where the parents could spread their bedding for the night (while their children slept in beds), or retire to watch television undisturbed, or sit in kimonos to keep New Year's Day.

*

'Don't run away with the idea that the Japanese are human beings like you and me,' urged a New Zealander who had been there for several years, and who spoke the language fluently. 'Because they're not. They're extensions of the trees and flowers. That's how they see themselves, as a part of nature. It's only the rare exception who thinks of himself as an individual, in the way that we think of ourselves as individuals. Most Japanese see themselves as members of the group – of the family, of the company they work for. They don't know how to act or think outside the group.

'And they haven't really changed – that's the mistake people make. They're not rich; they're still well down the league table for per capita income. You see the streets jammed with traffic – but you have to remember that only one in sixteen owns a car.

'And they don't understand how we think! They're masters of appearance, of taking over a style. They've taken over the forms of Western culture just as they took over the forms of Chinese culture way back in the Middle Ages. But they don't understand the ideas behind the forms that make them work!'

Other resident foreigners I met who knew Japan well talked about 'them' (the Japanese) in a similar way. But when I put this thesis to Miss Ishiguro, who had understood the ideas of Western philosophy well enough to become a rather distinguished commentator in the West on Leibnitz and Wittgenstein, she could not recognise any truth in it at all. She found it easy to think of other Japanese scholars who had achieved international recognition for their contributions to mathematics, physics, and other areas of purely conceptual thought, and she took me to various coffee-houses in Tokyo where students paid to listen to carefully chosen programmes of Bruckner and Albinoni and Carl Philipp Emanuel Bach in stereo while they worked.

It was this – the total absorption of European music – that I found the most surprising thing of all. I was with the Okamotos on the overnight boat to Hiroshima. As we leaned on the rail and watched the summer lightning flicker over the polluted Inland Sea, Mrs Okamoto sang Schubert songs in her small true sweet voice. There were some, she said, that she could never sing without tears coming to her eyes.

When Schubert wrote those songs, Japan was still in the two centuries of total isolation from the world which she had imposed upon herself, an inward-looking feudal society based upon authority and devoted to the conservation of her own ancient traditions. That she should since then have digested the structure of European science and economic organisation with such rapidity and success is astonishing enough. But that both the ritual grimaces of the kabuki actor and the delicate dislocations of early nineteenth-century European tonality should move Japanese to tears I found beyond any easy comprehension.

*

Look out of the living-room window of even the most comfortable middle-class house in Japan and the next house is never more than a few feet away. Or the next factory. And beside the bamboo fence of the last house on the outskirts, beside the wall of the last factory, the rice paddy commences.

Four-fifths of Japan is uninhabitable mountain, so that 108 million people have to live, manufacture, and grow their food in an area about the size of the Irish Republic. This dense civilisation must have thickened almost in front of the eyes during the last 120 years, since Japan – then an impoverished feudal society with a population, limited by famine, of some thirty millions – was forcibly reopened to the world by the great imperial Powers.

And not only thickened, but changed, and changed again. Working in timber rather than stone or brick, the Japanese have never built to last. Then nearly half of Tokyo was reduced to ashes in the great earthquake of 1923, and well over half of it destroyed again in the fire-raids carried out by the Americans in 1945. Miss Ishiguro, who had been back to Japan for only two short visits in the last five years, was constantly astonished, as she showed me round Tokyo, by the sight of new buildings, and baffled by miles of new subway line. The population has increased by half since the war, and shifted like sand; the great majority of Tokyo's inhabitants were born elsewhere.

It's been difficult to build upwards for fear of earthquakes, though clumps of high-rise buildings are appearing now in Tokyo which are designed to resonate freely in time with the shockwaves. In Osaka they have escaped downwards, and dug out a huge underground shopping centre two floors deep, with its own decorative subterranean river. (An earthquake expert I talked to was very gloomy about what would happen down there when a big quake shattered the exits and extinguished the lights.) The dense, low urban sprawl on the surface is dominated by towering wire cages like gigantic aviaries, inside which you can take out your frustrations on a golf-ball, to keep sane while you work to become rich enough to hit it out in the open (I saw advertisements in the *Japan Times* offering up to £27,000 for membership of a real golf club).

I felt an almost physical sense of being pressed in upon. At sunset one sweltering Sunday night I found myself waiting in the centre of a rather scruffy little commuter town near Tokyo while a friend went to make a phone-call. We and a million other people had been walking round Kamakura all day, looking at temples and hydrangea-viewing, and we were just about to join what looked like a twenty-five-mile traffic jam back to the city. The shops were all open still, loud pop music was playing, and there was a noise like steel rain coming from a pachinko parlour, where a hundred or more men were standing shoulder to shoulder playing banks of quickfire vertical pinball machines to win domestic provisions.

I suddenly became aware that somebody huge was staring at me. I looked up – and there on a hill outside the town was a gigantic Buddha gazing placidly down through the tangle of overhead electric wires. Suffering from either cultural shock or severe sensory overload, I took refuge in a charming riverside prospect across the street, with little bridges leading to a little garden beyond. There in the river below me, when I leaned on the balustrade, were the remains of five bicycles, one on top of the other, all thrown in from the same point. And over them, like a fountain playing upon a piece of statuary, gushed an abundant spring of pure, odoriferous sewage.

*

The roads are clogged with the nation's products; the rivers and seas with its waste-products. Miss Ishiguro begged me to make great efforts not to write yet another article about pollution, or the economic miracle, or employees singing company songs. But the subject of pollution it wasn't possible to avoid. Entire pages of the English-language papers were full of nothing but pollution news; conversations returned to it again and again.

At Minamata (the place which gave its name to Minamata Disease, a form of mercury poisoning), the fishery co-operative was being commissioned by the local authority to fish the bay – and bury whatever it caught. In Saeki, fishermen occupied the offices of a company discharging waste-products into the bay until a company executive knelt before them in apology. In Kobe, the president of a fish transportation company whose business had been hit by the scare burned himself to death on the tombs of his ancestors. Ten thousand fishmongers met in Tokyo to protest. The Prime Minister instructed all the members of his Cabinet to set people's minds at rest by eating fish for lunch every day. The government announced that it was safe to eat up to 10.2 sardines per week, plus 1.8 flatfish, 1.6 yellowfin tuna, and 12 horse mackerel; then, under heavy pressure from the fishery industry, revised this to 38.6 sardines, 6.7 flatfish, 6.1 yellowfin tuna, and 46.2 horse mackerel.

Whether any Cabinet Minister ever managed to get through 46.2 horse mackerel in a week was not reported.

*

Stewing in the damp Pacific heat (though of course it snows in winter), surrounded by a tight-packed mass in a state of agitated and rapid transformation, I sometimes felt as if I was inside some kind of pressure-cooker.

It seemed to me that people did work hard, as the legend has it. Most companies still work a six-day week. Wives complain that their husbands get home so late that they scarcely see them. Miss Ishiguro made a point of undermining all these generalisations by taking me to see a university computer centre which could be run only eight hours a day because it was staffed by government employees who refused on principle to work overtime. She introduced me to an executive in a pharmaceutical company who worked from nine to six, five days a week (and who sang not company songs but the B Minor Mass and the Verdi Requiem with a local choir). His firm was just going over to a system whereby office staff put in 160 hours a month arranged in any way they chose.

But a Swedish woman I met in Kyoto, who had lived in Japan for a number of years, and worked in the offices of Japanese companies (she spoke fluent Japanese), was very vehement about the effect which 'the company' had on life for its employees. 'The effect?' she cried. 'The company is life! And the real slave of the company is the boss. He has to work long hours – till nine, till ten – and the system *is* that no one else feels able to leave before he does. Men feel that they have to demonstrate their strength by working until they drop. And sometimes that happens. Every now and then in the office where I was working, late in the evening, a man would literally collapse and have to be taken home.'

Mrs Okamoto, while I was staying with her and her husband near Osaka, painted me a sombre picture of a Japan full of lonely wives sitting at home all day with nothing to do except to entertain lovers, or to denounce their neighbours for doing so. Or else reduced to watching the wives in all the 'home dramas' on afternoon television having illicit affairs on their behalf. Most marriages are still arranged, and Japanese husbands have always been expected to have affairs. Many older men, said Mrs Okamoto, died what she translated as a 'death on the body' – of a heart-attack while making love to a girl. It was a very good death, she said. Not quite so good for the girl, I suggested; at which Mrs Okamoto laughed in surprise. I don't think she'd ever thought about it from the girl's point of view.

A teacher from a university in Nara told me that it was the men in their thirties and forties who were the real force behind the economy. The younger people were more interested in leisure, and the economy would slow down as they took over. All the same, the pressure still begins early in life. A young school-teacher from Yokohama who looked in for fifteen minutes one evening brought a bottle of whisky as a calling present, and dismissed my protests by saying that he had hundreds more at home – the parents brought one every time they came to discuss their child's progress.

A scientist who happened to be present, Professor Seiya Uyeda, said he could easily imagine that this was true, and not merely an elaborate politeness. 'You should

see the children working in the evenings and on Sundays,'
he said. The State schools were unstreamed and unsetted,
but ambitious parents got round this by putting their
children into 'sideways' schools as well – supplementary
coaching establishments which crammed them outside
school hours (sometimes in the morning, before school
started). 'When registration day for these sideways
schools comes round,' he said, 'the parents literally take
blankets and queue on the pavement all night to get their
children in.'

You need to get your child into the crammers in order
to get him into one of the particular State or private high
schools which can get him into a university which can get
him into one of the big companies . . . If necessary,
wealthy parents rent flats for their children to live in, so
as to be near a successful high school; various people told
me about a boy who'd been so desolated by the loneliness
of living like this that he'd committed suicide. Professor
Uyeda, exhausted by three years of political disruption at
the Earthquake Research Institute in Tokyo University
where he worked, had made a bet with his family: if their
son didn't pass into one of the handful of high schools
able to get pupils into Tokyo University (still, out of all
the 562 universities and graduate schools in Japan, the
narrow gateway to the top) the family would move to
America. The boy passed; the family stayed.

What surprised me was that children ever learned to
read and write, no matter how many hours they worked.
Think of the difficulty a lot of English children have in
mastering the twenty-six characters of the Latin alphabet,
and then look at what a Japanese child faces. The Ministry
of Education has standardised a selection of some 1,900

ideograms (out of a total of about 20,000) for everyday use, of which more than 800 have to be learnt in elementary school. Nearly all of these ideograms (*kanji*) can be read in two separate and unrelated ways, one Japanese and one deriving from the original reading in Chinese.

There are also two syllabic 'alphabets': *hiragana*, a set of forty-six characters for writing out the phonetic values of the *kanji*, and for articulating the grammatical inflections which make Japanese such an entirely unsuitable language to be written in ideograms in the first place, and *katakana*, another forty-six characters, expressing the same sounds as their *hiragana* counterparts, but mostly unrelated in appearance, for transcribing foreign words.

The imagination fails. But most Japanese plainly take in Latin script as well. Advertisers and pulp magazine publishers are confident they do, at any rate. Legible words sprang kindly out of the deserts of public print to relieve my unfamiliar parching illiteracy: 'Sex', 'Fantastic Escape', 'Gimmick Productions Limited', 'Sainte Neige 1967, Château Haut Yamanashi.' Advertisers' mood phrases: 'New Life,' 'Dear Summer'. Even the names of products – 'Cedric', 'Sony'. Imagine the scene at the London advertising agency where the client agrees to give his Dog-i-Meet a more up-market appeal by posting it all over the Underground as Δογ-ι-μιτ, in Greek characters!

'But don't be fooled by all those claims you hear about universal literacy,' said my Japanese-speaking New Zealand sceptic. 'The average housewife can remember only about 900 *kanji*.' I put this thesis to various Japanese, and they all denied it sharply. But even highly educated friends agreed that they would need a dictionary to read a nineteenth-century novel, and Miss Ishiguro was shocked to find that people on the subways were no longer reading books, as they did a few years ago, but stories told in comic strip form. She blamed television. I secretly sympathised with them.

*

Some of the most familiar symptoms of social pressure, though, were remarkable by their absence. There's little crime on the streets, and no feeling of potential aggression. The only beggars I saw were monks. 'Homelessness,' a city planning official told me wryly, 'is solved by overcrowding.' The signs that differentiate rich and poor are comparatively subtle. Even the dropouts look rather presentable ('Japanese first, hippies second,' said an English resident.)

All the same, dark currents of violence stir beneath this self-respecting surface. Suicide is much discussed and written about. It's not, by international standards, much practised (if the statistics are right), but more and more schoolchildren are killing themselves, for reasons which no one is very clear about.

There is a race problem, with the Korean immigrant community cast as the blacks. And if I wanted to get myself stabbed, said a computer scientist, I should try going to Osaka and thrusting four upraised fingers in people's faces. The reference would be to four-footed beasts, and would imply being a *burakumin*. The word is a euphemism ('special community person') for a caste of untouchables, estimated to be some two million strong, concentrated particularly in Osaka, and isolated in many outcast villages. They are also referred to as *hi-nin* ('non-persons') and *eta* ('full of filth'), and are the descendants of a community designated in the feudal past for certain trades repugnant to Buddhist sensibility, such as slaughtering, tanning, execution, and grave digging. Now they work usually as day labourers and garbage collectors, despised by the rest of the community, unable to marry outside their caste or get a job with a company, the subject of grotesque sexual canards.

Shareholders' meetings are occasions to stay away from; companies hire *sokaiya* (translated to me as 'shareholders-meeting experts') to intimidate leftist hecklers. There was also a fashion among certain students, I was told, for beating up people in the street who 'looked' at them. At Kokushikan University in Tokyo, which has a reputation for being rightist, students this summer had been beating up a variety of victims, including a woman of seventy, but concentrating chiefly on Korean highschool children. At Waseda University in Tokyo eleven students were injured when forty members of the Revolutionary Marxist faction attacked fifty members of the Anti-Imperialist Student Council with iron pipes. Some thirty students, also thought to be members of the Revolutionary Marxist faction, raided a number of apartment houses in the Ikebukuro district, looking for members of a rival leftist group called the Centre Core faction. They beat five students about the head with iron pipes, seriously injuring four of them (not, apparently, members of any group at all).

When I went to meet Professor Uyeda at the Earthquake Research Institute they politely denied all knowledge of his whereabouts, and he appeared only later, on another part of the campus, summoned from his second, secret office by a phone call from an employee at the institute who was still co-operating with him. The institute, he explained, had been immobilised for the past three years by a dispute between faculty and technicians, with students intervening, which began after a technician claimed that he had been struck by a professor.

The professor in question, it turned out, was a Communist, and the Communist Party – constitutional, nationalistic, politically effective – is particularly loathed by the Left. The dispute had escalated into a kind of violent farce. At one confrontation between faculty and demonstrators, the director of the Institute had been hit forty times. At another point the Institute had agreed to continue paying the allegedly struck technician for time spent lying on the ground outside on hunger strike. In the end the intimidation had become so severe that the faculty had withdrawn from the building, since when research had been carried out only by clandestine arrangements with complaisant technicians, like the illicit affairs of the home dramas.

*

And one day the whole tightly pressed structure will burst apart. But literally, physically. All wealthy societies wait for their doomsday; in Japan the expectation is scientific and specific. This year is the fiftieth anniversary of the great earthquake which destroyed almost half of Tokyo and killed 100,000 people; and all the time the earth is storing energy towards another one. If it occurred now, said Professor Uyeda, it would be one-third of the 1923 strength. The longer it's delayed, the stronger it will be.

It has been estimated, he said, that a major earthquake would start some 30,000 fires, of which, if all the emergency services were working, they could extinguish perhaps 300. It was fire which did the damage in 1923, and he expected the fires next time to be worse, because there were more fuel and gas-pipes to fracture, because modern plastic building materials would give off poisonous fumes as they burnt, and because people would try to flee the cities in cars, which would burn 'like fuel'.

He admitted that he worried about it personally. So did many other people I talked to. The papers were reporting popular omens – snakes in the streets of Tokyo, sharks off the coast – and trying to trace the source of a rumour which had swept through Chiba Prefecture among the schoolchildren, predicting a big quake on 11 June. There were interviews with celebrities about the preparations they'd made; most of them seemed to have laid in emergency food supplies at least. At the top of the bestseller list was a science-fiction novel called *The Submersion of Japan* (cleverly and plausibly based upon modern theories of plate tectonics, according to Professor Uyeda) which postulated the total disappearance of the whole archipelago as a result of earthquakes and volcanic activity.

Each time I saw the fine wires holding the pots down in museums, or the torch waiting by the bedside in hotels, I felt a faint apprehension. 'Forget pollution,' said a Japanese diplomat who had just been told by a geisha that a big quake was on its way. 'Pollution we can solve. Earthquakes we can't.'

(1973)

Wild West Eleven

On the frontier in Notting Hill

We found the first flat we had when we got married only after a long and depressing search. It was in Notting Hill, situated almost exactly on the front line between the advancing middle classes and the desolation of unreclaimed slums. This was at the end of the 1950s. The middle classes had stormed the south side of the ridge that runs through North Kensington, and captured the summit – then, awed by the panorama of Notting Dale, Wormwood Scrubs, and Willesden beyond, halted to consolidate. Our road, which crossed the ridge from south to north, was a living spectrum of English society. Starting off with the houses of the unquestionably rich, it reached a point next to us, just over the top, where by longstanding custom the milkmen stacked their empty milk-crates and everyone else dumped their unwanted sofas and bedsteads.

'It's the classlessness of it that we like,' said our middle-class neighbours. 'You feel you're not being pigeon-holed.'

The flat was in a jerry-built Victorian house covered in white stucco, with a small false balcony on the first floor and a round Dutch gable capping the front elevation. It was one of the ugliest houses I have ever seen. It would have been the ugliest without qualification, but for the fact that it was in a terrace of four which were all identical. Or almost identical. The architect who lived in one of them had tried to improve the maddening wrongness of its appearance by amputating the false balcony and trimming the Dutch gable back to a triangle, and on another the stucco had degenerated into a patchwork of various shades of brown, like some sad urban camouflage. Because of these slight but oddly confusing variations, the four together were rather more than four times as horrible as any one of them.

The house had just been derequisitioned by the council, and when we came upon it the new landlords were in the process of converting it into four middle-class flats. This involved the application of large quantities of white gloss paint and Regency stripe wallpaper on the communal staircase, and of a vast, pointed knob of stainless steel like a medieval armoured kneecap to each of the four front doors. Inside the lower three flats the landlords had with elaborate fantasy built the kitchens in the corners of the bedrooms, and been lavish with thin cardboard walls. But the top flat, which had presumably once been the servants' bedrooms, had already been converted by the council, along simple but practical lines, and it had a distant view, through three tiny round-topped windows like a triptych, of the sun going down behind the White City dog-track. Moreover, if you climbed into the dusty attic, out through a trap-door on to the slates, and up to the pitch of the roof by the chimney, you could see Wormwood Scrubs prison. It was really the views which decided us to take the flat. Perhaps that doesn't sound a responsible reason for choosing a home. But the prospect of White City, and the knowledge that there was another of Wormwood Scrubs from the chimney-top, kept us attached to the flat long after the roof had started to leak and the kitchen ceiling had begun first to sweat and then to rain a slimy yellow liquid like bicycle oil.

Later, when we began to think about buying a house of our own, I became obsessed with the financial aspects of the place. The landlords had bought the house from the council for £4,000, and they were renting the four flats for £320 each. Assuming that the cardboard and the Regency stripe wallpaper had cost them about £1,000, they would have recovered their outlay in four years, after which they could put the rents up by another hundred pounds each (as they in fact did) and look forward to taking some £1,600 a year almost clear profit until the house fell down. By this time, moreover, the capital value of their investment had shot up. The architect next door who had shaved off his Dutch gable sold his house, still unconverted, for £10,000 (buying another, deeper in the slums, for £4,000, and using the balance to educate his two children at public schools).

Still, £320 was cheap for any sort of flat in West London. We signed the lease and got married. By the time the furniture had been carried in, a good deal of the shining white paint on the front door had come showering down like blossom, revealing the council's more durable chocolate brown beneath.

*

Soon we had a neighbour in the flat below – a young man with tinted spectacles who put up curtains designed to fit windows several feet shorter, and who slept all day every day for several weeks.

'You a university man?' he asked me affably with a slight Australian accent when we met on the stairs after he had emerged from this period of hibernation. I told him I had been at Cambridge.

'Really?' he said. 'Well, surprise, surprise! I'm a Cambridge man myself! Trinity. Listen, do you know the Chief Constable?'

'The Chief Constable? Of Cambridge? No.'

'Oh, I thought you would, being an old Cambridge man.'

He said he was in business, and a few weeks later he came up to a party we gave, where he managed, as a special concession, to let an old friend of mine have an unusual opal ring for £10. It was indeed an unusual opal ring, in that on valuation it turned out to be worth 12/6d, and I was deputed to undo the deal.

'My friend's decided he doesn't want the ring,' I said when the front door opened a crack, and the tinted spectacles looked cautiously out. I found the mission profoundly embarrassing – almost worth £9 7s 6d to avoid. But the Trinity man was very genial.

'He doesn't like it?' he asked, surprised. 'All right. If he doesn't like it, he doesn't like it. Up to him. Hey, if you hadn't come today you wouldn't have caught me. I'm off. On business. Sad, really – it's been a real pleasure to have a chance of parleyvooing with an old Cambridge man again. Never mind – I expect we'll meet again one of these days at some old Cambridge men's dinner, or something of that sort.'

Some weeks after he and his shrunken curtains had

departed, the landlord's manager came round. Had our neighbour really gone for good, he asked, or had he just taken his furniture and fittings on holiday with him? When I said I thought he had gone for good the manager grew very bitter. I tried to cheer him up by reminding him that under the terms of our leases he had six months' rent in advance, but this made him more bitter still. Apparently the man had agreed to take the flat only as a special concession, provided he could pay the rent retrospectively. I began to wonder whether I had got as much out of my time at Cambridge as I might have done.

We had a card from the man the following year. He was in Tahiti. 'Wow!' he wrote. 'The girls here are luscious! Give my love to Trinity.'

*

For some time the march of middle-class colonisation seemed to have stopped with us, in spite of all our landlord's efforts with the doorknobs. On one side of us was the architect. But the house on the other side of us remained what it had always been – some kind of Slavonic religious institution, from which on Sundays the calm chanting of the Orthodox liturgy could be heard. The head of this establishment was a man with a beret and a blond beard who was known locally as 'Peter the Painter'. I assumed at first that the sobriquet referred to artistic leanings, or to part-time work as a decorator. But, as I discovered, it was neither houses nor pictures that he painted; it was himself. He would go out in the middle of the day and come back reeling drunk, singing, and uplifted with ecstasy, then paint his hands, face, clothes and hair a brilliant pillar-box red. When he discovered I could speak Russian – he knew no English – he button-holed me in the street, where I was washing off the various synonyms for genitalia and sexual intercourse written in the dust on my car by his housekeeper's fat son, and explained at some length that red was the dominant colour in the universe, and that from it all power and goodness flowed.

Across the road, directly opposite us, was a house which appeared to be dying of some wasting disease. Larger and better sited than the ones in our terrace, it was presumably worth at least £15,000. And yet for the three years we were there it was scarcely lived in. The stucco dropped off the facade, and some old body shuffled about inside, shifting derelict lumps of furniture from one dusty room to another, covering odd windows from time to time with ragged bedspreads to prevent anyone seeing in.

Next to this was a house crammed with coloured families. The white landlord took a close interest in his property. He was an unhealthily overweight man who always wore an unbuttoned overcoat, had sparse hair plastered back over his head with water, and chain-smoked. He used to call every few days. He would drive up in his Vauxhall Velox, heave himself out with an effort, laboriously climb the front steps, ring the bell, then turn round and gloomily survey the rest of the street, from time to time extending his arm and tapping the ash off his cigarette, as if the act were symbolic of the unhappy responsibilities brought by wealth. Faces would inspect him covertly from various windows. He would ring again, then turn back once more to gaze at the street and cope with the never-ending accumulation of the ash.

Eventually, with the utmost reluctance, the door would be opened, and two or three of the tenants would come slowly out and set to work to clean, service and maintain the landlord's car.

The landlord would help them, transferring his cigarette to his left hand and polishing some small chromium trimming, the grey folds of flesh around his neck shaking with the motion. He liked to help. One week he came every day, to watch and make suggestions for hours at a time while one of the tenants painted the house, covering cracks, stains, and window-frames with one semi-transparent coat of dilute whitewash, ribbed with tidemarks indicating the end of each day's work. But in spite of the redecorations his tenants never seemed to stay. They tended to move house at about eleven o'clock at night, quietly loading their children and oil-heaters into borrowed vans. Finally the whole house fell upon evil times at once. No one would open the door to the landlord or to anyone else. Every day dour, official-looking men forced the ground-floor windows and climbed in. Two middle-aged men and two young men, their hands thrust into the pockets of unbuttoned overcoats with turned up collars, drove up in an old American car. They wore that vacant air of suspended animation that bodyguards and strong-arm men have, and after a great deal of standing about on the pavement, they repossessed what appeared to be half-a-hundredweight of sand.

In the top flat of another house opposite us lived a middle-aged man of vaguely benign appearance who played the violin to my wife. Each evening he used to open his curtains about a foot, then stand well back into the room so that he was invisible to anyone but my wife as she stood by the kitchen window preparing dinner, and fiddle away. At that distance, of course, through two layers of glass, it was inaudible, but my wife was touched by the thought. Then one evening there was an abrupt change in the nature of the serenade. He laid his violin aside and unzipped his flies instead. From then on he continued to expose himself fairly regularly, though as soon as I came to look he vanished. We would forget about it for weeks at a time. Then my wife would happen to look out as she washed the lettuce or sliced the beans – and there he would be, still demonstrating his genital equipment, like one of those indefatigable salesmen in department stores who go on showing the world their new wonder potato peeler whether anyone is listening or not.

All these people in the houses opposite formed a ready-made audience for the fights that used to occur in a house on our side which was hidden from us by the curve of the street. On hot summer nights they would lean out of their windows and watch a middle-aged man who used to come home drunk and fight it out with his wife at the front door. We could hear the shouting and screaming perfectly well, but we could see the fighting only at secondhand, like the shadows in Plato's cave, as reflected in the expressions of the audience. It wasn't easy to infer what was going on. Black or white, the faces mostly remained completely impassive. Come to think of it, I expect ours did, too.

*

A trickle of fellow pioneers from the middle classes began to arrive. Into the old Trinity man's flat moved a newly married couple – he in razor-blades, she in advertising; and into the flat below them another newly married couple – he in advertising, she in women's mags. The advertising man on the ground floor rebuked the character of the neighbourhood with a rolled umbrella, dark suit, carefully puffed pipe, and specially phlegmatic English walk, like the aristocrats in the past who carried a stuffed orange to hold off the stinking breath of the mob. The advertising girl on the first floor was American and dedicated.

'No, but seriously, Michael,' she would say, when we ran into one another among the Regency stripes, 'you simply have a terrible, terrible misconception about advertising. I'd like you to come in and spend a week or two at our office, going from department to department, chatting it over with the account executives and the copy chiefs – really finding out what makes us tick. Would you do that for me, Michael?'

A welcome note of social variety, however, was struck by the tenant in the basement flat, a young man who seemed not to be in advertising or any allied profession. He looked like a ballet-dancer, but he worked at home. Endless and everchanging relays of petulant-looking young men in impeccable lightweight suits drove up in expensive cars and picked their way delicately down the basement steps to his front door. Rolls-Royces, Lotuses and AlfaRomeos regularly spent the night outside the house among the rusting Minis and Ford vans. The cars commanded a certain respect in the neighbourhood; the fat boy from the religious community never, so far as I know, laid his scatological finger on the Facels or the Ferraris.

Now that all the flats had gone we took down the To Let sign. We rocked it gently back and forth to break the strand of wire attaching it to the front railing, and uprooted all the railings from their foundations.

*

There were sometimes other watchers in the street – relays of men in tidy raincoats who stood on the pavement doing nothing in particular, looking at nothing in particular, for three, four, five or more hours at a time. Were they detectives, watching the comings and goings from our basement? I don't know. Don't detectives try to make themselves inconspicuous?

It was one sunny afternoon when there was no one watching that I heard panicky screams of 'Help! Police!' from downstairs. I snatched up the coal shovel and ran all the way down to the street, scared sick already by that croaky note in the voice. On the basement steps stood a golden-haired young man wearing a white tee-shirt and skin-tight jeans, wild-eyed and trembling.

'Help me!' he croaked as I appeared. 'Please help me! It's down here!'

Oh Christ, I thought, starting to shake with fear too, there's been a murder. I looked up and down the street, but there was no one else in sight. The young man ran down the steps. I followed him, grasping the coal shovel as if it were life itself.

'Quick!' cried the young man, motioning me into the front door of the basement flat. 'In here!'

The curtains were drawn, and as I came cautiously in from the sunlight, shovel upraised, it was difficult to make anything out. Gradually I perceived that the floor was covered with a tangle of blankets. There was no sign of the owner of the flat, but among the bedclothes stood a young West Indian, cowering back before me in evident expectation of being beaten to death with the coal shovel.

'That's him!' sobbed the young man in the tee-shirt. 'He stole my watch!'

'He give me the watch!' gasped the West Indian. 'He ask me to this place and he give me the watch!'

We gazed at each other, all three of us completely panic-stricken.

'Where is the owner of this flat?' I cried in a terrible voice, unable to get it out of my head that there was a dead man about somewhere – probably under all those bedclothes. But it appeared that the owner was out for the afternoon, and had lent the flat to the other two. Gradually we calmed each other down, and began to discuss the ownership of the watch at a more appropriate level of feeling – they addressing their arguments to me as arbiter, making me feel like a magistrate adjudicating the disputes of some strange, frightening tribe, with the coal shovel as my emblem of authority. Eventually they sat down on the bedclothes and began to discuss the matter between themselves.

'Honestly, if you'd just *asked* me for it I'd have given it to you.'

'I thought, hell, he leave it here on the floor – he want me to have it!'

'It's just this going behind one's back that one can't stand.'

I edged towards the door, feeling a little superfluous.

'Well, then,' I said, 'I'll be shoving off.'

'What?' said the young man in the tee-shirt. 'Oh, must

you? Thanks for looking in, anyway.'

We shared a party line with the man in the basement.
One day a team of Post Office engineers came down the
road, making adjustments to the cable, as a result of
which he began to get all my calls as well as his own. He
had to come bounding lithely up the three flights of stairs
every half-hour or so to inform me that the third paragraph of my piece was thought to be libellous, or to ask
me to write twelve humorous advertisements for industrial cotton waste, until, at the urgent request of both of
us, the Post Office men returned to correct the fault. In
fact, they over-corrected it, and not only restored to me
my own calls, but added all the calls for the man in the
basement as well, so that for the next day or two I had to
keep running downstairs to tell *him* that Nigel was coming on Thursday instead of Wednesday, and that Lance
had simply sent his love.

When we complained about this arrangement, incred-
ible as it seems in retrospect, the Post Office engineers
came back and reconnected us so that we *both* got each
other's calls.

We got to shouting up and down the stairwell to one
another.

'Oh, Michael! Could you be a pet and cut nine lines
out of your article thing?'

'Tell them to cut somebody else's piece for a change.'

'I'll try, Michael. But they're being frightfully, you
know, insistent about it.'

'Well, you be firm, too. Put your foot down. And can
Steve come on Sunday at three, bringing a friend?'

'Who's Steve?'

'I don't know. He said you'd know.'

'Does he sound, you know, *nice*?'

'He sounds all right, I suppose.'

'Tell him I can manage six-thirty.'

*

The most socially cohesive event during our tenancy occurred one autumn evening, just as it was getting dark. The ex-advertising wife of the advertising man a couple of houses uphill and upmarket of us left her station wagon parked outside the house with the hand-brake off. After she had shut the street door, the car started to move, ran with the slope in a great arc across the road and crossed the invisible frontier into still uncolonised territory. There it jumped the pavement, crashed through the railings in front of the decaying house with the bedspreads at the windows, and half-dived into the basement area. There were a few moments of absolute silence, and then the entire population of our little world appeared, class alongside class, natives and colonisers together – ourselves, Peter the Painter, the fat boy who wrote on cars, the architect and his family, the man from our basement and his current guest, the violinist, various members of the advertising industry, and twenty or thirty others.

A bald head rose from the area beside the upended car and stopped a few inches above pavement level.

'I was just having my tea,' it said, 'when I heard this crash. I looked out – and there it was!'

The bald head was as much a surprise to all the rest of us as the car was to him; no one had known there was a bald man, or indeed any other sort of man, living down there.

It was like the Blitz, a moment when neighbours discover each other's existence and make common cause. It was also the grand finale of our time there. We moved a few months after that; we needed a third room for our new baby daughter. It was a grey February day when the van came, in the middle of the great cold spell of 1960, and after the furniture had gone the flat looked bleak and seedy beyond belief. But for months afterwards we missed it painfully, as one does miss places in which one has been happy, and to which one will never return.

(1964)

House 47, Block 2, Entrance 5

In Moscow with Sofya

The sun's shining, and it's 17 degrees below freezing, and I've just been swimming in the famous open-air pool, and the food is all right, and the service is greatly improved; and out of my room in the Hotel Metropole I have a charming view over the Lubyanka, the headquarters of the KGB.

A lot of things have changed since I was here last, in the late fifties. The smell of the place, for a start. There is a Paris smell, and a New York smell, and there used to be a Moscow smell, of low-octane Soviet petrol, men's scent, *papirosi*, hot pies and pickled cucumber. One breath of it (in Cuba, for instance) and at once I was back in this world of delicately colour-washed classical façades seen across dull streets as wide as parade grounds, of blank buildings looking inwards on to muddled, touching yards, of a gross inert marble rhetoric of stars and sheaves and scrolls and banners, of unmade-up roads lined with old wooden houses warped to improbable drunken angles.

Anyway, now it's gone. So have the war-wounded beggars who used to work the streets and Metro trains, thrusting the raw stump of an amputated arm at you. So have the spittoons in the streets. So have the really terrible crushes aboard the buses; I can recall taking a foot off the floor in the south-western district and not being able to get it down again before the centre.

Nobody cared this time where I went or what I did. There's been no one telling me that a visit to the Red October piano factory had been arranged, and that people would be very hurt if I declined to go. I walked into various offices and university departments just like that, just like you might anywhere, and there was no grim old woman sitting inside demanding to see a pass. The queues are fewer and shorter. The people who came up to me in the street wanted dollars, pounds, bubble-gum and gas lighters, but not, this time, my clothes. The reason's plain enough; this time I'm the shabbiest person in sight.

Traffic pours along the streets, through new underpasses, across new overpasses. Old Moscow has disappeared a little further even from the names of the streets. Mokhovaya Street and Okhotny Ryad, for example, have been run together as Marx Prospect, while Manège Square has become the Square of the 50th Anniversary of the October Revolution. (One of the world's great songs that somehow never got written: 'Goodbye, Marx Prospect! Farewell, Square of the 50th Anniversary of the October Revolution!')

And yet it doesn't feel quite like a city, in spite of all the cars. There are no conflicting voices. In the architecture, in the illuminated slogans, in the shop windows, only one voice speaks – flatly, moralisingly, on and on, unanswered and unanswerable. Even the faint illusion of competing claims in the weekly advertising magazine that's published now, *Reklama*, comes as a relief. 'Gennady

Pavlovich, where did you get your artist from? – What artist? – The artist who did this poster. – I drew it myself. – It's come out marvellously . . . – That's because I did it with an "Etude" pen . . .'

The rest of the press hasn't changed much. *Musical Life* has the words and music of two new songs about Lenin. 'Our corn-fields burst furiously into ear,' goes one of them, *molto largamente con festivo*. 'Towns and villages look young again. We shall all live still more happily, more happily . . . (*Poco a poco crescendo*) Lenin's words inspire towards the great labour. The Party leads towards new summits, joyous paths await us.'

*

Outside the centre, district after district of new housing has appeared. You travel along broad prospects and highways from snowbound horizon to snowbound horizon, and pass nothing but new apartment blocks in every direction; here raw brick post-Stalinist, set parallel to the roads; now mid-sixties international public housing set slantwise, with small trees growing between the blocks. Every now and then the pattern is varied by the wide window of a neighbourhood provision-shop running across the ground floor of a block, casting at night a staring fluorescent white forecourt of light on to the packed snow outside.

In these districts you navigate by numbers. 'Take the 23 bus 4 stops,' people tell you. 'Then the 55 trolley 2 stops. It's house 47. Block 2. Entrance 5. Floor 14. Apartment 61.' You follow the figures as blindly as a pilot in cloud. At 20 degrees below, with the windows of the bus frosted over, and the sounds of voices and traffic

remote through fur earflaps, the outside world becomes
unreal, a gleaming white numerical dream.

When I was last here the municipal notice-boards were
still full of advertisements offering to exchange corners of
rooms. Now nearly every family has its own apartment.
You ride up in the rickety little lift, and find yourself in
what might almost be a council flat in London. Self-contained, with wood-block floors, and just enough space in
the living-room for everyone to squeeze round the table,
or sit on the sofa and watch television. Only one of the
apartments I saw was markedly different – more Span
than council. This was in one of the new co-operative
blocks which are being built in the South-West district,
on the Lenin (late Sparrow) Hills. It was occupied by a
designer, who had knocked through between the two
small bedrooms, and ripped out the simple plumbing,
installing in its place an elegant decor of white tiles and
chromium. The large L-shaped living-room was furnished with a few well-chosen antiques. Windows ran the
length of one wall, giving on to a balcony with the lights
of Moscow shimmering in the frozen air sixteen floors
below. Another wall was lined with built-in bookcases,
and all the rest with icons – row upon row of sad-eyed
saints and Mothers of God, watching a skating competition on television.

I saw a lot of icons in the apartments I visited, and several collections of *pryalki*, the distaffs which Russian
peasant families used to carve, or paint bright red, with
flowers and figures, for their daughters' dowries.
Muscovites go round the villages and buy up all the old
stuff the peasants throw out. Some people showed me literary treasures they'd managed to accumulate – books in

the old orthography on freemasonry and Swedenborg. One man got down his guitar and sang me 'unofficial' songs – thieves' songs he'd learnt as a boy, when his father had been at the front and he'd run wild. I felt there was a hunger for something different, preferably old, and somehow dark. Some intellectuals have begun to go to church again for the same reason. Not many of them are believers, though, said a friend who was a believer himself.

So there I am, at the — s, let's say, with some of their old friends such as — and —. ('Go back and tell the truth about Russia,' they urge me, 'but please don't mention our names.') Surrounded by his icons and *pryalki*, the host puts on Soviet recordings of Tom Jones and Engelbert Humperdinck, and fixes drinks in tall glasses with straws. I suck mine up appreciatively, and ask what it is. His face falls. 'I thought it was a Martini,' he says sadly. As a representative Westerner, I'm hopeless.

We move on to a whole variety of drinks – whisky and gin and good-quality vodka, all of which have somehow found their way from the hard-currency shops – and nibble sausage and tinned salmon and pickled cucumber. They all refuse to accept that anything (apart from housing) has improved in the last fourteen years. 'Nothing has changed,' says a woman in her seventies, who lost her husband in the camps. 'They will be starving in the villages this year. Not in Moscow, because Moscow is never allowed to go hungry. But in the villages they will suffer.'

The tape-recorder is switched on, and people look at me to see how I react as a dark bass voice of indescribable melancholy fills the room. This is Galich. Once, they tell me, he was a playwright and Stalin prizewinner. But after *One Day* (the Year One of Soviet dissent – the publication in 1962, by Khrushchev's personal permission, of Solzhenitsyn's *One Day in the Life of Ivan Denisovich*) he began to write and sing songs instead. 'Galich and Solzhenitsyn', say my friends, 'are the first writers to speak to the whole of the Russian people.'

The recording has obviously been made under difficult circumstances – I find it hard to catch a syllable. The text, in *samizdat* ('self-published'), is placed in front of me. He is singing a funny song, about a man who hears on the radio that his aunt in capitalist Fingalia has died and left him her factory and fortune. He is drunk for days to celebrate, and sobers up just in time to see a TV news bulletin reporting that there has been a revolution in Fingalia, and that all private businesses there have been taken over by the State.

We drink. We dance to records of Soviet jazz, and a wavering tape of Western pop music. A blurred English voice is audible between numbers; Kenny Everett being beastly to his Gran. I admire a painting by my hostess on the wall, and restrain her only with the utmost difficulty from ripping the canvas off the stretcher and giving it to me. Russian generosity! How do you cope with it? And Russian drinking. One of my friends is by now almost too drunk to speak or to stand. Yet he continues to behave with dignity and correctness, dancing with each of the ladies in turn and mutely insisting that I dance with his wife. Later he gets right downstairs and into the back of a car before decorously passing out.

There are articles in the paper explaining what to do about drunks who go home and wake up the whole block of flats by hammering on the central heating pipes,

protected by the knowledge that 'in our country the invi-
olability of the home is strictly safe-guarded'. But all the
drunks I see behave with great sobriety. They sit in the
restaurants, two men together usually, dark-suited, with
neat, responsible haircuts, having long heart-to-heart
conversations about life, the vodka slopping out of
vaguely gesticulating glasses. In family parties they fall
quietly asleep at the table, and the conversation continues merrily all round them. One young man in the hotel
restaurant, very drunk, smashed his glass against the
table and cut his wrists. But he did it quietly, without
ostentation. And quietly, he and the bloody tablecloth
were bundled out of sight by the waiters.

Once or twice I went out to restaurants with friends.
But it's difficult: they refuse to eat anywhere where they
don't have '*svoy ofitsiant*' – their 'own' waiter. One has
to have a network of one's 'own' people everywhere, they
explain – not only in restaurants, but in shops, in
Government departments – who serve you first and keep
the best things back for you. 'Grigory Fyodorovich,
please,' murmured my friend in the lobby of one of the
most popular restaurants, crowded with people waiting
for tables. And when Grigory Fyodorovich appeared – all
poignant smiles, like a waiter in a film – he ushered us
openly past everyone waiting, found us a table, and
served us at once. No one complained.

And sometimes we walked. Along taciturn white
streets where a single old slatternly wooden house lingered on among the well-spaced rectilinear forest. Into a
church full of restless activity, where a corpse was being
carried past on a bier, the face like the grey stub of a
burnt-out candle, and tiny old women in grey head-

shawls were begging alms to pray for the departed soul. Past a silent psychiatric clinic where political deviants are detained. Into an open yard set aside as a pet market, where men with pickled faces crowded round, slipping puppies (all stolen, whispered my friends) out of the warmth of their overcoats, and unfolding tattered pedigrees (all forged).

Once, at night, we passed a car parked at the kerb with three men sitting inside. '*Spetsmashina*,' murmured my friends. 'A "special" car. The *kagebushniki* – the KGB. They're listening in to something. Someone's telephone, probably.'

Another evening, in the darkness outside the Yaroslavl Station, a woman's voice was suddenly shouting in alarm, and there, on the hard-packed snow, glittering in the light from the hot-pie kiosks, half a dozen bouquets wrapped in transparent paper lay scattered. My friends shrugged. 'Probably she was trading, and someone caught her at it.'

But several times, when my friends stepped out on to a highway to stop a taxi, the cars that picked us up had no meter inside. 'This isn't a taxi,' said one of the drivers, when I asked him about it. 'I'm a doctor. This is my own car. But a car's an expensive thing to run. I'm just trying to cover the cost of petrol and tyres and so on.'

At minus 20 degrees C, the women selling hot pies in the open outside the Metro stations worked on with bare hands. Rows of men stood eating them, all facing the same way, their backs turned towards the driving snow. Queues waited at the ice-cream kiosks. In Red Square the queue waiting to see Lenin in the Mausoleum still stretched out of sight.

'He's falling to pieces in there,' said one of my friends.

'Perhaps when he goes it will all go,' said another. 'This society can't last more than another ten years. People are empty.'

*

My meeting with the friend I'd most looked forward to seeing again was disastrous. When I'd known him before he was questioning, ironical, with a passion for truth. Now he worked in a government department, and he was plainly embarrassed to see me.

After one awkward session when I called unannounced, he excused himself from meeting me again. 'Best leave the initiative to him,' said some of my other friends gently. 'He's probably in the *nomenklatura*.' This is the Soviet establishment, the caste who occupy all the key jobs in every department, and who call one another 'comrade' still.

There are some other familiar constraints. On a suburban train we suddenly got up and moved into the next coach. 'Sorry about that,' said my friend, 'but that man sitting next to us looked like an informer.' 'Don't phone me from your hotel,' said someone else: 'go to a box in the street.' I asked someone inside the British Embassy if it would be tactful to avoid mentioning a certain writer's name when I phoned from the hotel. 'I'm afraid you've already mentioned it,' he replied, 'in front of these walls.'

Still, there are two well-known Russian ladies whose names I can put down with impunity – Galina Borisovna and Sofya Vasilyevna. Galina Borisovna I never met, which was just as well, since she is a euphemism for the (K)GB. But Sofyushka was everywhere. She's the lady people mutter about when they get to the head of the queue and are told that supplies have run out – they've got the wrong form – they must apply at another department on the other side of town. She is SV – *Sovyetskaya vlast'* – Soviet power.

*

'Congratulations,' said the cool young Customs officer at the airport when I arrived. 'You're a rich man.'

A cheerful welcome. The riches are the royalties from a book of mine which was published here three years ago. You can't take the money out of the country, of course, and you have to pay for your hotel in advance, in Western currency, so there's not too much you can do with the money, except to put it in the savings bank, or give it away. Still, riches are riches. Unless the lovely Sofyushka is involved in the deal.

If only they'd known I was coming, said the man at my publishing-house, when I arrived in his office, perhaps they could have done something. Well, I had written three weeks ago. The letter hadn't arrived, he said. I'd cabled, too . . . Yes, but they'd passed the cable on to the Union of Writers. The Union of Writers are the people I must deal with. And the man there, when I got hold of him, was very optimistic. 'I think you will get your money,' he told me cheerfully. 'When? Oh, in some days . . .'

In some days? But I'm only here for a week! I'm only here for a week because the Intourist office in London said they couldn't get me a visa for longer. 'They think there's not enough to do in Moscow to last more than a week,' the clerk explained.

Anyway, the Intourist bureau in the hotel arranged an extension for four days, so that I was still here when the man from the Union of Writers came round, three days after I should have left, to report progress. 'Well,' he demanded, with courteous interest, 'did you get your money?'

Did I . . . ? But *he* was supposed to be getting it! Oh, he explained, regretfully, he couldn't do anything, because he didn't have the telephone number of the publishing-house. I let him into this secret, and he promised to ring me back at midday today, three hours before I have to leave for the airport.

So here I sit, waiting for the phone to ring. Intourist say they can't extend the visa any further. 'There are many people who want to visit Moscow,' explained the woman, 'so no one is allowed to stay too long.' (There were two other tourists on the plane that brought me from London, it's true.) The sun is shining; there are seventeen degrees of frost outside; I've had my swim in the famous open-air pool; the Lubyanka looks lovely; and I'm all set to be rich for three hours before the car leaves for the airport.

The telephone rings. 'I think it will be impossible to speak to the director of the publishing-house until after three o'clock. What time do you leave . . .?'

Ah, Sofyushka, you strange, mysterious creature – you could drive a man crazy! I shall return, I swear! Provided you'll give me a visa.

(1973)

A Pilgrimage to St Trop

Burnt offerings on the Côte d'Azur

Laboriously accumulating excrement-coloured pigmentation in one's skin by day; parading one's accumulation about the streets and places of amusement by night. Is it possible to devise a more grotesque parody of the human condition?

Sunbathing is still only a cottage industry, and its machinery of reclining chairs and shades and windbreaks seems unnecessarily clumsy for our times. One day the Rotissomat spits which now broil chickens all the way along the Riviera will be extended to broil human beings in a scientific and labour-saving way.

Already the evening parade is becoming highly mechanised. In Cannes and Nice and Juan-les-Pins elegant traffic jams collect at *apéritif* time and continue until after midnight. Young men in the cars try to pick up girls on the pavement; young men on the pavement try to kiss the girls in jammed cars. The Citroëns gaze respectfully at the Mercedes; the Austin Healeys try to get themselves noticed by the Alfa Romeos.

In St Tropez they still walk. St Tropez is *très décontracté*, according to two young hairdressers I met here, by which they meant that one could walk about in bare feet if one wished, which is like saying Ascot is relaxed because you can take your top-hat off. It's difficult to know whether St Tropez looks like a film set because film people used to come here, or whether film people came here because they felt at home on a film set. The centre of the town, the quays of the port, are no bigger than the scenery for a reasonably expensive musical. On one side they are lined with cafés, restaurants and clothes-shops, on the other with the yachts of the rich. From the packed terraces of the cafés what appears to be a crowd of film extras looks out. From the luxurious after-decks of *Fibro*, *Katy*, *Bernina*, *Capitan Blood*, *Guimiery*, *Diana Marina IV* and *Gaudeamus V* a selection of character actors gaze down.

In between, more extras in St Tropez costume, plus gendarmes, US sailors etc *ad lib*, walk up and down with a brisk air of purpose, as if indeed on the way from one point to another. Animation is displayed. Rhubarb rhubarb is said. At any moment everyone will take up the tune of the big production number, 'In a Little French Town by the Sea', and the studio electricians will come out on strike.

'It's such fun – I keep meeting people like you!' says a sunburnt English girl hawking salted peanuts, to a party of sunburnt English salted-peanut eaters. Hey, she must be the second lead, just about to be fallen in love with by that darkly handsome millionaire leaning over the stern rail of *Guimiery* . . .

After I had taken an *apéritif* and eaten a dismal dinner at the tables on the terraces, and been refused a coffee in a café because the profit margin on coffee was too small, and walked up and down and up and down and down and up and up and down, a certain unaccustomed gloom about the whole nature of the human race seized me. Perhaps this was really what life was – walking up and down from nowhere to nowhere else, searching the passing faces to see if they belonged to Brigitte Bardot or Jeanne Moreau, and finding that they did not – and not having in any case the slightest idea what one would have done if they had.

I must report that the animation continues without strike or tea break far into the night. A Dominican priest once told a colleague of mine: 'St Tropez is like Lourdes. People come here looking for spiritual fulfilment, and because they have faith in the place they find it.'

*

I found some consolation among the sunbathing industry in the contemplation of other people's navels. It only occurred to me seeing so many massed together how much they differ from person to person. Almost as much as eyes. It's surprising that the police don't include them in their descriptions of wanted persons, and that novelists have never used them to suggest character.

Some are small and perfectly round. Some are elongated horizontally, some mere vertical slits. Some navels wink cheerfully at all the passers-by as their owners walk along. Others have disappeared for ever into obese rolls of flesh. A shallow or obtruding navel suggests to me a person not to be trusted. A deep, mysterious cavern promises tranquillity and thoughtfulness.

*

The whole Coast is being built up. A dense tropical forest of skyscrapers struggles for foothold in the untaxed soil of Monte Carlo. In Cannes, and Nice, and along the scruffy littoral between Nice and Antibes, block after block of flats is going up – the heaviest building programme in France outside Paris. Whole cliffs of fancy balconies are lifted up to the sun. Half the shops seem to be estate agents.

Some 12,000 habitations have been built privately along the Coast in the past five years, according to one estimate I was given. The prices of the flats I saw advertised in one agent's window ranged from £7,000 to £20,000, and probably two-thirds of them are bought as a second residence, or for renting out, by people who live elsewhere.

The film stars and the very rich are tending to move inland, to the still beautiful hill villages of the Maritime Alps. The builders are following them doggedly. There are blocks of luxury flats going up at Vence. IBM has built a magnificent research centre perched high above the valley of the Var near La Gaude. In every agent's window there are restored farms and manor houses for sale; at Cagnes they were offering an authentic Provençal hamlet complete for £35,000.

In spite of international retrenchment, the builders see no end to the boom. 'The needs remain the same,' one of them told me. 'The aspirations of the French and foreigners alike are more and more towards the sun.' Eventually the whole of Provence will probably become a sort of residential suburb of industrial Europe.

*

St Tropez, according to my private hagiographical researches, is called after St Trop, the patron saint of excess, who takes under his special protection those who charge too much. The good St Trop is everywhere on the Coast. I went with a number of English people one night to a sort of high-class roadhouse in a converted monastery. Exactly what faith it had been converted to I'm not certain. The old chapel was still open and available for customers' devotions, and there were also photographs of an American girl who made her small contribution to the sweet life one night by climbing into the middle of the fountains and stripping to her girdle. At the end of the evening we were brought a bill for ten times the correct amount, which we almost paid in the vague belief that it only looked so alarming because of the noughts after the decimal point. I felt constrained to slip into the chapel and burn a ten-franc note to clever old St Trop, who understood the decimal system, as a consolation prize for a good try.

*

The whole of the South of France is alive with modern art, in the way that Tuscany is with the art of the Renaissance. The most superbly housed of the many collections is undoubtedly the Maeght Foundation, which was opened last year. The buildings were designed by José Luis Sert, the professor of architecture at Harvard, and sit cool and complex and infinitely moneyed on the wooded hilltops above St Paul.

Modern art seems to be accepted as a tourist interest here in just the same way that classical art is elsewhere. The Matisse chapel at Vence is packed with visitors on the days it opens. Picasso authorised a pottery at Vallauris to copy his works, and now Vallauris has pottery the way Montélimar has nougat – over a hundred shops, mostly selling, on the strength of the Picasso association, pottery of that exquisite domestic nastiness at which the French surpass even the English.

Perhaps the most moving monument is the Renoir museum at Cagnes. It was the Impressionists who discovered the South of France as a place to paint, and Renoir who set the seal upon its reputation when he came here in 1903 suffering from the rheumatic arthritis which crippled his hands. The house he built among the olive and orange trees at Cagnes, and in which he worked for the last sixteen years of his life, has been opened to the public. In the calm rooms of the villa, the pink and cream breasts and thighs of the women he painted glow with a more enticing sexuality than all the charred flesh of the Riviera beaches put together. What on earth would Renoir make of the skin tones which any local model would present him with today – dark brown limbs, shoulders, and belly, and stark white breasts and bottom? It would be beyond even Renoir to make sense of it.

The only local artist entirely uncollected and uncommemorated seems to be Van Meegeren, the Vermeer forger, who settled at Roquebrune in 1932, and made half a million pounds. He died in prison after selling a Vermeer to Goering, and escaping a charge of collaboration only by proving that he had painted it himself.

I asked a dozen or so people in Roquebrune if they knew which house Van Meegeren had lived in. 'Van Migraine,' they all repeated dubiously; 'never heard the name.' Such is infamy.

*

Violence simmers in the sticky heat. Everyone drives too fast – cars turn over in the middle of towns, wrecks lie abandoned beside the main roads. At Toulon a man blinds his unfaithful wife with vitriol. At Contes a man hacks his brother to death with an axe, then pours petrol over himself and sets fire to it – a form of suicide which seems fashionable down here now. At Cannes, when armed robbers attack the tote office in a café, the customers drive them off and beat one of the raiders to death on the floor with chairs and bottles. At Golfe-Juan a girl is killed crossing the railway to get to the beach – the eighteenth death in ten years at the same spot. People say that crime was much worse before the police broke up the gangs at the end of last summer. They lived on prostitution and stealing works of art (£700,000 worth of stuff was stolen on the Coast last summer), and they used to shoot out their differences in the street, in the Chicago manner.

All disputes are violent. At St Raphael, the owner of an exclusive site built a wall across the beach to keep out the proletarians from the workers' camping site next door. All summer the workers, under Communist leadership, have been trying to remove the wall – attempting alternately demonstrations, bulldozers, and dynamite. This week one of the demonstrators was arrested and charged with *outrage*, *rebellion* and *violence*.

One form of outrage, rebellion and violence which the Englishman misses, however, is the sort perpetrated at English seaside resorts by Mods and Rockers. Anyone under sixteen here without his parents has to be able to produce a legally witnessed letter of authorisation from them, and the Ministry of the Interior has formed a mobile brigade 5,000 strong to enforce the law. Where there has been trouble, parents as well as children have sometimes been prosecuted.

A small island of authoritarian calm among the encircling hazards.

*

Some of the most moving of all the art on the Coast is amateur – the extraordinary collection of ex-votos in the Chapel of Notre Dame de la Garoupe, next to the lighthouse on the highest point of the Cap d'Antibes.

They were placed there in gratitude for deliverance from danger. The original offerings were mostly from sailors, who made elaborate models of the ships which had gone down under them, or painted pictures of the scene. Landsmen took the idea up and commemorated their escapes in the same way. There is a picture of a woman falling off a horse, dated 1805. There are scenes showing attacks by mad dogs, people falling off ladders and through roofs. In semi-literate French, one Jules Briand offers thanks for having escaped from prison at Toulon in 1812.

More modern disasters follow. A woman with her foot caught in a lift bleeds copiously on the floor. A bus dangles over a bridge on to the railway line below. A car lies wrecked in the ditch; the family kneel suicidally at prayer in the middle of the road.

Some of the pictures record not dangers but moments of intense experience. 'In memory of a night guard December, 1914,' says one, 'before the shelled church of Prunay (Champagne) – a sergeant has just been killed and lies covered with a sack on a tomb.' The amateurish technique strains to express something of the blackness of that night, and the horribleness of the body on the tomb. It fails; its failure is eloquent.

On one wall 'J.P.C.' has hung a little *petit-point* of some anonymous Oriental scene in commemoration of an unnamed soldier. 'In three years of war in Indo-China,' reads the inscription, 'he was neither victim nor executioner. Ave Maria.'

(1965)

Warm Red Socks

Talking money in Sweden

Useless, I suppose, to tell you that the suicide rate in Sweden is in fact lower than in (for instance) merrily waltzing Austria, or that the Swedes in fact drink less per head than (for instance) the sober, dog-loving British. You have your own ideas about Sweden. You know that all their famous wealth and peace and social justice have, gratifyingly, led to nothing but drunkenness and the highest suicide rate in the world.

So you'll be pleased to hear that within a few days of arriving in Sweden I was sitting comfortably and watching a new Swedish film about a man attempting suicide after a drinking bout. He had received a crushing tax-demand, and had also been mugged. The suicide attempt failed ludicrously, and the film ended in a very long, passionate embrace – the hero kissing the receipt for the tax he had finally paid off.

I must add that the director of the film, who also played the lead, was thirteen years old. He had mastered not only all the basic technology and visual vocabulary of the cinema, but also a very funny right-angled running turn on one foot derived from Chaplin. It was a funny film.

This was one Sunday in the country, after a great Sunday lunch with eleven of us at table, including children and grandparents. It was an old wooden house on the edge of the forest, all odd angles and unexpected rooms. Painted country furniture glowed dark green and red against the cool grey floor timbers. The old tiled stove in the corner filled the room with a sleepy warmth. The younger children played quietly. The projector murmured hypnotically on.

Outside – the long winter night, the empty leagues of snowbound forest, and all the moral ghosts we were laughing at within. *Trygghet* – security; the warm enclosing uterine reassurance against all ills to which the whole of Swedish politics seems bent on giving expression.

Or so it seemed to me. But into the mild transparent complexity of Sweden you can read almost any interpretation you like.

*

The Social Democrats have been in power continuously now for forty-two years. While I was there Gunnar Sträng, the Finance Minister, presented his nineteenth budget. The trains leave on time, and run quietly past neat wooden houses painted dark Dalarna red, past concrete cliffs of habitation rising from landscapes of trees and rock outcrops, where no streetlamps are broken and no old cars lie dying, past inviolate forest and lakes and ploughland. There are no waste lots, no vague areas on the edge of towns, no slums, no derelict industrial landscapes, no nothingness. Everything (as Bishop Butler said) is what it is, and not another thing.

But this air of changeless prosperity is deceptive, for

the whole experience of modern Sweden has been one of continuous and dislocatingly rapid change. God did not create Sweden rich and progressive. Until far on into the nineteenth century it was one of the very poorest and most backward countries in Europe – the Balkans of the North. Between 1860 and World War I nearly a fifth of the population fled hunger by emigrating to America.

The common shared experience of this century has been the bewildering move off the land into the towns. The drift continues, particularly out of the economically bleak North; up there the initials AMS, which designate the Swedish equivalent of the Department of Employment, are said to stand for *Alla Måste Söderut* – Everyone Must Go South.

It was only in the 1940s that Sweden caught up with the rest of Europe. Well over half the housing in the country has been built since then. Progressive social ideals – in marriage, in pensions, in education – have been applied almost as fast as the flats have been built. 'Social democracy,' said the Prime Minister, Olof Palme, in a speech once, 'has been able to be radical because it represents stability. That is not a contradiction in terms.' In Sweden change has been the norm, the status quo.

A lot has changed even since I was first here in the 1950s. The awkwardness and stiffness have gone out of social life. (I used to think then that the British disliked Sweden because they saw in the Swedes people just like themselves, only disconcertingly more so.) The complex sequence of toasts which had to be observed at dinner-parties has disappeared (though some people told me their parents never failed to notice the moments when the glasses should have been raised to them and weren't). So has the curious usage whereby strangers were addressed by their 'title' in the third person ('Would Writer Strindberg like another cup of coffee?'), though in the telephone directory, maddeningly, *Svensson* Lennart Bus-driver would still be listed as alphabetically prior to *Svensson* Arvid Cabinet Minister. The polite plural form of 'you', moreover, has completely vanished from social life, and '*du*' has become almost universal. I couldn't help thinking of the leftists I met in Germany who were strug-gling to call strangers '*du*', but who confessed privately to feeling very awkward about it. In Sweden change is wholesale.

A certain old-fashioned country quality persists, all the same – a kind of thrifty homeliness. I went to see an old friend of mine who now lives in one of the new suburbs of Stockholm – Tyresö, a twenty-five-minute ride aboard an uncrowded bus out beyond carefully preserved forest. Tall blocks among pines; hard-packed snow; a short day; then only the neighbourhood policeman patrolling the shopping centre with his Alsatian, and children playing ice-hockey on little rinks among the pedestrian walkways and woodlands of the estates, beneath floodlights that swung and creaked in the wind. But all around you, through the trees, like little illuminated stage sets, domes-tic interiors uncurtained against the winter night; a thou-sand theatres side by side, or stacked above one another, each playing the warm, bright drama of *trygghet*.

Foreigners misconceive Swedish domestic style. They have a picture of pale bland functional objects made of birchwood and stainless steel against a background of austere white emptiness. But these rooms glow. Their keynote is solid masses of warm colour – deep reds, and the dark, flowered greens of traditional painted country furniture. Silver and steel are reflected in dark veneers. Bowls of tulips stand beside blue armchairs. Climbing plants cover walls and half-obscure windows.

My friend flung her arms round me when I arrived and hugged me impulsively. (Swedish nature is as misunderstood abroad as Swedish decor.) But a little later she was reminding me candidly that I owed her 9.50 crowns which I'd borrowed as change for fares last year, plus 1.40 for a stamp.

Money – this is what we talked about. We did everywhere I went, and half the stories in the papers seemed to be about money, too. I don't mean in any coarsely materialistic way. We talked frankly about how much we earned, and how much we paid in tax. We talked thriftily about how much things cost, and how certain cunning savings could be made. When we talked about politics, it seemed to be almost entirely in terms of contributions and subsidies. The main political issue which emerged while I was there was whether Stockholm's 'fifty-card' (a pass costing kr. 50 – £5 – valid for a month on all public transport in Stockholm county) should be extended to the rest of Sweden. 'It would be great,' declared smiling citizens in front-page interviews.

Money, it seemed to me, was the medium of all political thought and action. Sweden is the richest nation in Europe, of course, and a high proportion of her wealth passes through the fiscal system – over 45 per cent of the gross national product is absorbed in taxes and social service premiums. Two school-teachers who went through their accounts with me in some detail were earning £5,000 and £6,000 a year, and repaying 44 per cent and 50 per cent of it in tax respectively. Almost every-thing – including the arts and even the practice of politics itself – has become dependent upon the closely negotiated redistribution of these central funds.

The political parties (including the Communists) are subsidised by the State in proportion to their electoral strength; a supporter of the new Lapp party, Samernas väl, whom I met in the North, explained to me that it couldn't be expected to make much headway because it was too small to qualify for an adequate subsidy. Anyone recognised by the appropriate committee as a profes-sional writer receives a guaranteed income, from State compensation for library loans equalised out and supple-mented by additional grants, of £2,400, and a Royal Commission has just recommended that publishers should be required to distribute 1,250 copies of each book they publish at the State's expense before normal sales commence. Even the funds of the unions must some-times come to seem to their members to be part of this same financial system; the contributions are levied on a progressive sliding scale like tax, and like tax deducted at source by the management, who also pay the local branch chairman and provide an office for him.

Now the State has begun to accumulate huge sums in the pension funds. The pensions paid out are large by any standards – two-thirds of your income averaged over your fifteen best years. But the contributions levied (chiefly from the employers – 10 per cent of the wages bill) outbalance them. A Social Democrat party official told me that the party saw the surplus very much as an instrument of State influence over the economy. By the beginning of last year the funds had reached £5,600 million. Already they have outstripped the commercial banks as a source of credit, and they are now beginning to move into the risk capital market. By the end of the century they are expected to have reached about £70,000 million.

The community provides; the individual is provided for. My friend in Tyresö showed me round a new church youth club. It could have been the headquarters of some successful progressive advertising agency – suites of conference rooms and offices, each with its own carefully chosen warm colour scheme, its own complete set of matching furniture and equipment. The children hadn't yet been admitted; when they were, they wouldn't need to think about a thing. She also showed me the school where she taught; another warmly stylish new building. Here there were children, but only 250 of them in a building which in Britain would have housed two or three times that number. They were taught mostly in groups of not more than fifteen, in warm-coloured classrooms with fitted carpets and house phones. The fitted carpets were clean; when the discreet chimes sounded at the end of a lesson and the pupils moved out of a room, a team of cleaners moved in. The phones had not been vandalised. Nothing had been vandalised. There was very little sign, good or bad, of the children's presence.

When we came out into the snow at the end of the morning, however, and saw the bus we wanted just leaving the stop, there was a spontaneous scream of jeering laughter from two fourteen-year-old girls who happened to be passing, which struck a rather more familiar note. Later my friend showed me a newspaper cutting about the excesses of drunkenness and vandalism which had greeted the end of the last school year in various parts of the country. At one festivity ('arranged by a child welfare committee') in the west of Sweden, complained the writer, 'some intoxicated and naked pupils had public intercourse with each other'.

'None the less,' he added, 'a social worker said that "the result of our arrangements was better than expected".'

*

They don't drink much in Sweden, by international standards, but, as in all North European countries, the drinkers drink to get drunk. In Stockholm they then accumulate, perhaps by a natural process of gravitation, in the underground. In the evenings and at weekends the air down there is heavy with the exhaled fumes of grain alcohol. Old beer cans roll underfoot. Long-haired young policemen patrol in twos and threes and fives. Small groups of men transport fragile private worlds of geniality about with them like huge invisible parcels, staggering under the comical awkwardness of the load. But I couldn't help feeling, as I watched one young drunk with blond hair over his shoulders aggressively bum a light for his cigarette, then struggle halfway up the platform, against some powerful magnetic field which seemed to be trying to divert him from his goal, in order to dutifully deposit the empty cigarette packet in a rubbish-bin, that there was something rather homely about even these deviations from decorum.

In a restaurant one night I sat at the next table to a very respectable middle-class couple in their late forties who were both helplessly drunk. I had to eat with my left hand, because at frequent intervals the lady fell sideways and grabbed at my right arm, urging me to dance with her, or to come home with them for the night, and scrabbling about in my lap looking for a napkin to dab at the confusion of slopped coffee, beer, and akvavit which was accumulating on their table.

'Inge-Lisa, Inge-Lisa!' moaned the man, trying to catch glasses as they somehow lost their balance. She stumbled up to various tables in the restaurant, presumably with the same propositions. Everywhere she went, wine turned over, coffee ran into laps. She persuaded a bald young man with sideboards to hold her up for a few minutes on the dance-floor. Then she insisted, with determined wrong-headedness, on getting back to her place by squeezing round the side of the table against the wall, where no gap had been left. She was a tubby little lady, with thick spectacles and warm red socks. The table heaved and swayed. 'Inge-Lisa, Inge-Lisa!' complained the gentleman sadly, performing a dream-like slow-motion juggling act with the tumbling cups and glasses, the saucers full of cold coffee. Then they argued about which of them was paying. Then she somehow slipped down on to the floor, and disappeared between the tables. The discreet silver-haired maître d'hôtel, whom you would have taken to be the chairman of the Stockholm Enskilda Bank, raised a mildly disapproving eyebrow, but did nothing else. About half an hour after they were finally assisted to the door I passed them in the street outside. They were propped up against a shop, still arguing. And still about money, of course.

A year ago, a lawyer told me, brothels were taking full-page advertisements in the papers; but this was felt to be a breach of the traditional Swedish moderation in all things, and stopped after a new establishment run as a producers' co-operative in the elegant Östermalm district was successfully prosecuted. *Dagens Nyheter*, the leading quality daily, still carries advertisements for night-clubs offering 'Live show every hour', or 'non-stop on four different screens – animal-homo-spanking'. But most of the films on offer seem to be American, and the newspaper in its editorial columns is worried about the increasingly open allusion to intercourse which Swedish advertisers are learning from current British practice. And even in the sex-clubs there is a note of cosy good taste. 'Our sex-hostesses,' claims Sexy House, in an advertisement for its pornoshop, 'demonstrate everything in a beautiful porn-environment.'

There is something touchingly homely, too, about a lot of the public sexual frankness. I was struck by a letter in the advice column of one of the Stockholm evening papers from a woman who claimed that she had enjoyed 'hundreds of orgasms' simply by imagining herself naked when men looked at her in the street – a handy knack which, she couldn't resist adding, was 'free of charge'. Alongside was a letter from a man who was a little worried about a strange new technique he described which his wife had suddenly started trying out on him after thirty years of marriage. (It was fellatio, as the paper's medical correspondent explained.) She had first sprung this on him, he said, when she came home one night after hearing the ladies discussing it at a meeting of her sewing-circle. He signed himself 'Regular Reader'.

Some of the announcements in the Births column of *Dagens Nyheter*, too, have a certain broad rustic humour

which seems remote from *The Times*. A friend of mine at
Gothenburg University showed me a collection which she
and her children had made to amuse friends in Denmark.
I liked the verses best. Difficult to do them justice in
translation, but here are one or two:

'We're so pleased we could shout
Now ULRIK's come out.'

'That bulge in his mother
Is now Sven's LITTLE BROTHER.'

'Let the bells tinkle –
It's one with a pinkle.'

My friend's favourite was this one, celebrating the arrival
of a daughter in a family presumably much taken up with
boats and outboard motors:

'What did the long cold winter bring?
3.25 kilograms
Without a starter-string.'

*

August Palm, the tailor who brought the first notions of
socialism back to Sweden from Germany in 1881, returns
from the dead in a revue which opened in Stockholm
while I was there. They tell him that the Social
Democrats have been in power for forty-two years.
   'Hurrah!' he cries. 'Socialism is here!'
   'For some reason,' said the critic in *Dagens Nyheter*
next morning, 'a violent laugh bursts forth.'

Ten years ago they wouldn't have laughed. 'Ten years ago,' said a Social Democrat friend, 'there was a real feeling that things were going forward and changing in the right direction.' Now the mood is one of disillusionment. I met a number of people who said they were lifelong Social Democrats, but who at the elections last autumn had voted for the Communists or the Centre Party. In the new Riksdag which sat while I was there the Social Democrats have retained power only in a dead heat.

Many people felt that it was the Kiruna strike in 1970 which had changed the whole atmosphere. The workers in the State-owned iron mines in and around the Lapland town of Kiruna came out unofficially, and stayed out for three months. It was the most serious breach of the industrial peace since 1938, when the unions and employers signed the Saltsjöbaden agreement outlawing strikes and establishing the famous system of collective wage negotiations for the whole of industry. For the Social Democrats it was an alarming demonstration that they were losing the contact with the working class, and the control over it, on which their forty-two-year reign is based.

It was the Green Wave that washed many voters to the right. Exactly where this all-purpose catchphrase first came from no one could tell me – some people thought from the hippies. It gives expression to a widespread yearning. Sweden was a rural society until much more recently than most other European countries; if you weren't brought up in the countryside yourself your parents or grandparents probably were. A lot of people have always managed to keep one foot on the soil – some little cottage or cabin in the forest, or on an island in the skerries, where they could go in summer to fish, or to grow fruit and vegetables.

There is a wave of nostalgia at the moment for the style known disparagingly as *snickarglädje* – carpenter's delight. You can see it all over the inner islands of the Stockholm Archipelago – deliciously elaborate wedding-cakes of houses built for the newly rich in the late nineteenth century, all timber balconies and turrets and cut-out patterns of curlicues and leaves and hearts. Or you can in summer. Most of the boats that ply among the 24,000 islands of the Archipelago are tied up now. The Green Wave swells in the bloodstream only from June until September.

I suspect that in the Swedish imagination it's always summer. Certainly in films and novels it usually seems to be. (Think of the buzzing midsummer insects in *Elvira Madigan*.) One of the most simply and immediately evocative first sentences in any novel is the opening of one of those very engaging thrillers by Sjöwall and Wahlöö: 'At a quarter to three the sun rose.'

Stockholm in summer, in eight words.

*

In theory, the fate of Sweden now turns upon pure chance; any vote in the Riksdag in the present state of the parties ought to end in a tie, when the Constitution requires that it should be decided by lot. But it will never happen. The Opposition party leaders don't see it as their duty to embarrass the government and bring it down; on the contrary, they have all indicated their intention of helping it out.

This is the Swedish way: to avoid the overt confrontations and symbolic violence with which other nations conduct their affairs. This extends even to the courts. A prosecutor told me that 90 per cent of criminal prosecutions succeed. It's difficult to find a lawyer who will put up a serious fight; most see it as their duty to persuade their clients to plead guilty, and then to present a case in mitigation. Jan Myrdal has spoken about a conspiracy of silence in Sweden, a tacit agreement to keep all fundamental questions out of public discussion. The Royal Commission on civil rights, he told me, was sitting in camera, because the government claimed that questions about civil rights aroused 'high feelings' which would make the necessary compromise difficult.

The Riksdag, it's generally agreed, is not an arena of real debate. It cannot question the day-to-day administration of the country, which is in the hands not of the Ministers and their Ministries, but of the Directors-General and their Departments – a bureaucratic world apart. Much of the real debate takes place between the government and the 'central organisations', which represent people in their different functions, as Employers, Consumers, Landlords, Tenants, and so on; 'one bureaucracy talking to another', someone complained to me.

Consensus doesn't mean unanimity, of course. Pretty well everyone I met seemed convinced that the country was going to hell in a handcart; but as to who was pushing the handcart I found little agreement. Leftists know that the country is run by the Wallenbergs, and a handful of other wealthy families in banking and industry (it's still possible to be rich in Sweden; tax stops at 80 per cent). Conservatives know that it's a Leftist conspiracy which has taken over – one showed me charts illustrating how the Leftists had moved in on the traditionally Liberal *Dagens Nyheter*, and told me that the whole of the Left was in the pay of the Russians. Liberals say that the country is run by a small establishment of Social Democrats in the bureaucracy. A spokesman for the Social Democratic Party assured me that what they were worried about was the contrary – that so few civil servants were Social Democrats, and that the party was helpless in the hands of a predominantly Liberal or Conservative administrative machine.

I found the sheer volume and diversity of gloomy warnings about the future rather reassuring. Intellectuals are worried that the recent attempt to suppress revelations about the intelligence services signalled the end of free speech in Sweden. The universities are certain that the proposals for higher education will mean the end of academic freedom. The new Constitution, which the Riksdag is due to finish voting into force this year, has come under attack all round. A movement called With the People For the King protests that it will deprive the sovereign of all his traditional powers; the Left claims that it will enable the government to cancel most civil rights at a stroke by a simple majority vote in the Riksdag.

I put this to Professor Jacob Sundberg, a right-wing lawyer at Stockholm University. He dismissed the anxiety briefly. The new Constitution didn't really alter anything, he said, because 'civil rights have always been a joke here'. A rather metaphysical joke for Hasse and Tage – Hasse Alfredsson and Tage Danielsson, the two best-known satirical comedians in Sweden, who started their career as undergraduates at Lund and Uppsala respectively (Tage has a disconcerting resemblance to Jonathan Miller). In their marvellously stylish revue at Berns, the Stockholm nightclub, one of the characters applies to God for a permit to exist. 'What do you want to exist for?' murmurs God reproachfully back from the rococo gilt-and-crystal vastness of Berns. 'Look at Walter, the man who isn't standing next to you. He doesn't exist, and he's not complaining.'

Roland Huntford, for ten years the *Observer*'s correspondent in Stockholm, has written a book called *The New Totalitarians*, in which he argues forcefully that Sweden has become a Brave New World where people have been persuaded by skilful 'social engineering' to accept the servitude which other totalitarian States have been obliged to impose by force. He quotes the Deputy Ombudsman as advancing this theory: 'All people want security. Now you in England, in America, and I might say in most Western countries, get your feeling of personal security from the rule of law. But the Swedes get it entirely from social welfare. So that our people regard welfare as you regard the law.'

Security: *trygghet*. The word – and its opposite, *otrygghet* – recur again and again in the newspapers, and in the utterances of politicians. The anxiety about it seems chronic, unappeasable. 'Insecurity is dangerous!' announced a headline in *Dagens Nyheter* while I was there. Beneath it was a review of three new sociological works which had insecurity in welfare as their central theme. 'Is Sweden more insecure than other societies?' asked the author, Kerstin Vinterhed. 'No, obviously not. But our relationship to security is, I think, of a more complicated sort than in other countries. We have, that is to say, believed for a rather long time that security is possible. When it is shown to be impossible, here as in other States, we feel ourselves disillusioned, alarmed, and abandoned by the State, by the economy, by social democracy, by capitalism . . . The form of insecurity we now feel contains, moreover, an element of frustration: we are insecure in spite of material prosperity.'

The National Board of Health and Welfare commissioned a survey of the country's mental health from a distinguished doctor called Hans Lohmann. He reported last year with a variety of disquieting statistics. Various studies among both adults and the young, he claimed, had found that 'about 25 per cent of the population suffer from mental inadequacies or neuroses of such a degree of severity that qualified help in one form or another was considered necessary'. Many people, commented *Dagens Nyheter* in its report on the survey, are so affected by functioning like machines during working hours that 'there is no room left for feelings of desperation or impotence. Just uneasiness, gloominess, and emptiness remain.'

I spoke to a psychologist who was rather cautious about such assessments. Ten years ago, he said, when people were asked if they were happy in their work they said yes, because it was the convention of the time to believe yourself contented. Now it was the convention to believe that you were not. He thought that it was not work but leisure which people often found most difficult to bear. Great value had always been placed upon hard work. And it had been important while Sweden was being urbanised and brought out of backwardness. Now that period was over; but still people couldn't relax. They often took a second job, claiming they needed the money. What they needed the money for was to buy boats and summer cottages. What they needed the job for was to make sure that they never had the time to use them.

*

I found it difficult to convince myself that Sweden was in general any crazier, more miserable, or more oppressed than anywhere else. But, of course, I read my own moral tale into that quiet good order. I sometimes found myself thinking about all the old fairy-stories in which people are magically granted their wishes. They don't usually turn out very well, these gifts from the central authorities. A palace, a piece of sausage – the wishes become trivial, insipid, absurd even as they are realised. The very act of realisation destroys the fact of their being wished for which gave them meaning. This is in the logic of human experience, not in the nature of the Swedes or the short-comings of social democracy. There are no steady states in experience – only variation and contrast, motion towards and away. There is no enjoyment of security without the experience of insecurity; no pleasure to be gained from order without disorder beside it.

Turning these matters over in my mind I flew back to London, and dragged the great weight of books and handouts I'd acquired explaining what was right and wrong with Sweden on to the suburban train home. 'Owing to an industrial dispute,' announced the station loudspeaker immediately, 'no trains will be leaving this station until further notice.' The only taxi-driver I could find who would agree to take me into the suburbs com-plained unceasingly about it all the way . . . At home the phone still wasn't working properly, and the children had been standing outside their school in the cold for hours because of bomb-scares . . . No, no place like home. If my theory is correct.

(1974)

The End of the Dance

Forty years in a parallel England

Sometimes, when I pass the Quadriga, at Hyde Park Corner, I remember for an instant what has long since been too obvious to be noticed: how it felt to be grown-up. I suddenly catch the flavour of a sweltering summer's night in the 1950s, when I walked all round this part of London talking to a girl I'd just met at a party. It must have been nearly dawn. We walked down the middle of the empty roadways, and I felt that after all those unsatisfactory years of being young I had suddenly inherited the entire city as my rightful estate.

Sometimes, though, it's another memory that the Quadriga brings to mind – also of something that happened here after a party on a hot summer's night. But this one was in, I think, 1929, several years before I was born. On the edge of the pavement here, in Grosvenor Place, Kenneth Widmerpool confided to Nicholas Jenkins the agonies of love he had been suffering over Barbara Goring. They had just left the Huntercombes' dance in Belgrave Square, where Barbara had poured the sugar over Widmerpool's head. It was a disclosure that came as something of a shock to Jenkins, partly because he too had been suffering over Barbara, and partly because in those far-off youthful days he 'used to think that people who looked and behaved like Widmerpool had really no right to fall in love at all'.

Widmerpool, Jenkins, Barbara Goring, and all the events of that night are of course part of another world – the world created by Anthony Powell in *A Dance to the Music of Time*, the huge novel which is finally completed tomorrow with the publication of the twelfth volume, *Hearing Secret Harmonies*. 'People think because a novel's invented, it isn't true,' says X. Trapnel, one of the novel's several characters who are themselves novelists, in this final volume. 'Exactly the reverse is the case. Because a novel's invented, it is true. Biography and memoirs can never be wholly true, since they can't include every conceivable circumstance of what's happened. The novel can do that. The novelist himself lays it down. His decision is binding.'

I think (and I think Powell thinks) that the relationship of imagined worlds to perceived ones is more complex than this, particularly where, as with Powell's, they occupy objective space and time. But in essence Trapnel is right. The world remembered by Nicholas Jenkins (Powell's first-person narrator) is in many ways better established, more publicly accessible, more objectively *there*, than the worlds we ourselves remember (or imagine we remember). You don't remember my walking up Grosvenor Place, but (if you've read Powell) you remember the night that Widmerpool was there. In fact I remember it better myself. I've forgotten now who was at the party I'd come from, and I don't know what's become of the girl I was with. But I could tell you the names of quite a number of the guests at the Huntercombes' dance.

I know what became of Widmerpool. I remember clearly the sequence of events which now began to occur in Grosvenor Place, and the position they came to occupy in the larger pattern of events which developed over the next forty years. How Widmerpool stepped back to say good night, and collided with Edgar Deacon and Gypsy Jones on their way home from selling *War Never Pays!* to late travellers at Victoria; how all four of them went off to have coffee at the stall by Hyde Park Corner – Widmerpool already falling in love with Gypsy, already becoming entangled into forty years of increasingly bizarre political affiliations; how the air was full of the heavy summer night scent of the park; how at the coffee stall an elderly man in a dinner-jacket was very slowly practising the Charleston, the tips of his fingers in his coat pockets; how, as they drank the coffee, Charles Stringham, with whom Jenkins had shared a study at school, reappeared from the past, urbane and detached, and already in that state of curiously sober inebriation in which he was going to spend so much of his life.

For twenty-five years this world has been in the process of creation – the first volume appeared in the same year as the Festival of Britain. I didn't stumble upon it until somewhere in the early sixties, when it had reached the outbreak of the Second World War, and the threshold of my own conscious experience of life. It was like discovering a complete civilisation – and not in some remote valley of the Andes or the Himalayas, but in the midst of London, in the midst of my own life. It altered my perception of the world – and not only of Hyde Park Corner. I began to see in my own life the kind of patterns which were emerging in Jenkins's life; glimpsed how tremendous changes prepared themselves unseen beneath the surface of the apparently immutable course of events, and then quite suddenly deflected one's life into some new course, apparently no less immutable. Another world had been superimposed upon my own, refracting and reflecting it.

One of the pleasures of Powell's world is its sheer size. You can live in it – you can get lost in it. Its texture is close and fine, its population dense enough to operate as an autonomous society, with its own political and business life, its own books and paintings. And everything in it is in perpetual movement and evolution, from the first appearance of Widmerpool, like some legendary ancestor of the tribe, as he doggedly returns from one of the runs he imposes upon himself at school, on a bleak December afternoon 'in, I suppose, the year 1921', until his final disappearance from the stage, now in his late sixties and stark naked, on another self-imposed run in (*I* suppose) 1970.

You come across people you knew donkey's volumes ago, often in the most unexpected places, as when Charles Stringham, now dried out and burnt out, but as stylishly self-contained as ever, turned up in 1941 as Jenkins's mess waiter. Widmerpool, by now in a position of power at Divisional Headquarters, saved us all a lot of embarrassment on that occasion by having him smartly transferred to the Mobile Laundry Unit, and eventual death in a Japanese prison-camp.

The sharpness with which Widmerpool is seen as he first looms up out of that lost December dusk is characteristic. ('Two thin jets of steam drifted out of his nostrils, by nature much distended.') But so is the slight uncertainty about the date. In the background definite, date-able events occur – the Gold Standard is abandoned, Dollfuss suspends parliamentary democracy in Austria. But Nick recalls only that Maclintick, the music critic, was found dead 'three or four days' after he and Moreland visited him, and that he had lasted 'about eight or nine years' since the evening he'd talked about suicide in Casanova's Chinese Restaurant (and Barnby, charac-teristically, had got off with the waitress whom Moreland fancied).

The geographical locations, too, have this same careful mixture of definiteness and indefiniteness. They shade outwards from Grosvenor Place and the other London settings, always real and often identified by name; through Eton, unidentified but unambiguous; and Oxford, unidentified, and distinguished from Cambridge only (I think) by the presence of a Rhodes Scholar, to an outer landscape of purely fictitious great houses in unspecified counties.

A similar uncertainty hazes many of the events. Recounting, at third hand, the nocturnal encounter between the elderly father of Books-do-furnish-a-room Bagshaw and the naked Lady Widmerpool, in the hall of Bagshaw's house ('a bit north of Primrose Hill'), Jenkins speculates, with characteristic interest in practical minu-tiae, as to why Mr Bagshaw should have had to go through the hall to get to the lavatory. 'An upper lavatory may not have existed, been out of order, possibly occupied, in view of what took place later. On the other hand, some prefer-ence or quirk may have brought him downstairs . . . Perhaps sleeping pills, digestive mixtures, medicaments of some sort, were deposited at this lower level.'

Sometimes this measured diffidence borders on disin-
genuousness. 'Some sort of embrace may even have taken
place,' records Jenkins, describing his conversation with
Gypsy Jones, at the birthday party of Edgar Deacon's
which finished that unsuccessful painter off. I suppose it
may be possible to forget whether you kissed a girl at a
party; but, when Jenkins breaks off his career as a writer
to serve in the war, he tells us he has produced 'three or
four novels', which is as plausible a modesty as admitting
only to possessing one or two feet.

One of the ways in which Powell both suggests and
distances landscapes and faces is to see them through the
brush-strokes of particular painters; and what the receding planes of definition and knowability in his world
recall is an aspect of painting which he mentions more
than once: 'recession' – the receding planes of colour by
which perspective can be suggested. And, in the depths of
the picture, the world we are being shown opens into
other, half-glimpsed, worlds beyond, like the sunlit street
beyond the open door of the room in a Pieter de Hooch.

You can almost see the paintings and read the books
that Powell's characters are producing. You know exactly
the stiffness of poor Edgar Deacon's academic studies of
classical scenes (like the *Boyhood of Cyrus*, hanging on
the stairs at the Huntercombes'), and the coarseness of
Isbister's portraits of industrialists, which reflect only too
accurately the fashionable preconceptions of the
moment. If anyone, in a literary competition, produced a
quotation from the once-fashionable novels of E. St. John
Clarke – *Fields of Amaranth*, say, or *Match Me Such
Marvel* – you feel you'd place it at once, sight unseen.
Huge panoramas of critical tendentiousness open out

from the title-page of J. G. Quiggin's long-awaited *Unburnt Boats*; of knowingness from the wrappers of the novels by which Quiggin's wife, Ada Leintwardine, made her name in the fifties – *I Stopped at a Chemist* and *Bedsores*; of hideous campness from the Quentin Shuckerly title, *Athlete's Footman*.

Even the characters in the immediate foreground of the picture retain a rare inner privacy, a sense of being worlds in themselves, of having (as Jenkins says of Widmerpool) their being in obscurity. 'One passes through the world knowing few, if any, of the important things about even the people with whom one has been from time to time in the closest intimacy.' This is something he keeps coming back to – 'the difficulty in understanding, even remotely, why people behave as they do'.

Like the world we ourselves inhabit, and unlike most of the worlds fabricated in novels, the world in which Nicholas Jenkins lives is not fully interpreted. We have to make our own sense of its ambiguity, place our own constructions upon its events, just as we do with the world around us. Sometimes, years and volumes later, the most radical reappraisals become necessary of everything that Jenkins and we have taken most for granted. His love affair with Jean Duport at the beginning of the thirties is as absolute and unambiguous as anything in life ever is. You have a sense of the whole fabric of the world crumbling when Jenkins discovers, eight years and three volumes later, that she had in fact been simultaneously beginning an affair with the disconcertingly unimpressive Jimmy Brent. You can't help beginning to worry (though the thought doesn't seem to occur to Jenkins) that on that memorable day when Jean opened the door of the flat ('somewhere beyond Rutland Gate') to Jenkins dressed only in a pair of slippers . . . No, surely not! Not *then*!

But in fact we're left to make all sorts of connections without being prompted. It occurs to you only afterwards, and with an uneasy shock, why it must have been that Priscilla Tolland suddenly insisted on abandoning her lover without any coherent explanation in the middle of that wartime dinner in the Café Royal. And when, at the end of the war, Colonel Flores, the South American whom Jean marries after she has divorced Duport, tells Jenkins he was at the Ritz with all his family fifteen years before, you can't help wondering (though again Jenkins doesn't) if that wasn't the South American family Jenkins was idly watching in the hotel on that very day in 1931 when he met Jean with the Templers, and first became her lover.

Powell's, of course, is not the only imaginary world relating to this particular piece of space and time. Evelyn Waugh's novels are another extensive comic projection of the upper classes over the same period. Yet they might be about different planets. Waugh's world is besieged by middle-class barbarians of grotesque pretension and threatening loathsomeness; Powell observes his *arrivistes* (like Ted Jeavons, the former car-polisher who is taken up and married by Lady Molly Sleaford) with exactly the same steadiness and detached sympathy as everybody else (though I suppose Widmerpool is never forgiven the middle-class laboriousness of his efforts to rise).

In Waugh's world the comedy arises from the puppet-like helplessness of the characters in the grip of external forces that they cannot control, and internal codes of behaviour that they cannot abandon. Powell's world is driven by human willpower; the comedy arises from the success which the characters have in imposing themselves upon their material.

Another related and powerful current, too, charges Powell's world: eroticism. Genuine erotic feeling is surprisingly rare in English fiction (perhaps in all fiction), and at the very end of *The Music of Time* the sexual interest of the narrative coarsens to take in voyeurism and necrophilia, and finally an entirely unconvincing excursion into mystical orgiastics. But the earlier volumes are alive with fascination for the complexity of sexual behaviour – 'the tangled strands of appetite, tenderness, convenience or some hope of gain'. The condition of marriage Jenkins passes over as too complex to be described at all from the inside, but in the affair with Jean Duport he touches the living nerve throughout. The evocativeness is heightened by the tact with which the affair is both conducted and described; from the first unpremeditated embrace, in the back of the Templers' car, just beyond the neon sign on the Great West Road of the girl forever diving; to the irritation displayed later by Mona Templer, 'perhaps due to an inner awareness that a love affair was in the air, the precise location of which she was unable to identify'; to 'that terrible sense of exhaustion that descends, when, without cause or warning, an unavoidable, meaningless quarrel develops with someone you love'; and the apparently simple observation that goes to the heart of the affair (and all affairs): 'There is, after all, no pleasure like that given by a woman who really wants to see you.'

I wonder if, when he passed the Quadriga in later years, Widmerpool (or Lord Widmerpool, as he later was) ever recalled that first meeting with Gypsy Jones (or Lady Craggs, as she later was, more dizzyingly but no less logically). Probably not. But then he almost certainly hadn't read the book; he was never one to waste his time on novels. Some of the other characters might have read at any rate the earlier volumes. You'd think Jenkins would have done – he's read everything else, from E. St John Clarke to Ariosto. He speculates on the relation between the fictitious and the factual in Proust, but says nothing about Powell. Professional jealousy, perhaps? He doesn't tell us much about his own work, after those 'three or four' pre-war novels, and a later study of Burton. Was he, too, writing his twelve volumes? Is there a complete Jenkins world, bearing upon Powell's world in the same way that Powell's world bears upon ours? And is there, in Jenkins's world, a writer who is producing a twelve-volume meta-meta-novel in his turn . . . ?

Sadder worlds than ours, if there aren't.

(1975)

The Smiling Faces of Paradise

Forwards backwards in Vienna

Sunday morning. A sky of unbroken blue, softened by a haze that will dissolve later in the first great heat of early summer. Up into the Gothic vaulting of St Stephan's Cathedral, as clear and pure as an ascending angel, soars the A of the oboe, attended by all the clamouring anticipatory voices of a great orchestra tuning up. All over Vienna, into other high medieval arches and painted baroque skies, the same note is rising, the same huge symphonic murmur is swelling and dying to the same taut silence.

And then the music starts. In the cathedral, the Bruckner Mass in F. In the Franciscan Church, Haydn's St Nicolai Mass. In the Canisius Church, Mozart's Coronation Mass. In St Michael's, Schubert in B; in the Votive Church, Schubert in G. Already, in the old Court chapel, they are into Haydn's St Theresa Mass. As the morning wears on, and the heat sets in, other churches will be joining in with more Haydn and more Mozart, with Beethoven and Liszt and Kodaly.

Paradise; the people I met in Vienna kept mentioning the word, with deprecating ironic smiles. 'An operetta paradise,' complained a modern composer. A 'work paradise', said a wry leader in *Die Presse* on the economic situation. At least a dozen times people reminded me (with ironic smiles) of what the Pope called Austria – 'an island of the blessed'. 'And,' said the editor of a conservative weekly unfriendly to the Socialist Government (smiling as he said it, of course), 'we think he may be right.'

It's just twenty years since the Allies finally signed a peace treaty with Austria. Twenty years of neutrality so profound that the fighters of the Austrian Air Force can now be overtaken by the DC9s of Austrian Airlines. Twenty years of industrial peace. Twenty years of such leisurely reaction to international economic disaster that Austria missed the last recession, and with any luck might get round to thinking seriously about the present one only after it's over. Or so a government spokesman suggested to me, with a disarming sardonic smile.

For a hundred years Austria was racked by the ever-increasing strains of Empire; and then, for another thirty years or more, after all her non-German territories (and 87 per cent of her population) were severed from her in 1918, by the trauma of the loss of Empire – a bleak syndrome of hunger, civil war, fascism, defeat, and hunger again. Now the calm is almost unnerving. Mothers happily let their daughters walk home through the city at night. And although Austria is structurally the most socialist country in Europe outside the socialist bloc, with most of primary industry nationalised, and a lot more controlled through the State-owned banks, the most radical criticism that the conservatives I spoke to could produce was that the government wasted money.

According to a survey published while I was there,

only 7 per cent of Austrian women confessed to any interest in politics. The student elections took place, and surprise was expressed when the poll turned out to be as high as 39 per cent, and when the Conservative students managed to get only just over twice as many places on the central committee of the national student organisation as the Socialists (with the parties to the left of the Socialists once again almost nowhere). Big business (so someone assured me, grinning with pleasure at the paradox) supports the Socialists, as the guarantors of industrial peace and economic expansion.

What other great imperial Power has achieved at last a retirement of such implausible serenity? And at the same time managed to hold on to so much of the loot? Vienna remains an imperial capital – a monstrous mass of stone demonstrating to the peoples of Central Europe the power and permanence of the Habsburgs; the caryatids groan almost audibly under the sheer weight of it. There are rooms in the Schönbrunn Palace which are literally encrusted with wealth. Such stockpiles of European art were amassed by the Habsburgs that the State museums (according to a critical news magazine) don't know what they've got. When I was talking to Dr Wolfgang Kraus, the director of the Austrian Society for Literature, at their offices in some unconsidered palace in the Inner City, he picked up the mass-produced ashtray by his chair to demonstrate. 'Look,' he said, 'this cost money. That Gobelin tapestry on the wall cost nothing. We borrowed it from the Kunsthistorisches Museum. There are many such tapestries in Vienna.'

It was 'the city of dreams and fantasy', said Dr Kraus. The fabric of the city is these dreams made concrete, from the *Scheinarchitektur* of the High Baroque, the 'appearance architecture' that made flat ceilings look domed, to the heroic historical daydreams which were specified by the authorities for the Ringstrasse, when the street was built in the space left by the demolition of the city walls in 1855.

From the later years of the Empire survive counter-fantasies even more grandiose. In the Berggasse, behind a ponderous facade supported by the ubiquitous corps of caryatids, a consultant's waiting-room has been restored to the solid respectable comfort of the Belle Epoque. Beyond the inner door, Freud conducted his patients on tours of the baroque underworld of suppressed sexuality. In the Kundmanngasse, a baldly square house has been saved at the last minute from a development site. It's the one that Wittgenstein designed for his sister, and its undecorated angularity echoes the neat logical grid defined by the world of facts in his *Tractatus*.

From the Ringstrasse outwards, the city is ancient with trams. You don't notice at first that they are as smooth and swift as a Japanese monorail, only that their bells clang of top hats and trailing skirts, that their grinding iron bogies rasp of railway shares and assignations with actresses. Beneath the Inner City they are building an underground system: in the narrow streets above cruise open horse-drawn fiacres, the gondolas of the tourists, trailing in their wake a delicate, sharp, half-forgotten odour that tints every perception as distinctly as the sepia in an old photograph – the stale of horses.

'Heave! – into a good future,' say the hoardings which the Socialist Party has put up all over the city in preparation for the elections this autumn. And there in the

picture, heaving smilingly upon a rope in pastoral surroundings, is a group of happy young folk advancing into
that good future firmly backwards.

*

'An essential cleavage between appearance and reality'
marked the Empire in its closing years, according to
Allan Janik and Stephen Toulmin in their book
Wittgenstein's Vienna. The new forces at work in Europe
boiled beneath a thin baroque pie-crust of archaic social
forms and brittle constitutional formulae. It was in this
structure of contradictions that the astonishing intellec-
tual life of the late Empire flourished.

Now both Dual Monarchy and Jewish intelligentsia
have gone. But a structure of formal appearances, a
ghostly baroque castle of complex social forms, lingers in
the air like the smile of some sardonic Cheshire cat.
People are not ashamed of liking a certain amount of
social frontage to protect themselves from the world – or
of conspiring to preserve a decent frontage on others.
Even in the arts, men who have known one another for
years are still on *Herr* and *Sie* terms. An astonishing
number of the people I met were professors. Most of the
others were doctors, and I regretted not finding the
opportunity to meet the publisher of the radical libertar-
ian journal *Neues Forum*, and having the pleasure of
addressing him by his correct title of Dr Dr.

Aristocratic titles were abolished in 1918, when
Austria became a republic. But everyone knows who the
aristocracy are. 'She's a socialist,' people explain, 'and
also, of course, a countess.' While I was there, Princess
Marie Hélène took a quarter-page in the paper to

announce the death of her 'immeasurably good and noble husband', who was also, as she went on to remark in fourteen-point type, 'His Imperial Royal Highness Franz Josef Karl, Archduke of Austria, Duke of Madrid, Grandmaster of the Carlist Order of San Carlos Borromeo, etc., etc.'

Waiters in the cafés are supposed to know the surnames of all their regulars ('*Grüss Gott*, Herr Moosbrugger!'), and the customers the Christian names of all the waiters ('*Grüss Gott*, Herr Josef!'). When a strange customer comes in, the waiter confers a title on him – '*Herr Baron*', sometimes still, if he's reasonably well-dressed, or '*Herr Direktor*'. (And without the satirical intent of the English 'squire' and 'captain'.) The socialist countess, a journalist by trade, told me that she'd been in a café with a photographer, and the waiter, his respectful imagination seizing hopefully upon the array of technical equipment round the man's neck, had addressed him as '*Herr Ingenieur*'.

People disappear behind the sheer smiling radiance of all that Viennese charm. I watched a teenaged boy ask his mother for permission to bake a cake, and having obtained it, bow, with grave irony. A taxi-driver insisted on getting out and walking a hundred yards to see if the shop I wanted was open. People present themselves, with modest irony, as characters of old-world inefficiency. 'Typically Viennese *Schlamperei*', cried one of the evening papers, when the Government failed to secure any sufficiently distinguished guests for the twentieth anniversary celebrations. *Schlamperei* – mess and slovenliness – the word cropped up in conversations almost as often as that ironic 'paradise'. Coming from present-day

Britain, I couldn't help feeling that *Schlamperei* in Austria (as the man in the old story said about sex in Burnley when he got back from his first trip to Paris) was still in its infancy.

I spent some time with a mathematics student from Berlin who was outraged by all this charm. Talking to her was like being back in Berlin again – a certain familiar directness and simplicity, an openness and seriousness, an articulateness about human relationships. And there, all around us on the café terrace in the sunshine, men with neatly curling hair and discreet suits would be smilingly laying their heads on one side and gesturing to wide-eyed smiling women with bouffant hair-dos. Trying to focus on these two German worlds simultaneously I found as disconcerting as looking at one of those optical tricks with a pattern of cubes that spring from convex to concave, but are never both at once.

Wittgenstein warned against the charm of hidden worlds beneath the surface of things. (He was talking about Freud.) Other qualities do exist, though, behind the smiling appearances – certain darknesses and inertnesses. They laugh in the *Heurigen*, the suburban vineyards where you sit outside on summer nights and drink the previous October's vintage – whole families, grandparents and adolescents, middle-class and working-class together. A happy sight. But when the *Schrammelmusik* comes round to the table – violin and accordion – and the violinist sings to you, gazing saucily and ironically straight into your eyes, what he sings of (explained the painter Georg Eisler) is mostly death. ('Look the other way!' urged the Berlin mathematician desperately, as the *Schrammelmusik* bore down upon our table.) The suicide rate is one of the highest in the world. (There are only three countries with higher rates – Hungary, Czechoslovakia and the DDR – and two of them were part of the Austrian Empire.)

'And don't imagine,' said Dr Theodor Prager, an economist working in labour relations, 'that the high membership of the Socialist Party – it's got almost as many members as the SPD in Germany – represents any great political enthusiasm. It's just the desire to belong. You pay your dues and you get protection.' You get (for instance) jobs. Some positions belong by tradition to the reds, some to the blacks (the Conservative People's Party). 'The famous social partnership', said Dr Prager (between management and labour), 'is really just the old tradition of leaving it to the high-ups to settle. There's no tradition of fighting for it.' If real economic disaster returned, people might still look for a strong man to settle things out of hand.

Still, they make up for this quietism in other ways. 'If you've got friends in Vienna, you don't need enemies,' said another couple who were both in newspapers. A lot of people told me the same thing. An American academic complained that he'd had to have dinner with various writers in three separate shifts one night, to respect the permutations of who wasn't speaking to whom. 'The first double-bass in the Vienna Philharmonic', said a composer, 'told me that when you had a solo, the next player wouldn't turn the pages for you. And when you sat down at the end of the solo you had to make sure he hadn't taken the chair away.' The newspaper couple thought it was a survival of intrigue surrounding the court.

Another musician told me that he had to work for

Austrian Broadcasting under seven different pseudo-
nyms. 'Everyone does it,' he said, 'because they don't like
the same name coming up too often.' In some institutions
there is an aversion to certain names coming up at all.
Freud was not mentioned in the psychology department
of the university until recently. Wittgenstein has had no
impact on the philosophy department; nor has the group
of logical positivists who are known all over the world as
the Vienna Circle. This is called in German
Totschweigentaktik – silencing to death. Peter Handke,
the playwright from Graz, who like many famous
Austrians was not taken seriously in Austria until he had
established his reputation abroad, celebrated the twentieth anniversary of the peace treaty by making a few
'passing remarks' on television in which he declared that
there were still powers maintaining a 'secret occupation'
of Austria and exercising a murderous violence.

'Broad interests don't go with narrow frontiers,' said a
journalist I met. All the same, wistful reports come back
to Vienna, like sensations in an amputated limb, of lin-
gering Austrian influence in the succession States. A correspondent in *Die Presse* while I was there reported back
from Cracow, in the centre of what used to be the
Austrian province of Galicia, that the city 'breathes
Imperial Royal good manners to an extent that can be
found scarcely anywhere still within Austrian frontiers.
From the *Jugendstil* coffee-houses with their red plush
tablecloths . . . to the kissing of hands, which is constantly practised – beginning with the taxi-driver . . .'
There is a wistfulness, too, for some kind of post-imperial role in world affairs. 'On Peace Patrol with Charm',
said a headline in the evening paper, over an article

reporting the diplomatic skill of the Austrian troops serving with the UN in Cyprus. (Remember the *savoir-faire* which was going to make Britain indispensable still as head of the Commonwealth?)

The policy of the Chancellor, Dr Bruno Kreisky, is to safeguard Austria's neutrality by making it as useful to the Great Powers as Switzerland's has always been. He is establishing Vienna as the third UN headquarters, after New York and Geneva, and the newspapers are triumphant over each international diplomatic encounter which takes place in the city.

Georg Eisler was very hopeful about the arts. German publishers, he said, were queueing up for books by Austrian writers. A glowing future was also foreseen by Otto Zykan, a composer who originally made his name as a pianist playing Schoenberg. Now he was making dramatic programmes for Austrian television, which he saw as the focus of a new artistic life in Vienna. He thought there was a growing creative friction between the young and the *Operettenparadies* in which they lived. 'I'll give you a secret tip,' he said. 'Vienna will be the next great place for the arts, just like Paris and New York and London were. In ten years' time.'

We were sitting talking over coffee in his garden, an orchard on the slopes of the Vienna Woods, with the city at our feet. Johann Strauss had lived there as a boy. Zykan, the interpreter of Schoenberg and critic of the *Operettenparadies*, was piously restoring the house, and fitting it out with appropriate Biedermeier furniture.

Of course, he said, smiling ironically, he was all for greater social freedom. But in practice he had to admit that he liked the correctness with names and titles, and

the sparing use of *du*. It gave the individual a certain
Spielraum – room for manoeuvre. 'I shouldn't go to
Germany – not for five times the money. We have almost
as good an economic situation as Germany – and we
don't work so hard. Here we are in Austria, sitting drinking wine in the sunshine.'

It did seem crazy, at that particular moment, ever to
consider being anywhere else in the world. And when I
left Zykan's house (half an hour by tram and bus from
the centre) I walked straight into the Wienerwald, up
over the Dreimarkstein and the Hermannskogel (mountains, by British standards – nearly half as high as
Snowdon), through deserted woods full of sunlight and
cuckoos and Schubert songs. The songs were being sung
by me, the only person around.

I stopped at a simple country inn on the road to
Birdsong Mountain, and had a plain country meal and a
quarter of local white wine at a rough wooden table in
the sunshine; and when I went to wash my hands the
water turned itself on automatically, controlled by a simple rural photo-electric cell. I stopped again and drank
strong black coffee in another wine-garden at a place
marked on the map as In the Sky (or possibly In Heaven),
with a view over Vienna and the rising towers of UN-
City, the new post-imperial dream. I couldn't help thinking of the Socialist Party's poster. We should all be
heaving away into the future, no doubt about it. And
there's a lot to be said for doing it backwards.

(1975)

Rainbow over the Thames

South Bank 1951

'In 1951,' wrote Evelyn Waugh, in the epilogue to his novel *Unconditional Surrender*, 'to celebrate the opening of a happier decade, the Government decreed a Festival. Monstrous constructions appeared on the south bank of the Thames, the foundation stone was solemnly laid for a National Theatre, but there was little popular exuberance among the straitened people, and dollar-bearing tourists curtailed their visits and sped to the countries of the Continent where, however precarious their condition, they ordered things better.'

Poor Evelyn Waugh. It was certainly not the Festival of his Britain. For those sections of the upper and middle classes of whose subconscious anxieties he is the curator the Festival marked the climax of a decade in which almost every single act of government had been inimical to their immediate interests. For a decade they had lived in unprecedented austerity – austerity which could have been ended for *them* years before if it had not been artificially prolonged by egalitarian theorising. For a decade they had been watching – or thought they had been watching – the gestation of a monstrous new state, in which their privileges would be forfeit, their influence dissolved, and their standards irrelevant. When they said – as they frequently did in the years that led up to the Festival – that there was pathetically little for Britain to celebrate in 1951, it was their own private Britain that they had in mind. Perhaps if they had realised that 1951 was to mark the end of this era, and the entry into a decade of stable, moderate Conservative government, when it soon became plain that the balance of power and privilege had hardly changed after all, they might have enjoyed it more.

On the other hand, it was scarcely the Britain of the working classes that was being feted. With the exception of Herbert Morrison, who was responsible to the Cabinet for the Festival and who had very little to do with the actual form it took, there was almost no one of working-class background concerned in planning it, and nothing about the result to suggest that the working classes were anything more than the lovably human but essentially inert objects of benevolent administration.

In fact, Festival Britain was the Britain of the radical middle classes – the do-gooders; the readers of the *News Chronicle*, the *Manchester Guardian*, and the *Observer*; the signers of petitions; the backbone of the BBC. In short, the Herbivores, or gentle ruminants, who look out from the lush pastures which are their natural station in life with eyes full of sorrow for less fortunate creatures, guiltily conscious of their advantages, though not usually ceasing to eat the grass. And in making the Festival they earned the contempt of the Carnivores – the readers of the *Daily Express*; the Evelyn Waughs; the cast of the *Directory of Directors* – the members of the upper and middle classes who believe that if God had not wished them to prey on all smaller and weaker creatures without scruple he would not have made them as they are. Perhaps this domestic split in the privileged classes, rather than any struggle between classes, is the basis of all democratic politics. Anyway, for a decade, sanctioned by the exigencies of war and its aftermath, the Herbivores had dominated the scene. By 1951 the regime which supported them was exhausted, and the Carnivores were ready to take over. The Festival was the last, and virtually the posthumous, work of the Herbivore Britain of the BBC News, the Crown Film Unit, the sweet ration, the Ealing comedies, Uncle Mac, Sylvia Peters . . . all the great fixed stars by which my childhood was navigated.

*

The idea of celebrating the mid-point of the twentieth century, and the centenary of the Great Exhibition, was one which had naturally been in the air for a long time. The Royal Society of Arts, which had been closely concerned with the 1851 Exhibition, put it to the government privately as early as 1943. In September 1945 Gerald Barry, the editor of the *News Chronicle*, urged the project in an open letter to Sir Stafford Cripps, the President of the Board of Trade, and followed it with a campaign to whip up support among industrialists. Cripps scribbled a reply to Barry in his characteristic red ink, saying he thought it might be quite a good idea. Presumably the Board of Trade had been thinking about it already, for, eleven days after Barry's letter appeared, the government set up the Ramsden Committee to consider the question.

The idea had now been fed into the official government processing machinery, from which ideas habitually emerge squeezed to the pips by the intermeshing teeth of incompatible political expediencies. But it did the Festival project nothing but good, reducing the grandiose pretensions that mar most undertakings of this sort to the modest and practical functionalism which was in the end its greatest virtue. Again and again pure expediency deflected the plans from the dismal disaster towards which they seemed naturally disposed to gravitate. The Ramsden Committee, for example, reported in favour of a 'Universal International Exhibition, to demonstrate to the world the recovery of the United Kingdom from the effects of the war in the moral, cultural, spiritual, and material fields', in Hyde Park. Unwilling to deprive Londoners of their main open space, the government set up an interdepartmental committee to find another site. It recommended using 300 acres of Osterley Park, in the outer western suburbs, and the scheme was only abandoned when the government discovered that it would cost the taxpayer £70 million, and absorb a third of London's building labour for three years. So, by the spring of 1947, the universal international exhibition had been ground down to a national one, and Cripps, now that the Board of Trade was no longer concerned, handed over responsibility to Herbert Morrison, the Lord President of the Council.

By this time the project had a name, and was sufficiently mature to begin breeding a profuse genealogy of organisational units. The Cabinet begat the Great Exhibition Centenary Official Committee. The Great Exhibition Centenary Official Committee begat the Festival of Britain

Office. The Festival of Britain Office begat the Festival Council and the Festival Executive Committee. The Festival Executive Committee begat the Presentation Panel. And the Presentation Panel begat the Design Group, which was to bring honour upon the entire family.

Expediency still ruled. The government had failed to find a site big enough to hold an international exhibition; the Festival Council and the Executive Committee, respectively the Lords and Commons of the new organisation, were almost defeated in their search for a site big enough for a national one. The main exhibition halls at Earls Court and Olympia, they discovered, were already booked for the British Industries Fair. They proposed putting it in Battersea Park, under 'recoverable standard shedding'. The government rejected this awful idea for fear of upsetting the people of Battersea, but, having saved the Festival from a living death in recoverable standard shedding, went on to propose a fate worse than death – housing it in the museum buildings at South Kensington. It was only the inexpediency of turning the regular museum-goers out for two or three years that persuaded the Festival Council to refuse.

By the summer of 1948 complete deadlock had been reached. If the London County Council's plan to build a concert hall in time for 1951 on the South Bank had not come up for endorsement by the Festival Council at this point, the deadlock might never have been broken. Afterwards it was widely supposed that it had been Morrison who swung the South Bank on the Festival as a way of getting the area redeveloped – a project in which as an old LCC man he had long been interested. In fact it had been first suggested by the Ramsden Committee, and overlooked in the excitements of recoverable standard shedding and remote, mysterious Osterley. It was now revived, not by Morrison, but by the Festival Council.

It had taken three years to find a home for the Festival. There were only another three left in which to find a Festival for the home. It is difficult to know whether it made the task easier or harder that no one had ever clearly explained what the whole undertaking was *for*. But then, apparently, no one thought it necessary to ask. There seems to have been a mixture of motives taken for granted. It was intended partly to fulfil the abstract but curiously compelling task of marking the mid-century and the 1851 centenary; partly to be a sort of national prestige advertisement; partly as an attraction for tourists. Under attack, Gerald Barry, who in March 1948 had been appointed Director-General, sometimes tried to justify it on the purely materialistic grounds, which, he must have hoped, even a Carnivore would understand, that it would make people work harder; there was, he insisted, an appreciable increase in national production after the pageantry at the wedding of Prince Philip and Princess Elizabeth. Still, a certain vagueness about its purpose lingered to the end; as Noël Coward wrote, in his song 'Don't Make Fun of the Fair', in the Lyric Revue in 1951:

Take a nip from your brandy flask,
Scream and caper and shout,
Don't give anyone time to ask
What the Hell it's about.

Coward was for a time a member of the Festival Council, and if he didn't know what the hell it was about one can only wonder if anyone else did. Morrison probably made the closest guess afterwards when he described it as 'the people giving themselves a pat on the back'. After five years of war, and a disillusioning peace which had brought nothing but continued austerity, continued restrictions, and the threat of war again, the nation craved a brilliant holiday as some sort of tangible reward for its labours and sufferings.

What sort of holiday, though? The strange thing is, looking back on it from a Carnivorous age, that at no point was it ever suggested that the people should be given what Carnivores usually allege they want – a gigantic national booze-up, perhaps, with hostesses giving away free washing-machines, and gigantic, gas-filled facsimiles of chorus-girls' legs floating over all the major cities, picked out at night by searchlights.

But then the whole tone of public life was curiously different in those days; and besides, the Festival was securely in Herbivorous hands. The Press identified it with Morrison, particularly after he was given a convenient handle by a member who put down a question on the Festival for the Lord President, and by a spoonerism addressed him as the Lord Festival. It was the Lord Festival's energy that pushed the project through, and his surprising tact and statesmanship that brought it through the criticism in the House still looking something like an all-party undertaking. The actual making of the Festival, however, he left entirely to the Executive Committee. They were a purely Herbivorous herd – two civil servants, a scientist, an industrial designer, the former general manager of the Stratford Memorial Theatre, a representative from the British Film Institute, Huw

Wheldon from the Arts Council, a public relations officer from the Coal Board, Hugh Casson the architect, and Barry himself. These were the men who were to administer the national pat on the back – with not a Val Parnell, not a Billy Butlin, not a Herbert Gunn, not a shadow of a giver-of-the-people-what-they-want among them. In this Carnivorous age, the mind boggles at the idea.

More than anyone else, it was Barry who set the tone of the Festival. Appropriately enough, his appointment had been suggested by Max Nicholson, the Secretary to the Office of the Lord President, who was well known for his interest in the profoundly Herbivorous pastime of bird-watching. Barry himself was the son of a clergyman, and was educated at Marlborough and Cambridge. An anxious, sensitive, conscientious, rather dry man, he had spent his life as a radical journalist. The tone of the Festival was not unlike the tone of the *News Chronicle*, which he had edited for eleven years – philanthropic, kindly, whimsical, cosy, optimistic, middlebrow, deeply instinct with the Herbivorous philosophy so shortly doomed to eclipse.

The Committee met for the first time in May 1948 for a weekend session at Barry's house in Sussex. It must have been something like a Fabian house-party; they sat on the terrace in the sunshine, or paced the lawn in pairs, discussing the First Principles of Festivity, before a background of rolling English parkland brilliant with the first translucent green sheen of summer. It was the pastoral prologue to three furious years, in which waking hours were working hours. Barry recalls them as a period of almost continuous elation – even when, in the later stages, he would be still reading official papers in bed at three in the morning. The Festival, he wrote afterwards, was made not only in committee rooms. 'It was made on hill-tops, in gardens, round a log-fire, wherever half a dozen people could foregather and talk. It was made clambering among rubble and cement mixers, amid the uproar of cranes and pile drivers, in over-heated railway carriages and under-heated motor-cars, tearing through the English landscape. It was made in mayoral parlours, on fog-bound airfields, in dingy studios, on visits to experimental building stations, in lecture halls, youth centres, and standing on street corners waiting for a bus. I sometimes think that those who jostled us in a queue might have detected a special smell, for all that time we breathed, thought, imagined, willed, inhaled, and exuded – Festival.'

There is something about this exuberant toil that makes one think of putting on a school play – a super-colossal school play, perhaps, to mark the end of a super-colossally long and trying term. But the daily contact with bus queues and youth centres kept the reality of Britain's reduced circumstances perpetually before their eyes. 'One mistake we should not make,' wrote Barry: 'we should not fall into the error of supposing we were going to produce anything conclusive. In this sceptical age, the glorious assurance of the mid-Victorians would find no echo.'

All the same, the theme which the Executive Committee worked out that summer of 1948 had a fairly sonorous ring when Barry announced it to the press in October. It was to demonstrate Britain's contribution to civilisation, by way of showing 'what the Land has made of the People, and what the People have made of them-

selves'. 'We envisage this as the people's show,' said
Barry, 'not organised arbitrarily for them to enjoy, but
put on largely by them, by us all, as an expression of a
way of life in which we believe.' It is the true voice of the
forties speaking; not even the most Herbivorous of men,
in our age of more highly sophisticated class consciousness and guilt, could stand up in public and announce
that a committee consisting of a former newspaper editor,
two senior civil servants, an architect, a theatre-manager,
a cinéaste, a palaeontologist, a public relations officer,
and Huw Wheldon, was the People. 1951 was also to be
a year of 'fun, fantasy, and colour', of 'the fun and games
which the bitter circumstances of the last few years have
denied us', a year in which 'we can, while soberly survey-
ing our great past and our promising future, for once let
ourselves go, and in which the myth that we take our
pleasures sadly will finally be disproved'.

These were the first details to be published; but the
criticism which was to be a running accompaniment to
the whole project for the next three years had already
begun. When Morrison had first announced in the
Commons, in December 1947, that he was examining the
possibility of some sort of national exhibition in 1951,
the Opposition had offered its full support for the project. Not a voice was raised in protest anywhere in the
House – or anywhere in the country – despite the fact
that the announcement coincided with the news that
Britain was just beginning to spend the last £400 million
of the American loan.

Now the Carnivores fell upon it, led by the
Beaverbrook Press. Exactly why Beaverbrook took so
violently against the Festival it is not easy to say.

Anything with such a Herbivorous tone would naturally be antipathetic to him – yet the prospect of patriotic exultation in the achievements of British industry, with fun and fantasy thrown in, is one which might easily have struck him as being almost as admirable as the *Daily Express* Boat Show. A bookmaker might well have offered evens on whether Beaverbrook would put the Festival in the same category as the Boat Show or as the heinous British Council.

Anyway, at the beginning of August 1949, Beaverbrook's *Evening Standard* opened fire on 'Mr. Morrison's multi-million-pound baby'. The initial shots were two articles by Charles Wintour, complaining principally about the probable cost; though their effect was somewhat offset by Low's cartoon in the *Standard* a day or two later, which showed Barry explaining to the press: 'We've now cut expenses down to twenty-five quid – and we hope to knock off another ten by not having gates so that visitors can't get in.' From then on the *Express* and the *Standard* kept plugging away at it. They called it 'Mr. Morrison's Monument', 'Morrison's Folly', and 'This gigantic waxworks cum circus cum carnival', and sniped at it day after day with stories bearing headlines like 'Resort-Guide Paper Taken For Festival', 'Up Up Up Go Hotel Prices', 'Festival Badges Muddle', 'Up Go the Costs of the Festival'. Considering what a wide range of novel undertakings the Festival involved, and the speed with which they had to be pushed through, it is remarkable how little effective material the Beaverbrook papers were able to dig up. When, at the opening of the Festival, the *Evening Standard* reporter was reduced to writing: 'In one corner stood an object which may be thought symbolical of Mr Morrison and his planners. It was a brand-new twopenny slot machine. The shelves were bare. And on the machine was boldly draped a label reading NOT WORKING' – it was clear that Beaverbrook's plans, like Barry's, were being held up by a certain shortage of raw materials.

The campaign was, anyway, showing signs of wilting towards the end. Again one can only speculate on the reason. In January 1951, when the *Express*, like other papers, was wondering whether the situation in Korea would lead to a world war that year, it invited readers to submit postcards explaining either 'Why They Should Go Ahead With The Festival' or 'Why They Should Call It Off'. None was ever published. But a fortnight later the *Express* ran a leader on the Festival, saying: 'What should be the public attitude towards it? It should be one of support. It is too late to say that £11,000,000 of public money has been needlessly spent. It is too late to say that the men and materials could have been better used building houses instead of a monument to Mr. Morrison.' Had the *Express* discovered that it was not carrying its readers with it in its opposition to the Festival? (A Gallup Poll taken at about the same time found 58 per cent in favour of proceeding with the Festival, 28 per cent in favour of postponing it.) The Beaverbrook campaign tailed off still further in the spring – perhaps because by this time Morrison had become Foreign Secretary, and was taking a firm line, of which the *Express* approved, on Persian oil nationalisation.

The rest of the Conservative press stayed closer to the line followed by the party in the House, which was to give its general support, but to exercise its constitutional privilege of making political capital out of it whenever the chance arose. At Question Time certain of the more ancient pieces of ordnance entrenched in the rear of the Opposition would regularly discharge themselves against the whole enterprise. Now and again the Opposition in general was struck by the natural suspicion that the Festival might be used to advertise the record of the Labour government. Morrison handled them with great tact in the House, and took considerable pains to avoid overt party propaganda in the Festival. One of the only two occasions when he intervened in the actual planning of the Festival was to remove all mention of free school meals from the Schools Pavilion. (The other occasion was when the *Sunday Pictorial* alleged that Mitzi Cunliffe's projected group of statuary, representing the Origins of the Land and the People, was obscene, and Morrison sent Barry up to Manchester, to walk solemnly round the maquette with Mrs Cunliffe, and pronounce it decent viewed from every possible angle.)

A much heavier monkey on the Festival's back was the antipathy of the senior Carnivores, for whom Evelyn Waugh spoke. Something of the savagery of the resentment felt against the Labour government and all its doings, of the rage to bring the nation down in their own fall, is reflected in a letter to the *Spectator*, written in 1950 by one J. Dupont, of Kittery Point, Maine, at a time when Britain's need to earn dollars was desperate. 'Private letters from Britain', he wrote, 'urge American friends not to come to Britain during the Festival . . . Many Americans who made tentative plans to visit England next year have changed their minds for two reasons, one being the possibility of a general war, and the other being the dismay and distaste with which they regard the Festival.' (Two weeks later another member of the *Spectator*-subscribing community at Kittery Point wrote to say that she found the Festival advertising 'essentially un-British'. Americans, she said, 'want England to be the same, battle-scarred but beautiful'.)

Professor Albert Richardson, the Georgian-type architect, declared that the South Bank site was too small, and predicted a terrible catastrophe as thousands of visitors were pushed into the Thames by later arrivals. Sir Thomas Beecham described the Festival as a 'monumental piece of imbecility and iniquity'. Cyril Osborne, the Conservative MP, declared himself against holding the Festival on the grounds that the divorce courts were choked and the prisons were crowded. The Russians were against it, too; they thought it was a disguise for war preparations.

The government did its best to square the Establishment by empanelling a representative selection of them on the Festival Council, along with R. A. Butler and Colonel Walter Elliot, the hostages from the Opposition. There were Sir Kenneth Clark, T. S. Eliot, John Gielgud, Sir William Haley, and Sir Malcolm Sargent; a general, an earl and a few lords. The Council was put under the chairmanship of General Lord Ismay, Churchill's war-time Chief of Staff. An authority initially less enthusiastic about its task can rarely have been constituted. 'I think we all started this job in rather a lukewarm way,' said Sir Alan Herbert, one of the Council members, later. It was an understatement. Lord Ismay later told Barry that he had accepted the post partly out of relief that it had not turned out to be, as he half feared when he was summoned to Number Ten, 'a more distasteful offer'. Barry stirred their interest by having huge imaginary visualisations of the still unvisualised Festival drawn and hung up around the Council's walls. 'The Council warmed to its task gradually,' he wrote, 'passing – dare one say? – from a state of reserved scepticism on the part of some of its members, through various degrees of conversion, to final unanimous conviction.' After all, as Sir Alan Herbert pointed out, surviving 'five years of war and five years of His Majesty's Government' was certainly something to celebrate. Members of the Council, though, came under considerable pressure from their friends, and, at awkward junctures, as late as 1950, some of them were privately of the opinion that the whole thing ought to be called off. But open criticism of the Festival among the Establishment was dampened down still further when the King and Queen became patrons in March 1950.

All in all, the Festival might have had rougher handling. The critics seem to have suffered all along from the uncomfortable suspicion that they were on the losing side. The criticism was certainly mild in comparison with the torrent of abuse and ridicule which was rained down upon the 1851 Exhibition, when its opponents predicted divine retribution for the presumption of the enterprise, a disastrous influx of Papists bent on ruining the country with idolatry and schism, the turning of Bayswater into one giant brothel, an epidemic of venereal disease, and the return of the Black Death.

Meanwhile, the Design Group was trying to give the Festival some concrete shape. The group, which was led by Hugh Casson, consisted of two display designers,

James Holland and James Gardner, and three architects, Casson, Ralph Tubbs, and Misha Black. For a start they used to meet in the footman's bedroom of one of the massive red-brick houses behind Harrods, wearing overcoats on account of the shortcomings of the heating system, and taking Bisodol to keep at bay the dyspepsia to which exhibition designers are said to be martyrs. Here they sat and thought, with the despairing blankness that comes before one has actually got anything down on paper, about the South Bank site – a derelict slum, low-lying, marshy, and heavily blitzed, bisected by the arches carrying the busy mainline out of Charing Cross. And when their brains were beaten dry they went to Waterloo and walked the site, often at night when everything was still, picking their way among the hopeless heaps of rubble.

Early in 1949 they had a master-plan ready, and began to appoint architects for the individual buildings. The men they chose were mostly Casson's contemporaries. Casson (another true Herbivore – the son of an Indian Civil Servant, educated at Cambridge, with a spell in the Ministry of Town and Country Planning under William Holford) was then thirty-nine. The climax of the period that had formed them all was the Paris Exhibition of 1937, and after a decade of nothingness, given the chance to work with like-minded colleagues on a project whose temporary nature encouraged them to risk boldness, they took up architecture again where it had been left twelve years before. But the fundamental decision, which affected the characteristic appearance of the Festival more than anything else, had already been taken by Casson. It was Casson who had decided that the South Bank was not going to be laid out in the formal avenues and vistas of earlier exhibitions, but as a modest and informal complex of interlocking neighbourhoods, each with its own character – like the piazzas of Venice, or the courts of Cambridge – and peculiarly appropriate as a microcosm of life in an overcrowded island.

It was a terrible time to build an exhibition. When they started work steel was in short supply, and they were urged to use wood wherever possible, but by the time their plans were ready steel was plentiful, and it was timber that had to be avoided. To allow for these and other fluctuations in the supply of materials, plans had constantly to be redrawn. And when the designs began to come in, in the summer of 1949, the consulting engineers declared they were too novel and too complex to be built in the time available, and all but two had to be either scrapped or modified.

The Festival authorities set up home in the forecourt of the Savoy Hotel, in offices formerly occupied by the Free French. Here, as the pace grew hotter and the exotic oddments collected for the Festival piled up, there grew what Barry called 'an irresistible mood of sharrawaggy and slightly unhinged romance'. A complex organisation extracted, filtered and bottled the outstanding achievements in every department of life. A 'Lion and Unicorn Pavilion' was planned, to demonstrate the glories and whimsicalities of what, on these occasions, is taken to be the British character, and, on the truly Herbivorous grounds that someone who is used to the pithy intensity of poetry would be the right man to serve the state by writing captions, Laurie Lee was appointed chief caption-writer. He appealed for oddities, and was overwhelmed with collapsible rubber buses and smoke-grinding machines. A certain melancholy British whimsy crept in elsewhere uninvited. The Ministry of Pensions asked that room should be found for 'a modest display of artificial limbs'. A Midlands firm wondered if space could be found for some shrouds and coffin fittings. Another manufacturer sought permission to exhibit a model of the South Bank made out of toilet rolls.

The South Bank, of course, was not the only manifestation planned for 1951. There was to be a Land Travelling Exhibition stumping the provinces inland, and another exhibition was to tour the seaports aboard the *Campania*, a mongrel ship laid down as a merchantman, and converted to an aircraft-carrier while it was still on the stocks. Towns and cities all over the country were to hold festivals of their own – madrigals on the river at Cambridge, lectures on Non-Shakespearean Comedy at Oxford, Rudyard Kipling's relics at Rottingdean, a netball display at Colchester, and pageants of local history practically everywhere. Nor was this all. 'Spontaneous expressions of citizenship', said the Festival guide in positively Soviet tones, 'will flower in the smallest communities as in the greatest.' And the countryside duly sprouted rose shows and road safety weeks, new paint and fresh whitewash, memorial bus-shelters, memorial street-lighting, even memorial repairs to the local war-memorial.

And there were the Pleasure Gardens and Funfair in Battersea Park. It was ironical that these, which were in a way the least Herbivorous item of the whole programme, should have proved its most vulnerable point. They were entangled in dispute from the very beginning. It was during the debate on the Bill which provided for them, in November 1949, that the Opposition first cut up rough about the Festival. Spending the taxpayers' money on doing the taxpayers good was suspect; spending it on entertaining them was a jar to Conservative propriety which was much harder to explain away – though at that stage the money involved was little enough, an estimated loss of £100,000 to be shared between the government and the LCC.

The Gardens were intended to recall the glories and fantasies of the eighteenth-century pleasure gardens of Vauxhall, Ranelagh, and Cremorne; a shakily nostalgic basis compared with the rest of the Festival. They were to be run by the Government and LCC jointly, through a company in which they were the sole shareholders, called Festival Gardens Limited. It was intended originally to spend £1.9 million, and recover it by keeping the Gardens open for five years. But, in the summer of 1949, Chelsea and Battersea councils made it clear that they were not prepared to have them open for more than one year, and considerable alterations had to be made to the plans to bring the gross expenditure down to £770,000. The following year there was a bitter debate about whether the amusement section should be allowed to remain open on Sundays. The Advisory Committee of Christian Churches for the Festival was vigorously opposed to Sunday amusement in the amusement park, though it had no objection to Sunday pleasure in the pleasure gardens. In the end, it was put to a free vote in the Commons, and, by a large majority, the people's representatives voted to keep the amusement out of Sunday pleasure – so helping to nourish and increase the loss, cherishing it no doubt as a topic of discussion for later sessions.

On the site at Battersea the difficulties accumulated.

The work was hindered by an unending series of strikes, go-slows, and work-to-rules. The site flooded after the heavy rains of November 1950. The first five months of 1951 were the wettest since 1815, and the park was churned into a sea of mud that resembled the battlefields of Flanders rather than the pleasure-gardens of Vauxhall. Finally Richard Stokes, the Minister of Works, went down to Battersea and harangued the construction workers himself.

But by this stage it was clear that the Gardens were not going to open on time. It was also clear that they were heavily over-spent. By the end of 1950 the estimated gross expenditure had leapt from £1,100,000 to £1,600,000. By March 1951 it had reached £2,400,000. In April the chairman and managing director of Festival Gardens Limited resigned. Stokes had two firms of chartered accountants appointed to investigate both Festival Gardens Limited and the work of the site contractors, and their report, which was published as a White Paper, put a considerable share of the blame on the Festival Gardens board for the way in which they had managed the work. In the end the Pleasure Gardens opened three weeks late, and in June Stokes had to ask the House to authorise the loan of another million pounds, and to hear Harold Macmillan grind the humiliation home with the over-rehearsed debating club locutions which the future Prime Minister affected at that time – 'a little gem of mismanagement, a cameo of incompetence, a perfect little miniature of muddle'. Princess Margaret cancelled the visit she was supposed to make to Battersea at the end of the season, telling Morrison that she refused to come and get involved in his maladministration.

While Pleasure was brought forth in Pain at Battersea, there was plenty of agony elsewhere. In the summer of 1949 the government's gross expenditure on the Festival (excluding the Pleasure Gardens, a grant of £2 million to the LCC towards the Royal Festival Hall, and various charges to fall on the votes of other departments) was estimated at £12 million, of which £2 million would be recouped from entrance money. That September, however, the government devalued the pound, and in the ensuing round of economies the Festival's budget was cut back by a million pounds. The following summer, when the Korean War broke out, the question was raised as to whether the Festival should be held at all. It could clearly not have been abandoned at this late stage without writing off the whole investment, but there were even members of the Festival Council who had cold feet. By the beginning of 1951 itself, after the great United Nations withdrawals in Korea, the Press was full of gloomy speculations about the possibility of world war before the year was out, and the abandonment of the Festival was discussed once more. It was not only the *Daily Express* that raised the question. 'The country, which formerly gave unanimous approval to the enterprise,' wrote Rainald Wells in the *Daily Telegraph* on January 19th, with masterly oversimplification, 'is now divided in its views. More and more people, indeed, are asking whether it should not be postponed, or even cancelled . . . The overriding question is whether or not the Festival will tend to aid or to hinder us in what is now our primary task – that is, the strengthening of our defences.'

A gay start to Festival year. By this stage, too, the prospects on the South Bank looked extraordinarily depressing. The plans were late. The materials were late. The phenomenal rainfall, as at Battersea, played havoc, and after the rains it froze. There was a series of strikes, and at the end of January work came to a complete standstill for a fortnight. For fifteen whole days the desperate rush to get the exhibition ready in time was halted, and the only sign of activity in the whole of that suddenly paralysed leviathan was the strikers playing football on the fairway.

The delay on the South Bank was made up – 'A good time-and-a-half was had by all,' said Casson. But the political background against which the celebrations were to be held went from bad to worse. In May 1951 the papers were still publishing the casualty lists from the Gloucesters' stand on the Imjin River. The saddest irony of all was that, by the time the Festival opened, the age of the Herbivores who made it was in its last and dimmest days. The General Election on February 23rd, 1950, had left the Labour Party with an overall majority of six, and they dragged themselves through their last painful months in the spring and summer of 1951 like an old, wounded animal, biting at its own injuries. On April 14th Bevin died. On April 21st Bevan resigned, to be followed by Harold Wilson and John Freeman, over the proposal to make a charge for National Health Service teeth and spectacles. Francis Boyd, the political correspondent of the *Manchester Guardian*, described the Commons debate on the 'teeth-and-spectacles' clause as 'a picture of a Government suffering severe internal haemorrhage and likely to bleed to death at any moment. For the greater part of three and a half hours Labour members got up one after the other to attack each other.

The Opposition might not have been part of the House of Commons.' And at the end of May, to add to the government's embarrassments, Guy Burgess and Donald Maclean disappeared.

Still, on May 3rd the King and Queen went to St Paul's for a Service of Dedication, and from the top of the steps in front of the great portico, with a fanfare from the trumpeters of the Household Cavalry, the King declared the Festival open. Barry had wanted the King to perform the ceremony on Tower Hill, and proceed to the South Bank by state barge, but the King had refused, saying that Tower Hill had too many bloody associations, and that anyway the state barge leaked. There was a sense of holiday in the air, and, after careful observation of the crowds lining the streets to see the Royal Family, *The Times* gave its verdict – 'People in joyous Mood'. At the South Bank they worked all that day – and all that night – and as the guests began to come through the front gates for the private view on the morning of May 4th, so the rearguard of the army of workers retreated before them across the city they had built and withdrew through the back gates. The South Bank, or at any rate, 95 per cent of it, was ready on schedule. By the time the official visitors had left and the first handful of the general public had been let in, it was pouring with rain. The visitors splashed dismally round, offering no visible evidence of enjoyment. It was the gloomy baptism without which no British summer festival could be considered properly launched.

But the sense of anti-climax did not last. It quickly became clear that the South Bank, conceived in austerity and shaped by expediency, was a knockout. For two or three evenings the police had to close the streets round the Embankment to traffic, as the crowds poured down to gaze at the floodlit dream-world breathing music on the other side of the river. 'People making for the South Bank', reported the London Correspondent of the *Manchester Guardian*, 'begin to smile as they come close to it.' The *Guardian* suggested that 'on bright sunny days it seems likely that a trip across the Thames to the South Bank will be as invigorating as a trip across the Channel, for in its final form the scene is quite as unfamiliar as any foreign seaside resort'. It certainly was. The crowds came in, and wandered round in a state of somnambulism, forming queues with such abstracted readiness that the attendants found difficulty in preventing the accumulation of queues that led nowhere at all. No one had ever seen anything like it before. Apart from the New Towns, it was one of the first concerted attempts at modern architecture in Britain in this century, a brilliant microcosm in which every single object had been designed for its job. For a few hours people stepped out of the squalid compromises of the everyday urban scene into a world where everything was made to please. There was music on the loudspeakers to walk round to. There were plenty of cafés to sit down at (though the chips-and-peas-type food provided by the catering firms failed signally to rise to the occasion). There were the two distinctive shapes by which cartoons and souvenirs of the Festival were instantly identifiable – the great closed scallop shell of Ralph Tubbs's Dome of Discovery and the Skylon, the luminous exclamation mark with which the young engineers Powell and Moya had won the competition for a vertical feature. Round every corner there was a new delight – a catwalk to look down from, or the superb water mobile by Richard Huws, which imitated the regular sequence of small and great waves on the shore. There was the river to look at. And, on the other side of the river, the magnificent sombre building line of the north bank, revealed for the first time as a back curtain to the colourful and extravagant outlines of the Festival architecture.

Barry was duly knighted. The team of huskies in the Polar Theatre melted a million fusible hearts. The Red Cross treated sixteen people who fell, presumably bemused, into the fountains. Later in the season balloonists took off from the South Bank and drifted with the wind, in the leisurely way of Edwardian high summer, to the open country outside the city. Charles Elleano crossed the river on a tightrope. And twice a week, when darkness fell, there was open-air dancing among the twinkling lights that studded the Fairway.

Someone, unfairly, described the South Bank exhibition as 'all Heal let loose'. Afterwards, the fashions it set in architecture and design were quickly copied, became clichés, and eventually looked vulgar against the growing affluence of the fifties. But now that the whole painful process of outgrowing an out-of-date fashion has been completed, we can look back and appreciate just what a box of delights the South Bank really was. Though, as with any box of delights, the most delightful thing was the packaging, and the air of surprise and excitement it gave to the contents. The contents themselves were a little more mundane. The exhibition was supposed to show Britain's contribution to civilisation. This, of course, is the sort of thing that museums are about anyway, and the

Festival could only do it in the same way that a museum would, with samples of fossils and steam-engines, and pictures of more fossils and more steam-engines, garnished with the hearty Herbivorous display in the Lion and Unicorn Pavilion. But what else can you have a national exhibition about? Still, the splendour of their housing carried the exhibits; and the radar screens, the craftsmen making cricket-bats, and the three-dimensional representations of the integral calculus gave point and a sense of importance to their surroundings. The best thing of all about the South Bank was just being there.

That year the Whit-Monday Fair at Hampstead was abandoned in favour of Battersea. There were queues at the Pleasure Gardens for nylons and Festival rock – and prosecutions for traders who sold the rock without points. But, after the South Bank, the Pleasure Gardens were disappointing. There was something too insistently whimsical about the Guinness Clock and the Emmet Railway, and something even worse about the orange-girls, dressed up as replica Nell Gwyns, articulating 'Come, gentle people, buy,' in sub-Roedean accents, like air-hostesses at a fancy-dress ball.

Over eight million people went to the Pleasure Gardens, and nearly eight and a half million visited the South Bank. But there can have been few people in Britain whose lives remained completely untouched by the Festival. The Festival symbol devised by Abram Games (its original stark nudity draped in bunting by the Festival Council) was ubiquitous. So was the word 'Festival'. The great programme of poetry readings, serenade concerts, firework displays, and children's sports rolled across Britain relentlessly, and, though the local

Festival Rose Show may have been remote in spirit from the pre-stressed concrete élan of the South Bank, it brought with it some suggestion of national identity and consciousness. The BBC – the most thoroughbred Herbivores of all – hammered the Festival into the national cortex with 2,700 programmes on the subject. Even the Druids made a Festival of Britain pilgrimage to Stonehenge.

At the end of September the Festival closed. On Saturday the 29th, large numbers of people fainted in the dense crowd that packed the Fairway on the South Bank, waiting for Gracie Fields in the farewell cabaret. At midnight the crowd still surged and boiled, sliced by the violet-edged beams from the television arc lights, and full of that strange nostalgic excitement which marks end-of-term ceremonies. In the Royal Pavilion champagne corks popped among the official guests, and Ministers stood listening impassively to everyone's ideas on how to dispose of the corpse of the South Bank. On the Sunday night, with a slight air of anticlimax, the Brigade of Guards beat the retreat, the crowd sang 'Abide with Me', the National Anthem, and 'Auld Lang Syne', and the Festival flag was hauled down. The King should have been present, but he was ill – dying, as it turned out. The curious summer was over; a way of life was ending, too.

What is one to think of the Festival? It was not quite the roaring popular success of the Great Exhibition, which was seen by six million people – a third of the population at that time. Nor did it generate the intense national enthusiasm of a piece of routine royal pageantry like the Coronation. Rainald Wells, who at the beginning of the year had suggested abandoning it, gave in the

Daily Telegraph a grudging but not crushing verdict on behalf of the Carnivores: 'It may perhaps be likened to a moderately successful party, but one held on the wrong day and at far too great a cost. We are none the sadder for it, but we might have been wiser to have kept the money in our pockets.' Far too great a cost? The total net expenditure, apart from the loans for the Festival Gardens, was just over £8 million – comfortably within the estimate, and working out at something over three shillings a head of the population. Not quite so satisfactory as the 1851 Exhibition, which made profits big enough to finance the building of the Victoria and Albert Museum (though to do it the organisers resorted to some pretty curious means, like leaving deliberately wide cracks between the floorboards, and letting out a concession to a private firm to keep whatever fell through; so much did that it paid for the whole floor) but cheap by modern standards of government expenditure, and not unduly expensive by the standards of major exhibitions; Paris 1937 and New York 1939 both lost around £4 million. Foreign visitors to Britain, moreover, for whatever reason they came, and even if they did not include some of the citizens of Kittery Point, Maine, spent £18 million more than they did in 1950.

In the summer of 1951 the Gallup Poll asked people what their impression of the South Bank was, from what they had seen and heard. 58 per cent said they had a favourable impression, 15 per cent an unfavourable one. More of the young were favourably impressed than of the older age groups; more of the averagely well-off than the very or less well-off; more Liberal voters than Socialists or Tories. By a not overwhelming majority, in other words, the country liked the Festival – the Herbivores, naturally, most of all. But the South Bank and Battersea were also paid a more striking compliment. The acid democratic test of housing estates and similar undertakings is whether or not they are smashed up by that section of the community which has no other redress for being treated with contempt or condescension; and at the end of the season the police were struck by the absence of hooliganism and other crime in both places. It was quite a tribute.

The Festival certainly absorbed building materials at a time when many were homeless. But it did provide some of the 'fun, fantasy, and colour' that Barry had promised at a time when the nation was parched for lack of them, and the intense concern with design, function and appearance which pervaded the South Bank has survived. It did not, as Barry had also suggested, exactly disprove the myth that the British take their pleasures sadly. Some nights at the open-air dancing on the Fairway couples went doggedly dancing on in heavy rain. Perhaps we took the pleasures of 1951 not so much sadly as desperately.

The Festival was a rainbow – a brilliant sign riding the tail of the storm and promising fairer weather. It marked the ending of the hungry forties, and the beginning of an altogether easier decade. But it was not, as its critics had feared, to mark the consolidation of the Herbivorous forces which had made it. To adapt Rainald Wells's verdict, it may perhaps be likened to a gay and enjoyable birthday party, but one at which the host presided from his death-bed.

What was to become of the South Bank? The Executive Committee wanted to run it for a second year. William Zeckendorf, a New York estate agent, offered to spend up to a million dollars on freight charges to get the Dome of Discovery and the Skylon to New York. The Marquess of Bath said he was interested in putting the Skylon up at Longleat, to add to the charms of that stately home. None of these proposals came to anything. At the General Election at the end of October the sad remnants of the once triumphant post-war Labour government were swept away, and a Conservative government came in, eager to prove its freshness and efficiency. With almost guilty haste they turned on the remains of the Festival. David Eccles, the new Minister of Works, took Barry on a brisk tour of the site, indicating the buildings to be torn down, like a dictator's henchman picking out prisoners for execution. With the exception of the Festival Hall itself, a café beneath Waterloo Bridge, the Telekinema, and the verandahs slung like the gondolas of a balloon high out over the Thames, the whole twenty-seven acres was efficiently stripped down to ground level.

And there, with what one would have thought was intolerable symbolism, it remained for a decade: twenty-seven acres, in the very heart of one of the world's great capitals, totally derelict and unused. Until at last the ground was ready to put forth a second crop, and where the Festival had once stood there grew one of the largest and ugliest commercial office blocks in Western Europe. And a car park for 700 cars.

(1963)